Teaching Composition

WITH

The Prentice Hall Guide
for College Writers

SIXTH EDITION

STEPHEN REID

Prentice
Hall

Upper Saddle River, New Jersey 07458

©2002 by PEARSON EDUCATION, INC.
Upper Saddle River, New Jersey 07458

ISBN 0-13-099294-1

Printed in the United States of America

Contents

Part I: Teaching Guide

Part II: Chapter Commentary and Answers to Questions

Part III: Background Readings

Writing Process

Rhetorical Backgrounds

Reading/Writing Connections

Collaborative Learning and Writing

Revising

Responding to Writing

Conferences

English as a Second Language

Permission

Thanks

The author is grateful for the contributions of the composition faculty and instructors at Colorado State University: Kate Kiefer, Mike Palmquist, Donna LeCourt, Sarah Sloane, Jon Leydens, Laura Thomas, Bev Atchison, Meg Gallagher, Trish Taylor, and Anne Gogela.

Acknowledgements

Ronald Barron, "What I Wish I Had Known about Peer-Response Groups but Didn't," English Journal, September 1991. Copyright © 1991 by the National Council of Teachers of English. Reprinted with permission.

Patricia Bizzell and Bruce Herzberg, "Research as a Social Act," from The Clearing House 60 (March 1987), pp. 303-306. Reprinted with permission of the Helen Dwight Reid Educational Foundation. Published by Heldref Publications, 1319 Eighteenth St., N.W., Washington, D. C. 10036-1802. Copyright © 1987.

Kenneth A. Bruffee, "The Art of Collaborative Learning: Making the Most of Knowledgeable Peers," Change March/April 1987, pp. 42-47.Reprinted with permission of the Helen Dwight Reid Educational Foundation. Published by Heldref Publications, 1319 Eighteenth St., N.W., Washington, D.C. 20036-1802. Copyright © 1987.

Donald A. Daiker, "Learning to Praise," in Writing and Response: Theory, Practice, and Research, Chris M. Anson, ed., NCTE, 1989. Copyright © 1989 by the National Council of Teachers of English. Reprinted with permission.

James L. Kinneavy, "The Basic Aims of Discourse," College Composition and Communication, December 1969. Copyright © 1969 by the National Council of Teachers of English. Reprinted with permission.

Richard Larson, "Making Assignments, Judging Writing, and Annotating Papers: Some Suggestions," in Training the New Teacher of College Composition, Charles W.

Bridges, ed., NCTE, 1986. Copyright © 1986 by the National Council of Teachers of English. Reprinted with permission.

Chris Madigan, "Applying Donald Murray's 'Responsive Teaching,'" <u>College Composition and Communication</u>, February 1988. Copyright © 1988 by the National Council of Teachers of English. Reprinted with permission.

Thomas Newkirk, "The First Five Minutes: Setting the Agenda in a Writing Conference," in <u>Writing and Response: Theory, Practice, and Research</u>, Chris M. Anson, ed., NCTE, 1989. Copyright © 1989 by the National Council of Teachers of English. Reprinted with permission.

Joy Reid, "Teaching Composition to Speakers of Other Languages: An Overview," from <u>Simon & Schuster Handbook for Writers</u> by Lynn Quitman Troyka, Simon & Schuster, 1993. Reprinted by permission.

Marie Secor, "Modes of Thinking, Modes of Argument," in <u>The Writer's Mind: Writing as a Mode of Thinking</u>, Hays, et al., eds., NCTE, 1983. Copyright © 1983 by the National Council of Teachers of English. Reprinted with permission.

Daniel Sheridan, "Changing Business as Usual: Reader Response in the Classroom, <u>College English</u>, November 1991. Copyright © 1991 by the National Council of Teachers of English. Reprinted with permission.

Frank Smith, from <u>Understanding Reading</u>, 4th ed. pp. 6-9, 16-19. Reprinted by permission of Lawrence Erlbaum Associates, Inc.

Jeffrey Sommers, "Bringing Practice in Line with Theory: Using Portfolio Grading in the Composition Classroom" reprinted by permission of Jeffrey Sommers. In Pat Belanoff and Marcia Dickson, eds. <u>Portfolios: Process and Product</u>. (Boynton/Cook Publishers, Inc., Portsmouth, NH, 1991).

Nancy Sommers, "Revision Strategies of Student Writers and Experienced Adult Writers," <u>College Composition and Communication</u>, December 1980. Copyright © 1980 by the National Council of Teachers of English. Reprinted with permission.

Josephine Koster Tarvers, "The Composing Process: An Overview," in <u>Simon & Schuster Handbook for Writers</u>, by Lynn Quitman Troyka, 3rd ed. Copyright © 1993, pp. AIE 1-7. Reprinted by permisson of Prentice Hall, Upper Saddle River, New Jersey.

Lynn Quitman Troyka, "Closeness to Text: A Delineation of Reading Processes as They Affect Composing." In <u>Only Connect: Uniting Reading and Writing</u>, ed. Thomas Newkirk, Boynton/Cook Publishers, Inc., Portsmouth, NH, 1986. Reprinted by permission of Lynn Quitman Troyka and Heinemann/Boynton Cook Publishers.

Part I: Teaching Guide

Teaching Guidelines and Assumptions

Most beginning teachers of composition are no longer handed a textbook, pointed toward a classroom, and given a wave of the hand and a cheery "Good Luck!" New teachers usually enroll in a class in the teaching of composition, take seminars on teaching, and have the support of composition faculty who teach composition themselves and know how to help beginning teachers. Even with a support group, however, beginning teachers should take advantage of the wealth of published information about teaching composition. If I could mail a care package to every beginning (or even experienced) teacher of composition, it would contain the following.

Composition Teacher's Survival Kit

Lindemann, Erika. A Rhetoric for Writing Teachers. 4th ed. New York: Oxford Univ. Press, 2001.

Villaneuva, Victor. Cross-Talk in Composition Theory: A Reader. Urbana: NCTE, 1997.

Corbett, Edward, Nancy Myers, and Gary Tate, Gary, eds. The Writing Teacher's Sourcebook. 4th ed. New York: Oxford Univ. Press, 2000.

Lindemann's book is an excellent introduction to the field of composition and to some of the practical concerns of teaching and evaluating writing. But there are so many first rate books that the package might well contain several alternatives or additions to Lindemann: Donald Murray's A Writer Teaches Writing, Thomas Newkirk's Nuts and Bolts, or Peter Elbow's Writing Without Teachers.

Villaneuva's collection of essays has both classic and contemporary essays on key topics such as the writing process, discourse, developmental schemes, voice, and rhetoric and ideology that provide an excellent background for discussing the theoretical concerns underlying classroom pedagogies.

The Writing Teacher's Sourcebook edited by Edward Corbett, Nancy Myers, and Gary Tate, contains a wide range of essays on both theoretical and practical matters. From it--or other excellent collections of essays described in the Bedford bibliography--teachers can quickly see major trends and assumptions about the teaching of writing. This collection provides teachers with an introduction to the major issues in the field and with good background reading for essays currently appearing in periodicals such as College Composition and Communication.

One other resource of increasing importance to both writers and teachers are the many excellent OWLs (Online Writing Laboratories) available on the internet. On these sites, you will find an incredible array of kinds of advice, resources for writers, and internet links. Colorado State University has an excellent site at http://www.colostate.edu/Depts/WritingCenter.

Finally, becoming a member of NCTE and attending one of the many regional or national conferences will continue the dialogue established in the teaching seminar on problems and questions about contemporary issues in composition teaching.

In the past four decades, composition teaching has transformed itself from a drab stepsister of literary instruction into a dynamic and even fashionable muse of thinking, learning, and writing. Good composition teachers no longer need to spend long nights in the cinders of ennui and despair, marking comma splices and spelling errors in five-paragraph essays; they teach critical thinking, cultural diversity, writing across the curriculum, computers and writing, collaborative writing and learning, internet researching and evaluation, and processes for integrating reading, writing, and learning. Lindemann's book, the Bedford bibliography, and the short bibliography in this teaching guide cite sources that fully explain each of these exciting dimensions of the field of composition.

Theory and Assumptions behind The Prentice Hall Guide

Theory is not separable from practice. Whether you care to recognize them or not, certain theoretical assumptions are behind any textbook or teaching strategy. Most teachers are more comfortable if they can articulate the assumptions and purposes behind their methods and the text they are using.

The capsules that follow list only the most obvious assumptions--especially those that diverge from the stated or unstated assumptions behind other popular textbooks.

• Writing should be taught in a rhetorical context. The writer's purpose or aim, the expectations of the audience or readers, and the conventions of genre or form should guide the writing (and evaluating) process.

• Purposes for writing relate both to the writer and the audience. Purposes for the writer include expressing, remembering, observing, learning, and discovering. Purposes related to the audience move on a continuous scale from informing to explaining to arguing or persuading. Entertaining or pleasing the writer or reader can be added to any other purpose. **The Prentice Hall Guide** is structured by a cumulative sequence of purposes for writing.

• Teachers should focus on both the process of writing (conceived of as both an individual and social phenomenon) and the product of writing. Although process is important from the writer's point of view, process should not be a goal in itself. Teachers should not "teach the writing process"; instead, they should use writing processes to teach students to solve problems as they write.

• Strategies for writing, such as comparison-contrast and process analysis, should be <u>means</u> for writing and thinking rather than <u>ends</u> or <u>purposes</u>. Essay assignments should set evaluation rather than comparison-contrast as a goal or purpose for writing.

• Writing courses even at the college level should draw on both expressive (or private) and transactional (or public) kinds of writing. **The Prentice Hall Guide** is structured on the assumption that transactional writing develops, naturally, from expressive writing.

• Writing courses should teach critical and imaginative thinking skills and careful revising and editing skills. Critical thinking is integral to good writing and learning; they occur simultaneously and are mutually interdependent. **The Prentice Hall Guide** stresses critical thinking throughout the writing process, but it does not neglect revising and editing skills.

• Teachers should develop their students' critical reading skills. **The Prentice Hall Guide** describes collaborative reading/writing activities and peer review exercises that reinforce the connections between reading and writing. Teaching tips, journal exercises, and questions following essays encourage students to annotate professional essays and then apply their critical reading skills to revising their own essays as well as their peers' essays.

• Teachers need to introduce students to new technologies that are a part of reading, writing, and communicating in the computer age. Networks, discussion forums, email, internet access, and evaluation of internet sources are all skills students need in the 21st century.

Basic Guidelines for Teaching Writing

These guidelines will make more sense as you gain experience and confidence in the classroom, so read these before you begin teaching and again <u>after</u> you have taught for a few weeks. The following sections of this guide develop each of these ideas with specific strategies and handouts for your class.

On Your Role as Teacher

• In the classroom, be absolutely honest about what you know or don't know. To be a good writing teacher, you don't necessarily have to assume the role of the Expert or Writing Guru. Students already know quite a bit about the language. Let them teach you--and the rest of the class--what they already know (or need to know).

• Resist the temptation to listen to the sound of your own wonderful voice lecturing. To be a good writing teacher, you don't have to lecture fascinatingly about the aesthetics of non-fiction prose or about the intricacies of verb tenses and dangling modifiers. To teach writing effectively, you do need to <u>listen</u> to your students and carefully <u>read</u> what they are writing.

• Writing teachers should be coaches, not dictators. A writing teacher helps other writers communicate their ideas. A writing teacher gradually makes himself or herself dispensable by teaching writers to recognize and solve the problems they confront during the writing process.

• Writing teachers should write. They should model for their students not just their completed essays or products but their own processes for writing--halting, recursive, or stumbling though the composing process may be. Writing teachers should be part of the community of writers that they guide.

On the Structure of Your Class

• A writing class should be more like a laboratory or workshop session than a lecture course. Simply transforming a class into a workshop, however, does not make it easy to plan and run. Spend your preparation time designing sequences of writing, reading, discussion, or workshop activities that will enable students to learn what you would like just to tell them.

• Be sure to connect any "lesson" or material to be covered to the students' own writing. If you are discussing professional essays, relate the essay's strategies or topics to the students' drafts. (The reverse is also true: What students write will help them "connect" with essays or literature they are reading.) If you are teaching a professional essay, review techniques and strategies and then ask students to apply what they learned to their own drafts. If you are reviewing punctuation or usage, cover a few rules and then ask students to look for those problems as they edit their own--and other's--writing.

• Writing improvement is achieved by both individual practice and collaborative writing and learning. Use collaborative groups to balance (but not eliminate) writing performed by a single individual.

• Use writing-to-learn as one of your teaching strategies. Before discussing an essay, for example, ask students to describe, in their journals, a similar experience. At the end of a discussion session, ask students to write one question they still have. When students read each other's papers, ask them to write a short summary of the paper before offering feedback to the writers.

• Remember that individual students have different learning styles. Some learn quickly by reading, some through discussion, some by hands-on experience, some by drawing or diagramming, some by reading aloud or listening, some by a combination of styles. Draw on a variety of these styles as you plan your classes.

On your Role as Audience and Evaluator

• Establish clear standards and criteria for your evaluation of writing (Students can help generate and articulate these criteria.) Encourage students to use these criteria as they revise their own and other students' writing. There should be no "hidden agendas" in the evaluation of writing.

• Give your most careful written responses to drafts, when students can test and apply your suggestions and comments. Your intervention during the writing and revising process should, along with peer responses, receive more emphasis than comments on final drafts.

• Let your responses to drafts and final products be guided by the writer's sense of purpose, audience, and form. Your evaluation should begin by estimating how successfully the writer has achieved his or her purpose for that particular audience.

• Although you may feel torn between your "enabling" role as a coach and your "judgmental" role as evaluator, the roles are not really in conflict. As a coach, you encourage students during the writing process by offering advice, pointing out weak areas, and suggesting revision strategies. As an evaluator of a written product, you praise strengths and note weaknesses. You work just as hard communicating your high standards for writing as you do encouraging students to do their best. Excellence is a single standard.

Course Syllabi, Policy Statements, Lesson Plans

Because each chapter in **The Prentice Hall Guide** contains writing process advice, the text adapts remarkably easily to a variety of course plans. The sequence of the chapters (from personal, informal writing to more formal, academic expository and argumentative writing) enables instructors to design a theoretically and pedagogically sound course. Instructors can emphasize the personal writing in the early chapters, the expository and argumentative middle chapters, or the final research chapter. An interpretative literary essay can be added as appropriate. Most syllabi begin with Chapters 1 and 2, then skip some chapters or assign selected readings and journal entries from those chapters not crucial to the focus of the course. In each of the plans described below, the number of total essays is kept low (four to five essays) so that students and teachers have sufficient time for critical reading of professional essays in each chapter and for several drafts of student essays.

Sample Course Syllabi
One Semester Course: Expository and Argumentative Writing

The focus in this syllabus is on expository and argumentative writing. Students read essays from each chapter to build critical reading skills. The problem solving or arguing essays involve some research, but the syllabus does not require a formal research paper. Instructors assign either an observing or a remembering essay. The reading and investigative chapters familiarize students with summarizing, interviewing, and surveying.

Week 1:   Course introduction; Read Chapters 1, 2; Assign diagnostic
          essay.
Week 2:   Discuss writing myths and rituals; Discuss purpose, process,
          audience; Read Chapters 3, 4 and do selected journal entries.
Week 3:   Assign observing or remembering essay; Model
          collaborative peer workshops; Begin collecting and shaping.
Week 4:   Collecting and shaping workshops; Observing or
          remembering essay due.
Week 5:   Chapters 5 & 6 and readings; Authority list; Summary-
          response journal entries. Practice interviews questionnaires
          for one topic on list.
Week 6:   Chapter 7 and readings; Assign explaining essay; Assign
          selected journal entries.
Week 7:   Workshops on collecting and shaping for explaining essay;
          Conferences; Editing workshops; Explaining essay due.
Week 8:   Chapter 8 and readings: Assign evaluating essay;
          Discuss interviews, questionnaires.
Week 9:   Do workshops on collecting and shaping for evaluating essay;
          Revised draft collected.
Week 10: Revision of evaluating essay, based on peer and teacher
          responses; Revision and editing workshops; Evaluating essay due.
Week 11: Chapters 9, 10 and readings; Problem solving or arguing essay;
          Workshops on generating and focusing topics selected earlier.
Week 12: Chapter 12 and readings; Discuss research strategies;
          Library research on topics.
Week 13: Conferences on topics; In-class discovery draft; Peer and
          teacher responses to draft.
Week 14: Workshops on collecting, shaping, documenting sources;
          preparing Works Cited page; Editing workshops.
Week 15: Arguing or problem solving essay due; Discuss final.

One Semester Course: Personal and Expository Writing

The following course outline requires, in addition to assigned chapters and readings, five essays (observing, remembering, summarizing, explaining, and writing about literature). It emphasizes journals, collaborative peer work, conferences and extensive revision.

Week 1: Course introduction; Read Chapters 1, 2; Assign diagnostic essay.

Week 2: Discuss writing myths and rituals; Discuss purposes and processes for writing; Assign selected journal entries.

Week 3: Chapter 3 and readings; Assign observing essay and journal entries; Model collaborative peer response workshops.

Week 4: Do workshops on collecting and shaping for observing essay Editing workshops; Observing essay due.

Week 5: Chapter 4 and readings; Assign remembering essay and selected journal entries.

Week 6: Do workshops and discussion of collecting and shaping for remembering essay; Revised draft collected.

Week 7: Revision of remembering essay, based on peer's and teacher's suggestions; Revision and editing workshops; Conferences.

Week 8: Chapter 5 and readings; Assign summary-response essay;

Week 9: Assign Chapter 6; practice interviewing and finding sources for explaining essay. Investigating journal entries due.

Week 10: Chapter 7 and readings; Assign explaining essay; Do selected journal entries.

Week 11: Do workshops on collecting and shaping for explaining essay; Revised draft collected; Conferences on revision plans.

Week 12: Extensive revision of explaining essay, based on peers' and teacher's suggestions.

Week 13: Chapter 12 and readings; Assign final essay: writing about literature.

Week 14: Workshops on collecting and shaping; Conferences; Editing workshops

Week 15: Interpretation of literature essay due; Discuss final exam.

One Semester Course: Argumentative Writing and Research

This syllabus concentrates on academic, research-based writing. Course is most effective when students select one or two topics to write on for the entire semester. Early investigating, explaining, and evaluative essays should focus on the topic used for research essay. In addition to practicing critical reading skills in each chapter, students write four complete essays with extensive revisions.

Week 1: Course introduction; Read Chapters 1, 2; Assign diagnostic essay and journal entries on possible semester topics.

Week 2: Discuss purpose, process, and academic audiences for tentative semester topics; Conferences on topics; Library intro.

Week 3: Chapter 6 and readings; Investigative essay; Journal entries on writing summaries and questionnaires. Practice interviews.

Week 4: Workshops on collecting and shaping for investigating essay; Library orientation; Editing workshops; Investigating essay due.

Week 5: Chapter 7 and readings; Assign explaining essay on limited aspect of semester topic; Library research.

Week 6: Workshops on collecting and shaping for explaining essay; Revised draft collected; Conferences on revision plans.

Week 7: Extensive revision of explaining essay, with reference sources cited in text. Explaining essay due.

Week 8: Chapter 8 and readings; Assign essay evaluating sources; Journal entries.

Week 9: Read Chapter 12; Review collected resources; start research log for major paper.

Week 10: Chapters 9, 10 and readings. Assign major research paper, either problem solving or arguing.

Week 11: Workshops on collecting and shaping of research essay; Conferences on topics.

Week 12: Summaries of research articles; In-class discovery draft of research topic.

Week 13: Workshops on drafts of research essays; Collaborative peer response; Conferences on revision plans.

Week 14: Extensive revision of research essay; Peer editing work on revised versions.

Week 15: Research essay due; Postscripts on essays; Essays sent to appropriate audience.

Two Semester Course:
First Semester: Personal and Expository Writing

Many college writing courses have a cross-curricular or academic writing goal. Personal writing is important, but ultimately, teachers hope the first-year course helps students learn to read critically and write analytically. Because students have difficulty writing for an academic discourse community, the critical research skills should not be left to one "research" essay at the end of the year, but should be taught bit by bit throughout a two semester sequence. The following two semester outline assumes that "research" (including the "I-search" of personal writing as well as field observation and library research) is an integral part of every essay.

Week 1:   Course introduction; Read Chapters 1, 2; Assign diagnostic essay.
Week 2:   Discuss writing myths and rituals; Discuss purposes and
          processes for writing; Assign selected journal entries.
Week 3:   Chapter 3 and readings; Assign observing essay and journals;
          Model collaborative peer workshop groups.
Week 4:   Workshops on collecting and shaping for observing essay;
          Editing workshops; Observing essay due.
Week 5:   Chapter 4 & readings; Assign remembering Essay & journals.
Week 6:   Workshops and discussion of collecting and shaping for
          remembering essay; Revised draft collected.
Week 7:   Revision of remembering essay, based on peer's and teacher's
          suggestions; Revision and editing workshops; Conferences.
Week 8:   Chapter 5 and readings; Write summary response journal entry;
          Assign selected pages from Chapter 6. Practice interviews and do
          library orientation.
Week 9:   Workshops on collecting and shaping for investigative essay
          Editing workshops; Investigating essay due.
Week 10: Chapter 7 and readings; Assign explaining essay; Do selected
          journal entries; Assign Chapter 12 and research log.
Week 11: Workshops on collecting and shaping for explaining essay;
          Revised draft collected; Conferences on revision plans.
Week 12: Extensive revision of explaining essay, based on peer's and
          teacher's suggestions; Documenting sources; Editing workshops.
Week 13: Chapter 11 and readings; Assign writing about literature essay.
Week 14: Workshops on collecting & shaping; Conferences.
Week 15: Interpretation of literature essay due; Discuss final exam.

Two Semester Course
Second Semester: Argumentative and Research Writing

This course begins with a review of Chapter 7, Explaining, and then moves through the argumentative and research chapters. Some research is required for every essay after the first, but there is no long "research paper" as such. If instructors wish to assign a complete research paper, they should combine the problem solving and arguing papers, thus giving students the necessary six weeks to do a thorough job with extended library and field research.

Week 1: Course introduction; Review Chapters 1, 2; Assign
          diagnostic essay and journal entries on cross-curricular topics.
Week 2: Review purpose, process, and academic audiences for cross
          curricular topics; Conferences on topics; Library
          orientation.
Week 3: Review Chapters 5 & 6; Assign explaining essay in Chapter 7;
          Journal entries on possible explaining topics. Read Chapter 12.
Week 4: Workshops on collecting and shaping for explaining essay;
          Library/field research; Editing workshops; Explaining essay due.
Week 5: Chapter 8 and readings; Assign evaluating essay; Library and
          field research.
Week 6: Workshops on collecting and shaping for evaluating essay;
          Revised draft collected; Conferences on revision plans.
Week 7: Revision of evaluating essay, with reference sources
          cited in text; Editing workshops; Evaluating essay due.
Week 8: Chapter 9 and readings; Assign problem solving essay;
          Journal entries; Library and field research.
Week 9: Workshops on collecting and shaping for problem solving
          essay; Assign research log.
Week 10: Revision of problem solving essay. Conferences on revision
          plans; Editing workshops; Problem solving essay due.
Week 11: Chapter 10 and readings; Assign arguing essay; Journal
          entries; library and field research; Assign research log.
Week 12: Workshops on collecting and shaping of arguing essay;
          Conferences on topics; Editing workshops.
Week 13: Summaries of research articles; In-class discovery draft of
          arguing topic.
Week 14: Workshops on in-class drafts of arguing essays;
          Collaborative peer responses.
Week 15: Arguing essays due; Discuss final examination.

One Quarter Course: Expository and Argumentative Writing

The focus in this syllabus is on expository and argumentative reading and writing. During a quarter, time for extensive library research is minimal, so students should rely more on personal experience, surveys, and interviews. Instructors assign either an observing or a remembering essay, and conclude the course with either a problem solving or arguing essay. Investigating essay familiarizes students with basic research methods.

Week 1:   Course introduction; Read Chapters 1, 2; Assign diagnostic essay; Discuss purpose, process, audience.

Week 2:   Chapters 3, 4 and readings; Journal entries; Assign observing or remembering essay.

Week 3:   Collecting and shaping workshops; Observing or remembering essay due.

Week 4:   Chapter 6 and readings; Investigating essay summarizing article or profiling a person; Practice interviews and writing summaries.

Week 5:   Workshops on investigating essay; Conferences; Editing workshops; Investigating essay due.

Week 6:   Chapter 7 and readings; Assign explaining essay; Assign selected journal entries.

Week 7:   Workshops on collecting and shaping for explaining essay; Conferences; Explaining essay due.

Week 8:   Chapters 9 or 10 and readings: Assign problem solving or arguing essay; Discuss field and library research.

Week 9:   Workshops on collecting and shaping for problem solving or arguing essay; Conferences.

Week 10: Revision and editing workshops; Problem solving or arguing essay due.

Two Quarter Course
First Quarter: Personal and Expository Writing

Many schools have a separate quarter course devoted to research paper writing, so the following course outlines incorporate only minimal amounts of field and library research. The first quarter emphasizes personal and expository writing and the second quarter focuses on critical reading, research techniques, and expository/argumentative writing.

Week 1: Course introduction; Read Chapters 1,2; Assign diagnostic essay; Discuss purpose, process, audience.

Week 2: Chapter 3 and readings; Assign observing essay and selected journal entries.

Week 3: Collecting and shaping workshops on essay; Editing workshops; Observing essay due.

Week 4: Chapter 4 and readings; Assign remembering essay and journal entries.

Week 5: Workshops on collecting and shaping for remembering essay; Conferences.

Week 6: Chapters 5, 6 and readings; summary-response journal article on profiling a person; Practice interviews.

Week 7: Assign Chapter 6 and readings; Practice interviews; Conferences; Investigating topic proposal due.

Week 8: Chapter 7 and readings; Assign explaining essay; Assign selected journal entries.

Week 9: Workshops on collecting and shaping for explaining essay; Conferences.

Week 10: Revision workshops on explaining essay; Explaining essay due.

Two Quarter Course
Second Quarter: Expository and Argumentative Writing

For the second quarter course, some instructors prefer to have students choose one or two topics for investigation for the entire term. Students can then write at least two papers on different areas (or different purposes/audiences) for each topic.

Week 1:   Course introduction; Review Chapters 1, 2; Assign diagnostic essay and journal entries on cross curricular or quarter topics.

Week 2:   Review Chapter 7; Assign explaining essay; Journal entries on possible explaining topics. Read Chapter 10; Library orientation.

Week 3:   Workshops on collecting and shaping for explaining essay; Library/field research; Editing workshops; Explaining essay due.

Week 4:   Chapter 8 and readings; Assign evaluating essay; Library and field research.

Week 5:   Workshops on collecting and shaping for evaluating essay; Conferences; Evaluating essay due.

Week 6:   Chapter 9 and readings; Assign problem solving essay; Journal entries; Library and field research.

Week 7:   Workshops on collecting and shaping for problem solving essay; Conferences; Problem solving essay due.

Week 8:   Chapter 10 and readings; Assign arguing essay; Journal entries; library and field research; Assign research log.

Week 9:   Workshops on collecting and shaping of arguing essay; Conferences on topics; Editing workshops.

Week 10: Arguing essays due; Discuss final examination.

Administrative Matters and Policy Statements

Any experienced teacher will tell you that Murphy's Law controls a composition classroom: Whatever can go wrong will go wrong. Essay assignments will not work; students will disappear and show up a month later; collaborative group projects will fizzle or explode in your face; and students will challenge your authority. One fact of life you can count on: Students will seem obsessed in general about grades and in particular about their grade on the last essay or their grade in the course. An explicit policy statement is the best protection against Murphy's Law and against grade complaints by students.

On the positive side, a thorough policy statement shows that you have carefully planned your course, determined which activities or essays are most important, and carefully communicated your standards to your students. Think of your policy statement as a contract between you and your students. It spells out the commitments agreed upon by both teacher and student.

As you write your own policy statement, pay attention to your tone and attitude. Remember that your policy statement should not be just a legal document describing a prison sentence for your students. Be sure to include your side of the contract: How you will grade, how much assignments are worth, and when you will return papers. Also, be positive about the value of the course and your willingness to help. Let students know that you are eager to help them improve their writing.

Use the following sample policy statement as a guide. Revise as necessary for your particular course and your students.

Policy Statement　　　　**English 101 Sec 19**　　　**Spring 2003**

Instructor: Ms. Norris
Office: 345 Aylesworth Hall　　　Office Hours: 2-4 MWF & by appt.
Office Ph: 221-6723　　　　　　Writing Center: 130 Johnson Hall
English Office Ph: 221-6420　　　Computer Lab: 300 Eddy Bldg.

Course Description

English 101 is a workshop class in essay writing designed to prepare you for the college academic community. It will improve your critical reading skills and teach you processes and strategies for writing expository and argumentative prose. You will learn to develop and support a main idea or claim for an audience. You will practice strategies for selecting and focusing on a topic, collecting ideas, shaping and organizing your thoughts, supporting your ideas with evidence, and revising and editing to strengthen your writing and clarify your style.

Required Texts and Materials

The Prentice Hall Guide for College Writers, 6/e (Prentice Hall), Reid
 (Bring this text to every class.)
Purpose and Process: A Reader for Writers 4/e (Prentice Hall), Reid
A College Dictionary
2 pocket folders for submitting essays
Journal, consisting of 1 pocket folder with loose leaf, lined paper. (Bring your journal to class every day.)

Prerequisites

To enroll in English 101, you must have taken the English Placement Examination and been placed in E 101. If you have not yet taken the placement examination, go to the English Department, 359 Eddy Bldg.

Course Policies

Attendance: In this course, you are expected to help others with their writing as well as revise your own writing. You must, therefore, attend all class sessions. Missing class on a day when an essay draft is due will reduce your essay grade by a full letter. More than three absences will lower your final course grade. Excessive absence will result in failure of the course. If you miss a class, you are responsible for getting the assignment from another member of the class. If you know you will miss class because of illness or another commitment, please call me and leave a message <u>before</u> you miss class. Please do not arrive late to class.

Late Papers: In order to treat all students fairly, late papers <u>cannot be accepted</u>. The grade will be zero and the paper is not revisable. In case of a legitimate problem, contact me at least one day <u>before</u> the due date.

Submitting Essays: On assigned due dates, remember to submit all required materials in a <u>pocket folder</u>: final draft (typed and double spaced), postscript, rough draft(s), workshop sheets, revision plans, photocopies of sources, collecting notes, and relevant journal entries.

Returning Graded Essays: I will return your graded essays within 7-10 days after you hand them in. Usually, I will ask you to respond, in your journals, to the comments made on your papers.

Workshops: All essays will be workshopped in class. Essays without workshop response will drop one full grade.

Conferences: Several conferences are required during the term. Please sign up and bring your text and folder containing all your notes and drafts. Missing a conference appointment is the same as missing class.

Journals: Please keep your journal entries on loose sheets of lined paper (not on spiral notebook paper) in a pocket folder. Place new entries (ones I have not yet read) in the left hand pocket; put old entries on the right side. I will collect your journal approximately every two weeks. Journals are graded S or U. Bring your journals to class everyday.

Plagiarism: You are expected to give and receive help in this class, but all written work must be your own. Read the section on plagiarism in the <u>PHG</u>. If you plagiarize, in whole or part, from library or field sources or from other student's essays, or if you fail to document properly, <u>the minimum penalty is an F for the essay</u>. You might also be placed on probation or expelled from the university. If you have any questions about plagiarism, ask before you act.

Writing Center: The Writing Center is located in 106 Eddy Bldg. The hours of the center are posted on my office door. Please do not hesitate to use the tutor's assistance. Remember to bring a copy of your assignment and your drafts to any Writing Center conference.

Computer Lab: English 101 is a computer-assisted course. If you are not using your own computer, sign up for computer times at the lab in 300 Eddy. If you cannot use a computer, please check with me at the beginning of the course.

Course Grading: Your grade in this course will be based on the following:

Remembering Essay	100 pts./10%
Summary/Response Assignment	50 pts./ 5%
Explaining Essay	150 pts./15%
Evaluating Essay	150 pts./15%
Problem Solving/Arguing Essay	150 pts./15%
Major Revision	100 pts./10%
Assignment & Reading Quizzes	50 pts./ 5%
Journal	100 pts./10%
Class Attendance & Participation	100 pts./10%
Final Examination (In-Class Essay)	50 pts./ 5%

Total pts. = 1000

A Final Note: I want you to use your time and effort in this class as positively as possible, to read and write about topics relevant to your personal and academic interests. Most of the members of this class are not English majors, so I am not expecting that you become literary critics. Wherever possible, I will encourage you to learn and write about all the other subjects you are taking. If at any time you have a question about your writing, please talk to me after class or at my office.

"Curiosity is my natural state and has led me headlong into
    every worthwhile experience . . . I have ever had."

--Alice Walker

"Writing and rewriting are a constant search for what it is
    one is saying."
                            --John Updike

Writing Lesson Plans

Your department probably provides a general syllabus outlining number and kinds of essays, required reading, due dates, and class topics. You may even have a detailed, day-by-day schedule to guide your own class. As the semester progresses, however, you will need to adjust this syllabus to meet the needs of your own students. Perhaps you need to stop and review or clarify an assignment. Perhaps students need more time collecting or researching. Perhaps they need an additional day for revision. Inevitably, you will have to modify your class plans, speed up, slow down, or change directions. When that happens, you'll need to design your own lesson plans more or less from scratch.

Writing your own lesson plans requires choosing from a variety of possible activities those most likely to help your students at that particular time. The main problem usually is not finding something to fill class time but finding activities and then <u>sequencing</u> them so that they benefit the actual writing that your students are doing.

To illustrate how to put a class plan together, first look at the <u>possible class activities</u>. Then think about a <u>sequence</u> for those activities that makes sense for your students. Finally, put the sequenced activities together in a <u>lesson plan</u> that is appropriate for your class.

Possible Class Activities

• Giving a <u>writing assignment</u>, explaining the assignment, and doing some prewriting.

• Reviewing and discussing some <u>feature of rhetoric</u>: purpose, audience, writing situation, shaping strategies, revision, or editing.

• <u>Reading and/or discussing</u> a professional or student essay from the text.

• <u>Modeling</u> for students how to annotate professional or student essays, how to do collaborative annotations, or how to give good advice during a peer workshop.

• Conducting <u>collaborative workshops</u> on some phase of the students' writing process.

• Asking students to do a <u>write-to-learn</u> entry in their journals about some topic under discussion.

• Reviewing <u>handbook</u> items on grammar, punctuation, or conventions of mechanics and usage.

• Allowing students time in class to <u>write plans</u> for their essays or their revisions.

• Giving students time to write a "zero" or discovery draft in class.

• Having students give a short <u>presentation</u> on some aspect of writing.

• <u>Conferencing</u> with students in-class about problems with topic selection, revision, or editing.

Sequences for Class Activities

As you select the activities most appropriate for your class, you need to think about sequencing them or ordering them so that the class is coherent and effective. You should choose a logical sequence within an individual class as well as a sequence for successive class sessions. Three logical patterns of movement are as follows:

1. The writing process sequence.

Writing processes for individual students are not linear or lockstep, but usually students will need help with invention and prewriting during the early stages, help with shaping, organizing, and cueing the audience (as well as additional collecting) in the middle stages, and help with revision and editing strategies toward the later stages. Have your classroom activities follow (or anticipate) the progress of your students' writing.

2. The concept/application sequence.

Following a concept with an application is a time-honored learning strategy. In a writing class, improving the student's writing is the ultimate goal, so all discussions, readings, small group activities should be related to the students' own writing. Every class should ask students to apply what they are learning to their own essays, by taking out their notes or drafts and revising based on what they've learned from the class discussion or group activity.

3. The individual/social sequence.

Experienced writing teachers alternate individual activities (reading essays, writing in journals, drafting, etc.) with social group activities (annotation of texts, peer revision workshops, whole class discussion and synthesis). For example, a class may begin with a short teacher-centered presentation. Then the teacher may ask individuals to write about a topic or ask small groups to do some activity. Then the class as a whole synthesizes and discusses the ideas. Finally, the teacher asks individuals to work by themselves again, applying ideas learned from the group as a whole. The individual-social-individual alternating pattern draws on the strengths of both individual and social strategies for learning and writing.

On the next few pages are lesson plans from a Monday-Wednesday-Friday composition class written by composition staff members for new teachers. These detailed instructions illustrate how to build a logical progression of classes as well as how to sequence activities within an individual class. Remember that estimated times for workshop activities will vary considerably from one activity to the next, or from one instructor to the next. Be prepared with additional activities should you run short of time. More frequently, however, beginning instructors <u>underestimate the length of time required</u> for workshop sessions. Revise the activities and the times in these models to fit your own class. (For specific advice about conducting workshop sessions, see the section on Collaborative Learning and Writing Activities in this instructor's manual.)

Class #8

<u>**Purpose of This Class:**</u>

To review, edit, and collect the Explaining Essay.

To introduce, discuss, and prewrite on Evaluating Essay assignment.

<u>**Activity Sequence:**</u>

(1) Preview; (2) Give assignment; (3) Write postscript; (4) Do editing and collect essays. (5) Introduce Evaluating Essay; (6) Do prewriting and discussion; (7) Make plans and notes.

<u>**Class Activities:**</u>

1. <u>Preview</u> for the students the purpose and activities for today's class.

2. <u>Give the assignment for the next class meeting</u>:

Students continue prewriting, selecting a topic for the Evaluating Essay.

Reading Assignment: Chapter 8, Evaluating. Do two journal entries from #1, #7, or #8.

3. Ask students to write a postscript for their Explaining Essay (5-7 minutes). (Use or adapt the Postscript at the end of Chapter 7.)   The postscript might include a statement of their main idea or thesis, the process they used to write the essay, and their assessment of the strengths and problems in their own essay. After students write their postscripts, discuss what they learned and answer any questions. Students must also have their statement of purpose and audience at the top of the first page.

4. Conduct a short (10 minute) editing workshop on the final drafts. Divide students into pairs. Ask them to concentrate on one aspect of editing (grammar, punctuation, usage, spelling) that you discussed the previous class period. Students should make editing marks (in pencil, using editing marks illustrated in the Handbook section and the inside back cover of **The Prentice Hall Guide**) on the final drafts. After 10 minutes, students should return essays and confer with the writer. If the writer or the editor have any questions, they should raise their hands so the instructor can answer individual questions. During this session, the instructor should be answering student's editing questions, asking students to write sentences with typical problems at the board, and referring students to appropriate sections in the handbook.

Ask students to hand in their essays in their folders, complete with ALL drafts, notes, workshop sheets, postscript, and final version.

5. Introduce the Evaluating Essay (10 minutes). Hand out a sheet with the assignment, schedule of important activities and due dates, and criteria for your grading of the essay. (Remember: the class should discuss and, as

necessary, revise these criteria during the next week or so. Note: See sample assignment sheet in the next section under "Designing Writing Assignments.")

Assignment: Write an evaluation of a campus or community service or organization. The purpose of this assignment is to evaluate the strengths and weaknesses of the organization or service. Possible audiences for this essay include a prospective member of this organization or user of this service, an administrator of the service, or a funding agency for the organization. First, you must use (or have used) the service. In addition, you must do some research for this essay. You must observe the organization or service in operation and you must interview at least one representative from this organization and at least one user of the service. You may also use a survey to collect responses from other members or users and you may use any written sources, including pamphlets and library sources. Be sure to cite your sources accurately in the text of your essay and on a Works Cited page. Copies of interviews, survey results, written sources, and pamphlets MUST be turned in with your final draft. Essay length is approximately 3 pages. Final draft should be typed, double spaced. Essay is due Class #14.

6. Discuss and explain this assignment. Do prewriting and discussion (20 minutes). Hand out copies of your list of local land campus agencies and organizations. Ask students to write in their journals (write to learn) for 5-7 minutes about a campus or community service or organization they have used or participated in. They should jot down basic who, what, when, where information and describe some strengths or weaknesses they've experienced. You may wish to have volunteers read from their journals and/or have two or three volunteers put their notes on the chalkboard or on an overhead so the class as a whole can discuss them. Choose one or two of the organizations and ask students to tell you how they might write their essay, using this service. You (or a student) can act as the recorder at the board. Be sure you cover the following for each possible topic: Purpose, audience, purpose of the organization or service, description of the service, examples illustrating strengths and weaknesses, and possible criteria for evaluating. Be sure to have students explain to you several possible audiences for their essay and how choosing a different audience will change their evaluation.
7. Have students make notes for themselves about what organizations or services they might evaluate (2 minutes).

25

Class #9

Purpose of This Class:
To continue prewriting/collecting on the Evaluating Essay

Activity Sequence:
(1) Preview; (2) Assignment; (3) Journal or advertisement activity; (4) Annotation of essay; (5) Peer workshops; (6) Individual work on plans/answer questions.

Class Activities:
1. Briefly, preview for the students the purpose and activities for today's class.

2. Give the assignment for the next class meeting:

Review collecting and shaping strategies from Chapter 8.
Assign Chapter 6, sections on interviews, surveys, and written sources.
Select a possible organization or service. Begin to gather basic information about the service. Set up interviews.
Hand out sample essay on the Career Services Center; ask students to annotate it as they will practice today in class.

3. Discuss and share journal entries (10 minutes). Ask student volunteers to read from their journal entries. Ask the rest of the students to take notes as they listen about key features of evaluating: purpose, audience, description of thing being evaluated, possible criteria, evidence. After volunteers read, ask other students to read their notes. Record at the board. Discuss process of evaluation.

3. (Possible or alternate activity): You might bring two advertisements for students to practice writing on. Have groups of three work on observing the ads, determining criteria, and gathering evidence (15 minutes). Be sure to spend sufficient time determining the intended audience for evaluation of ads and possible criteria: What are appropriate criteria for an effective magazine ad? How are the ad writers' criteria different from the general public's, or from a particular group, such as parents, social workers, feminists, and so forth? Note that you need several copies and/or large reproductions if the whole class is to respond. As an alternate activity, bring ads for each group

to have. Give group instructions, set time, appoint recorders or reporters, and synthesize following the group work.

4. Individual and group annotation of selected essays (20 minutes). Choose one of the assigned essays from the chapter, and model for students how to annotate the essay for key features of evaluating: Purpose, audience, description, overall claim, criteria, judgments, and data. (The Phyllis Richmann essay, "Hunan Dynasty," already has some model marginal annotations.) Then select another essay and ask students to make individual annotations for 10 minutes. Next, divide class into groups of three and ask students to collate their annotations on one student's essay or (preferably) on a photocopy of the essay you provide each group. (Give specific directions and set time limits, appoint recorder, etc.) Following the group activity, have recorders report to the class and synthesize results at the board. (Another effective strategy is to form new groups that each contain one member of each of the former groups. The new groups synthesize the findings of each of their former groups and report their findings to the class.)

5. Have students work by themselves or in groups of two or three on their own tentative topics (15 minutes). Give students specific instructions. For each student's tentative topic, students should discuss or select specific topic, audience, material needed for description, tentative criteria, possible supporting evidence they might find/have found. Specify exactly what you want them to do before you divide into groups.

6. Have students write out plans (5 minutes or remaining time): when they will visit the organization, whom they might interview, what they might find at the library, what personal experience of their own they might use. Answer questions that students have about the assignment or their topic.

Class #10

Purpose of This Class:
To make sure each student has a workable topic.
To continue collecting and practice shaping for the Evaluative Essay.

Activity Sequence:
(1) Preview; (2) Assignment; (3) Conference sign-up; (4) Workshop annotating student essay; (5) Three column log; (6) Individual work/answer questions.

Class Activities:
1. Briefly, preview for the students the purpose and activities for today's class.

2. <u>Give the assignment for the next class meeting</u>:

Continue to collect information; conduct at least one interview. Write out at least one page of a "zero" or discovery draft for their essay.
For Class #12, following the conference, rough draft of essay is due.

3. Conference sign up. Next class will be a conference over their Evaluating Essay. Announce that the regularly scheduled class will <u>not</u> meet. Students should sign up for 15 minute conference. (Hand out sign up sheet and conference sheet that asks students to write out their tentative topic, audience, what evidence they have done so far; what interviews they have conducted or scheduled; and what questions or problems they have. They should bring their notes and their "zero" draft.)

4. Collaborative workshop over sample student essay. Have students individually annotate copy of student draft for key features of evaluating: purpose, audience, overall claim, description, criteria, judgments, and evidence. Following individual work, have students work in groups of three to compare their annotations and produce a collaboratively annotated version of the essay. Based on their annotations, they should have a recorder write out a specific response to that student assessing strengths and weaknesses of the essay. Final comment should focus on two or three most important things the writer of the essay should do to revise the essay. (Give groups specific instructions and appoint recorder, etc., <u>before</u> dividing into groups.)

5. Discuss how to write a three column log (10 minutes). Have students draw up a three column log for the student essay they read. Then ask two or three student volunteers who have a possible topic for their essay to write a three column log for their own essays at the board. Other students should try to write one for their own tentative topic. (Explain that obviously students don't have the necessary evidence yet to make a clear judgment for each criteria, but they at least need to be thinking about possible criteria.) At the board, have the class critique the tentative three column logs.

6. Ask students to complete working on their own tentative three column logs for their own topics (remaining time). Answer students' questions about their topics.

Class #11

Purpose of This Class:
To conference with students about topics, focus, criteria, evidence, judgments, and problems with drafting.

Activity Sequence:
Give Assignment; Individual conferences.

Class Activities:
1. Give the assignment for the next class meeting:

Remind students that the rough drafts are due the next class meeting.

2. During your conferences, remember that students should do most of the talking. Ask them to explain what they have done and what they intend to do. Review what they have written on the sheet. Ask students how they intend to solve problems they are encountering. Give students suggestions, but don't appropriate their essays.

Class #12

Purpose of This Class:
To conduct workshop on the students' drafts of the Evaluating Essay.
To review grading criteria for the Evaluating Essay.

Activity Sequence:
(1) Preview; (2) Assignment; (3) Evidence and shaping strategies discussion/modeling; (4) Collaborative workshop; (5) Review and revise grading criteria; (6) Individual work.

Class Activities:
1. Briefly, preview for the students the purpose and activities for today's class.

2. Give the assignment for the next class meeting:
Revised draft due next class meeting, along with note and photocopies of sources. Revise introduction and overall claim.

Review paragraph transitions and hooks from Chapter 7.

3.   Shaping strategies and evidence discussion (15 minutes). In class discussion, review possible shaping strategies. (Use a write-to-learn journal entry about text's discussion of shaping, if appropriate.) At the board, outline possible methods for shaping the Evaluating Essay. Next, review kinds of evidence that are necessary or appropriate. Discuss how much description of the organization or service is necessary. Hand out the workshop sheet you will use in the next activity, along with a copy of your draft (or the draft of a student writer not in the class) of the Evaluating Essay. Make sure your draft is rough and has obvious problems. Ask students to use the workshop sheet to give you feedback on your essay. (See sample collaborative workshop sheets.) Explain what kind of advice is helpful for you. Show students how to give specific suggestions about organization or evidence.

4.   Collaborative workshop on organization and evidence (20 minutes). Following your modeling of the workshop sheet, divide students into groups of two or three to exchange drafts and write responses. Give specific instructions before dividing into groups. At the end of the workshop, synthesize their findings. What are the most common problems? How do they intend to solve these problems?

5.   Review and revise grading criteria (10 minutes). Hand out the grading criteria for this essay. [See section on Evaluating Student Writing in this teacher's manual.]   If the criteria are on the assignment sheet (as is suggested), have students review the criteria on the assignment sheet. What does each criterion mean? Which criteria are most important? What suggestions for revising these criteria do the students have? Record definitions of criteria at the board. Jot down the students suggestions for revising. Explain that you will revise the criteria later, based on their suggestions. (Don't change the criteria on the spot, but do revise the grading criteria later, if necessary.)

6.   Individual work on drafts (5 minutes or remaining time). Have students review their notes from class, the grading criteria, and their workshop responses. Based on that information, students should write out a plan for revising their drafts: What additional evidence is needed? How do they intend to reorganize the essay? Go around the class and answer students' questions about their drafts and their revision plans.

Classroom Management Strategies

In addition to having a clear and purposeful class plan, teachers need to develop their repertoires of management strategies to handle everyday activities as well as those occasional crises. Even inexperienced teachers can learn these tricks of the trade.

• Do <u>learn your students' names</u> and use them in class. Do whatever it takes to learn students' names <u>early</u> in the term. Keep a seating chart. Take snapshots of your class and post the pictures in your office. While students do a journal, quietly call on students, have them raise their hands, and write their names on a seating chart. Have students interview each other so you have a personality to attach to a face. Have a conference during the second or third week. Learning and using your students' names is crucial to a successful class.

• Do <u>organize</u> your class and your assignments as clearly as possible. State your expectations clearly. You don't have to be a tyrant or an ogre, but you most be firm, steady, and clear.

• Do work on developing a <u>community</u> in your classroom. Knowing your students' names is a help. Helping students to know each other, through interviews, outside group work, and publishing a list of names and phone numbers, is a good start. Also build on those words and phrases describing effective writing that are special to your class. Acknowledge personalities and special abilities in class. The clearer sense students have of each other and of the personality of the class, the more secure they will feel in class.

• <u>Make the students do the work</u>--and the learning. Students will continually pressure you for the answers. Whenever possible, ask students to give <u>their</u> answers. The more pressure you feel to perform, the more you need to deflect questions back to the students. In class, think of yourself primarily as an asker of questions, a recorder at the board, a designer of group activities, a consensus maker, or a problem solver.

• <u>Get regular feedback</u> from your class about what they are learning. When you hear yourself say, "Who has any questions about that?" and you face a stony silence, ask your students to do a write-to-learn entry in their journal explaining the main point of the preceding discussion. When you hand back

32

essays, invite your students to respond to your marginal notes. Assign regular journal entries asking your students to respond to what they understand about the class and what they find confusing or frustrating. Don't wait until the end of the class to get student feedback; at that point, it's too late to adjust an assignment or change strategies.

• Always plan for that extra activity in case you finish early. Every teacher has a story about finishing his or her lesson plan after only 25 minutes of class, and then, in a moment of panic, dismissing the class for the day.

• Don't use the class for your soapbox. Even though you may believe strongly in certain social, political, or diversity issues, your classroom should be an open forum that respects multiple points of view. Otherwise, half your students will "write what you want" while the other half will believe that they get low grades because you don't "like" what they think.

• Don't be afraid to say, "That's a good question. I don't know." Honesty is always preferable to making up a phony answer that your students will see through. A better strategy, to buy yourself time to think, is to ask the class for input: "What do you [indicating the class] think about that?" Or, "That's a good question. Who knows the answer to that question?"

• Avoid hidden agendas in grading. Regularly and openly, discuss the criteria for grading. Encourage students to give their input to these criteria. Make the students use these criteria as they give each other feedback in workshops.

• When the pressure builds, don't retreat into lecturing. Instead, ask yourself, "What could I have my students do that would help students learn the points I'm lecturing about?" Don't tell students what they should know; do show them by letting them learn.

Collaborative Learning and Writing Activities

Using collaborative groups in the classroom for reading, writing, responding, problem-solving, learning, revising, and editing activities has been the single most influential composition teaching strategy for the past two decades. Collaborative groups give students <u>ownership</u> in their ideas and their writing; they help students <u>learn by teaching</u> each other; and they create small <u>discourse communities</u> within the classroom--and thus imitate real <u>audiences</u> and real <u>response</u> for student and professional writing.

Collaborative groups in the composition classroom are generally of three types. The first and most common is the <u>collaborative workshop</u> or peer review group that focuses on some phase of the writing and revision process. Small groups of students give each other feedback on ideas for topics, for drafts, and for revising and editing. A second type is the <u>collaborative writing</u> group: A few students work together actually writing an essay. They select a topic, apportion collecting duties, pool their prewriting materials, and draft and revise a single essay. The third type is the <u>collaborative learning</u> group. In this third case, the group is not working on any particular essay, but they use the social, collaborative environment to study, describe, review, explain, evaluate, or argue course ideas or concepts. This third type employs write-to-learn strategies, but with the added advantage of social interaction as students write, discuss, interview, reach consensus, and report their findings and decisions.

Keep in mind that these three types overlap in the composition classroom. Collaborative groups often use collaborative writing in the process of giving feedback. Reaching consensus and agreeing on a collaboratively written draft also require collaborative learning. Usually, however, each type of group has a different final purpose. The collaborative workshops assist in the writing and revision process; the collaborative writing groups produce a single written document; and the collaborative learning groups use social interaction and consensus to help students teach each other or agree on key ideas or class policies.

Collaborative Workshops

Collaborative workshops have real advantages over the traditional lecture/discussion method. They bring the all important social dimension into the writing classroom. They encourage critical reading of drafts and positive peer response for effective passages. They give students practice in responding to multiple readers and multiple reactions. They demonstrate the reasons behind revision: The text is simply not communicating to the intended audience.

Although many teachers use collaborative learning and writing strategies, there are some real disadvantages to collaborative peer groups. Some students do not learn efficiently in small groups; uncooperative students often derail small group activities; and students in small groups can give misleading, wrong, and counter-productive advice. Simply adopting the methodology of collaborative learning does not guarantee good writing.

Teachers should use collaborative techniques but should design them carefully, sequence them logically, and supplement collaborative workshops with other learning strategies: some lecture-discussion, some individual writing, some one-on-one conferencing. Following the general guidelines and sample workshop questions below will make your workshop class more effective.

General Guidelines for Workshops

1. Collaborative group work, by definition, is not just any small group of people working together, but a group held together by mutual purpose and benefit. It assumes that <u>negotiation</u> and <u>consensus-building</u> are important; It usually relies on the combined efforts of people with <u>different</u> points of view or <u>different</u> areas of expertise working; and it focuses on some <u>common goal</u> or shared objective.

2. Small groups must respect minority opinions. Groups should agree about their suggestions, or agree to disagree. Recorders or group facilitators should make sure that minority views are recorded and represented to the writer or the class as a whole.

3. As a rule of thumb, use collaborative activities only when they provide some benefit <u>not possible</u> or not effectively achieved through lecture, discussion, or individual work. They should not be used unless students can see some real benefit (response from a reader, tips on collecting or shaping, help on editing, and so forth).

4. Don't limit peer response groups only to editing activities. They can promote critical reading and interpretation of texts. (See the collaborative learning activities suggested on the following pages.) They can help readers read with a writer's eye. They can be effective at the invention or prewriting stage of an essay. They can help students plan global revisions on drafts. They can help teachers revise and articulate evaluation criteria and grading sheets.

5. Collaborative groups work well when they are part of an overall <u>sequence</u> that has some individual writing, reading, or thinking, some small group collaboration, some synthesis with the class as a whole, and some application to the student's reading or writing. One possible revision sequence: Four students in a group each read one essay draft, noting responses to key parts; then the small group reaches agreement (or agrees to disagree) on key features; the group reports to the class about key features of the essay; finally, following class discussion, students individually revise or plan their revisions.

6. Collaborative groups should have a realistic <u>purpose</u> and a clear <u>role</u> for each member of the group. The group activity should promote some realistic goal: discovering ideas for writing, getting feedback on development or organization, or helping each other edit and proofread. Roles should also be clear: One group member may be the writer, another the recorder or person who reports to the class, a third a facilitator who keeps the discussion on track, and so forth.

7. For effective collaborative activities, the teacher is not an instructor but a planner, a writer of clear instructions, a coach or facilitator, a resource provider, and class recorder and synthesizer. Careful planning is crucial. Teachers should carefully define the <u>tasks</u> for collaborative groups. Except when the purpose of the group is to decide how to proceed, teachers should focus on <u>one part</u> of the writing process, set a <u>limited </u>number of questions or tasks, specify a <u>certain length of time</u> and indicate what happens <u>after</u> the group activity.   Teachers should not rely on verbal instructions for workshops, such as "OK, now, everybody get into groups and edit each other's essays!" Instead, they should write instructions at the board or, better yet, hand out workshop sheets (see following pages).

8.   Early in the course, <u>model</u> for the class how peer workshops should operate.   One effective method is as follows: First the teacher hands out a

sheet explaining guidelines for group workshops (see following pages). Then the teacher hands out a workshop sheet for that particular day and takes the class as a whole through the response to the draft. (Note: If possible, the teacher can model with his or her own draft.) Ask one student to be the recorder and write suggestions from the class at the board. Teachers need to show students how to be critical yet constructive. Show the difference between a vague response ("The introduction seems abrupt") and a constructive one ("Why not use a specific, narrative example about your experience as the lead-in?").

9. Collaborative groups of 2-4 are most effective, but larger groups (5-6) can be effective for invention, group brainstorming, or testing pros and cons of argumentative claims. Sometimes teachers choose groups at random, sometimes by common essay topics or interests, or sometimes by group diversity (a verbal student who may not be a good writer, a quiet but good writer, and a struggling writer).

10. Use a variety of types and kinds of collaborative activities. Not all workshops should be driven by consensus making. For example, you may wish to have each person in the group look at a different element in each essay. Person #1 might look just at the introduction or thesis; person #2 might look just at supporting evidence in one main paragraph; person #3 might look at paragraph hooks and transitions; and person #4 might concentrate on clarity of the sentences. Similarly, not all workshops need to have the writer of the essay in the group. Sometimes students are more comfortable writing honest and constructive responses if the writers of the essays are working in a different group. Finally, collaborative groups need not be restricted to the classroom. Some of the most productive sessions occur when students set a meeting time and place outside of class.

On the following pages are one instructor's guidelines for effective groups and another instructor's advice to students about workshopping. You are welcome to use or modify these handouts for your own class.

Hints for Successful Group Activities -- Courtesy of Kate Barnes

1. Write instructions on the board or on a handout.

    Written instructions will help you avoid answering questions about your instructions ten to fifteen times, and students can refer to the instructions if you are busy with another group.

2. Tell students what they'll be doing, why they are doing it, and how long it should take.

    Once students start moving, the thundering noise will prevent any additional messages from getting through, so describe the activity from start to finish before you put them into groups.

3. Instruct students to elect a recorder and a spokesperson before they begin the activity.

4. Lie about the time they have for an activity.

    If you have planned 10 minutes for an activity, tell the students they have 5 minutes. This will elicit groans, whines, and accusing looks, but it will keep them working because they have so little time to do ALL THIS STUFF. Meanwhile, you can stand by with a knowing smile, comforted by the thought that, with luck, you may get done in time.

5. Once the students have divided into groups, gentle but firm reminders like "You all should be reading at this point" will prompt them to stop visiting and to start working.

    Gentle but firm reminders early on will help you to resist the temptation to scream later. Also, staring at your wristwatch intently and remarking, "Gee, there are only two minutes left," can be helpful. (Of course, if you applied hint #4 above, there will actually be four minutes left.)

6. Have your students write the results of the activity in a journal or on a sheet of paper to hand in.

Even though the activity may not be graded, students will often pay more attention to the activity if they know you'll be looking at their work.

7. <u>In addition to the main activity, plan for additional "If you have time" tasks.</u>

This will help prevent groups who have finished their work quickly from sitting (and talking) idly by while other groups are still working.

8. <u>If you ask the students to present their group's work to the class, have the class applaud after each presentation.</u>

Applause not only helps to ease the discomfort, but it also promotes enthusiasm, and it prevents you from having to give well-meant but lame comments in the awkward silence following a presentation.

The sample handout on the following page gives advice to students before they begin collaborative peer workshops. Be sure to follow this handout (and discussion) by **modeling** critical but constructive responses with a student sample or, even better, with a draft of your own essay.

SOME WORDS ON WORKSHOPPING -- courtesy of Dave King

** APPROACH EVERY EDITING JOB AS IF YOU WERE A READER ENCOUNTERING THE WORK FOR THE <u>FIRST</u> TIME. If you become confused as a reader, you need to tell the writer about it. When the reader doesn't understand, the writer hasn't done his or her job.

** WHEN YOU EDIT, DON'T JUST MARK WHAT IS WRONG--FOCUS ON HOW TO HELP THE WRITER <u>SOLVE THE PROBLEM</u>. If something looks or sounds wrong, and you really do not know what the problem is, seek a second opinion. Raise your hand and ask me for help. Between us, we should come up with some helpful advice. If I'm not immediately available, write in the margin, "I think you should see Mr. King about this." Otherwise, give <u>specific</u> advice on how the writer can improve the section of writing.

** "I DON'T WANT TO HURT THE WRITER'S FEELINGS" SYNDROME: Remember: If you say it's good when it isn't, you will hurt this writer's feelings even more when he or she is surprised by a low grade on the essay. He or she will remember that you weren't honest or competent enough as a reader to help him or her revise the draft adequately. But <u>be honest, not cruel</u>.

** HOW CAN I CRITICIZE WITHOUT BEING CRUEL? First, explain how you understood the passage and compare that with the writer's explanation. Next, ask questions: "I'm not sure if you mean X or Y at this point. Could you clarify this for me?" "You seem to be saying . . . here. How does this fit in with your main idea or claim? Make that connection clearer." Finally, give specific advice about problems: "Look again at the essay in the text on p. 148. Why not try that approach for a lead-in?"

** WHAT IF I THINK THE ESSAY IS GREAT? No essay is perfect (ask any professional writer!). You should still be able to offer some advice to strengthen the piece. Where the essay is strong, be sure to point that out; writers learn by recognizing their strengths. But be sure to finish your worksheet by explaining carefully how and why certain parts are strong and how and where they could be even stronger.

Sample Workshop Questions

Below are sample types of questions followed by actual worksheets used to accompany The Prentice Hall Guide. As you design your own workshop sheets, you might select among these types of questions as you write questions appropriate for your particular assignment and for your own students' problems. (For samples of specific Peer Response workshop questions, see Chapters 7-10.)

Writer's Questions Often the writer knows where the problems are and can ask for reader's reactions. Workshop sheets should provide room for the writers to ask one or two questions and the readers to respond.

Writer: What one question would you like your reader to answer?
[Writer writes out his or her question here.]

Reader: Answer the question the writer asks.
[Provide a place on the workshop sheet for the reader to answer the writer's question.]

Reader-response Questions These questions simply ask peer reviewers of an essay to react honestly, as a reader, to the writing. Sample questions are as follows:

The best part of this paper was _____ .

When I finished the essay, I wanted to ask you one question:

One place I disagreed was where you said _____ .

One experience or idea I had that was similar to this was _____ .

When you said _____ , I thought about _____ .

At the beginning of the essay, I thought you were going to discuss _____ , but after I got to the end, I realized that you were discussing _____ .

Descriptive Prompts These questions encourage readers to describe or summarize the passage. Evaluation is never wholly absent from any response, but the purpose of these prompts is primarily to hold a mirror up to the piece of writing. Some possibilities:

The intended audience for this paper is:

The main ideas of this paper, in order, are:

This essay has _____ paragraphs (or sentences).

This essay is written from the point of view of a person who
is _____ . (Profile the narrator.)

Identification or Labeling Questions Students in a group often give conflicting advice because they do not recognize or properly name a rhetorical feature, strategy, or error. Identification questions encourage students to simply label or name features <u>before</u> they judge the effectiveness of the passage.

Write "Lead-in" in the margin next to the writer's lead.

Put ** in the margin next to sentence(s) that contain the
writer's main idea, thesis, or claim.

Write "hook" next to hooks and transitions used at the beginning
of body paragraphs.

Label one example of each of the following uses of the senses:
sight, sound, and touch.

Find a passage containing definition and write "Def" in the margin.

Write "C/C" next to a comparison or contrast that the writer makes.

Write "Fragment" next to one sentence fragment.

Write "Passive" next to one passive voice sentence.

Evaluative Prompts   The responses to these prompts or questions should, ideally, indicate specifically what the reader is reacting to, refer to some stated or implied criteria ("Essays for this audience should/should not have a catchy lead-in"), and suggest a revision. The responses may take the form of pointings (see below), comparisons between the writer's intended purpose and audience, or short written suggestions about focus, development, coherence, or style.

Pointings: Underline any nouns, verbs, details, phrases that are memorable, striking, or effective. Put a wavy line under any words or phrases that are excessively wordy or ineffective. Put parentheses ( ) around sentences that need revision for clarity. Put carets (^) where additional details or examples are needed.

Purpose and audience: One way to evaluate an essay is to compare it with the writer's plans and intentions. Does the paper do what the writer hopes it will do? First, have the writer explicitly state his or her intended purpose and audience. Then have the reader read the essay, without looking at this statement. Then the reader should compare those statements with the actual essay. The reader should then indicate specific passages in which the essay illustrates or fails to illustrate that purpose. The reader should also identify specific passages in which the essay addresses a different audience.

Evaluations of focus, development, coherence, or style: Ask questions that encourage readers to focus on specific passages and to offer concrete revision suggestions.

Show where the writer could use more showing details, images, facts or description. Suggest a revision.

What details are not relevant to the main idea? Explain why they are not relevant. Suggest a revision.

Find one passage where the paragraph hooks and transitions should be clearer. Suggest a revision.

Advice for revision plans: Ask peer readers to locate one or two main areas to concentrate on during a revision.

As you revise this paper, concentrate most on
    a) collecting more examples,
    b) shaping your main paragraphs,
    c) revising sentences for clarity, or
    d) editing and proofreading.

Explain your choice. [Peer reader should explain his or her choice.]

Revision Plan Questions At the end of workshops, ask your students to spend a few minutes writing about the advice they received or about their plans for their revision. If time permits, encourage students to begin revising their essays, based on the workshop responses.

<u>Writer</u>: After you have discussed the suggestions with your other group members, work for 10 minutes on your essay, first planning the changes you want to make and then actually revising your draft.

A Word of Caution Often, teachers design workshop sheets with <u>too many</u> questions for a 20 or 30 minute workshop. Limit your workshop questions to those most appropriate to the writer's stage in the writing process (brainstorming, collecting, shaping, revising, or editing) or to the problems that your students are having with this essay.

Sample Workshop Sheets

On the following pages are sample workshop sheets from instructors who use <u>The Prentice Hall Guide</u>. Note that their prompts combine several types of questions from the samples above. As you write your own workshop sheets, adapt these samples to your own assignments and to your own students. (You will need to give students more space to respond than is provided in these samples.)

Observing Workshop Sheet

Writer _____   Reader _____

Instructions: The writer should fill out the top part of two workshop sheets for the other members of the group. Then each group member should exchange papers and read the drafts of the other two members in your group. Write your responses on this sheet and on the draft itself. You will have 20 minutes.

Writer: In the space below, write two questions that you would like to have your readers answer:
    1.   2.

Reader:

1. Read through the draft twice. Without looking back at the essay, explain what you liked best about the description. Then explain where (refer to specific paragraphs or sentences) you were confused or could not visualize the subject being described.

2. Without rereading the draft, write one sentence stating your perception of the writer's dominant idea. Now look at the draft again. Underline the phrases or sentences that most clearly express the dominant idea.

3. List three observed details that support the dominant idea.
    List one detail that is not relevant to the dominant idea.

4. Make the following "pointings" on this passage: A. Underline vivid words, phrases or images. B. Put a wavy line under vague, abstract, imprecise, or "telling" language.

5. Describe what you think the writer should do first when he or she revises this passage:
    a. Reobserve the subject and add more vivid description.
    b. Try writing from another point of view.
    c. Use more sensory images.
    d. Revise sentences for clarity.

6. Answer the writer's questions, above.

Remembering Workshop Sheet -- Courtesy of Carol Forseth

READER #1   Name: _____
Reader #1 will have 10 minutes.

1. Read the essay.
2. Most essays can be brought to life with dialogue. In the space below, write one or two bits of dialogue for this essay. (For help in punctuating dialogue, see the Walker essay.) Make a note in the writer's draft to show where the dialogue belongs.

3. Pass the essay and this sheet to the next person in your group.

READER #2   Name: _____

Reader #2 will have 10 minutes.

1. Read the essay.
2. What is the main change, contrast, or conflict in the essay? (See Chapter 4 for explanation of change, contrast, or conflict.)

3. Suggest ways to SHOW the central change, contrast, or conflict more clearly. Show by using vivid details, the five senses, images, and emotions. Write your suggestions below.

4. Give the essay back to the writer and discuss, with reader #1, the changes you both suggested.

Writer: After you have discussed the suggestions with your other group members, work for 10 minutes on your essay, first planning the changes you want to make and then actually revising your draft.

Workshop: Observing/Remembering -- Courtesy of Shelley Reid

Instructions: On a separate sheet of paper, write your name and the name of the author whose essay you're reading. Write the answers to the following questions on that sheet, except for those questions which ask you to write directly on the author's draft. At the end of the workshop, return the draft and the evaluating sheet to the author, to be handed in with the final draft. Keep this sheet and answer the final set of questions in your journal. You will have 20 minutes to respond to one other student's draft.

1. Read the FIRST PARAGRAPH ONLY, then stop. What is the general topic with which this essay begins? What dominant idea is stated or suggested? If the first paragraph does not suggest a dominant idea, suggest what the author might do to improve this opening.

2. Read the essay all the way through. Then turn the essay face down, or put it to the side. What specific examples or descriptions are most vivid in your memory? Identify them.

3. Go back through the essay and circle all the words that only TELL rather than SHOW. With a star (*), mark at least three places where the author should add more specific, sensory details to SHOW what he or she means. On the separate sheet of paper, make some suggestions about what kind of information the author should add to these places.

4. Put a question mark (?) in front of any sentence of group of sentences that seems to get off the topic or contradicts the dominant idea suggested in the opening paragraph.

5. If the author were to make only one change, what should it be? Explain your choice.

FOR THE AUTHOR

1. Evaluate the workshop in your journal, focusing on the following questions:
    --Did your reader's interpretation of the dominant idea differ from your own? What might you do to make your main idea clearer?
    --Which of your reader's comments were most helpful? Which least helpful?

--Complete these two sentences:

"Having someone else read my essay was ... because ...."

"Reading someone else's essay was ... because ...."

2. Revise this essay for Tuesday. Think about the suggestions you got today. Add showing details where appropriate. Go back and do another observation for more details if necessary. Rearrange the order. Change your mind. Decide not to change your mind. Whatever. At the very end of the revising process, check for punctuation, spelling, typos, and computos. Put everything--notes, drafts, evaluations, responses, and final copy--in your folder to hand in.

Investigating Essay Workshop

Writer _____   Reader _____

Instructions: The writer should fill out the top part of two sheets for the other members of the group. Then exchange papers and read the drafts of the other two members in your group. Write your responses on this sheet and on the draft itself. You will have 25 minutes.

Writer Fill Out:
The central question that I am investigating is:
My main sources of information are:
One question I'd like my readers to answer is:

Reader Fill Out:
1. Which of the techniques for reporting does the writer most successfully use? Cite examples of each from the writer's draft.

   * Beginning with an interesting title and catchy lead-in

   * Stating the main idea, focus, or key question for the investigation

   * Summarizing or quoting information from sources

   * Readable and informative style and tone (Essay should
       not be argumentative or editorialize.)

2. What I learned from reading this draft was

3. One place where I needed more information was

4. One additional source for information you might investigate is

5. When I read your draft, I realized that I needed to do _____
    in my own essay.

6. For your revision, concentrate on

7. My answer to the question you asked above is

Explaining Workshop Sheet

Writer _____   Reader _____

Writer: Briefly, describe your purpose and your intended audience for this piece of writing.

   In the space below, write the most important question that you still have about your essay.

Reader:

1. Does this essay focus mainly on explaining <u>what</u>, explaining <u>why</u> or explaining <u>how</u>? Refer to specific paragraphs in the draft to support your answer.

2. Identify the paragraph that best explains its subject. Identify the paragraph that least clearly explains its subject. Suggest how the writer might improve the weaker paragraph.

3. Identify the body paragraph that begins with the clearest hook or transition. Identify a body paragraph that lacks a clear hook or transition. Suggest how the writer might improve the hook and transition in the weaker example.

4. Where is the explanation likely to be too simplified (or too complex) for the intended audience? Suggest how the writer might fix this problem.

5. Put a wavy line under sentences that do not read clearly or smoothly. Put parentheses ( ) around sentences that might be omitted. Put a caret (^) where additional detail or explanation is needed.

6. Answer the writer's question.

Evaluating Essay: Interview/Questionnaire Workshop

--Courtesy of Kimberly Miller

Your Name Here _____ (Keep this sheet.)

Instructions: First, all group members should review sections on Interviewing and Writing Questionnaires in Chapter 5.

Then, each group member will explain his or her topic, including the subject(s) evaluated and criteria used. DO NOT REVEAL YOUR CLAIM. Next, the presenter should read each of his or her interview or questionnaire questions aloud and then solicit feedback from the other group members about the questions listed below. Presenters may reveal their claim during the feedback session.   Presenters should record the groups' responses to the questionnaire or interview questions below.

1. Give an oral explanation of your topic, the subjects you are evaluating, and the criteria you are using.

2. Read questionnaire or interview questions aloud, slowly. Other members of the group should listen and take notes.

3. Write down your group member's responses to the following questions:

Interview Feedback

A) Are there other experts or participants I could interview? List them.

B) Are any of my questions biased? Does my opinion show in the interview? Note how the questions might be reworded.

C) Have I asked any "yes/no" questions that will not be productive?

D) What other questions could I ask?

Questionnaire Feedback

A) Are there other sample populations I could use? List them.

B) Are any of my questions biased? How might these questions be reworded to avoid bias?

C) Have I used a good balance of closed vs. open questions?

D) What other questions could or should I ask?

Evaluating Essay Workshop: Collecting and Shaping

Writer _____   Reader _____

Instructions: The writer should fill out the top part of one workshop sheet for his or her essay. Then pass the essay with the worksheet to the other two readers for their responses. After each group member has responded to two essays, discuss your responses with each writer. (Time: 25 minutes)

After each group has discussed each draft, the writer should spend an additional five minutes making plans for a revision. If you have questions about your essay, please raise your hand for help. If time runs out and you still have a question, stop by my office after class.

Writer Fill Out:

Person/Event/Place/Thing Evaluated:

Intended Audience:

Tentative Overall Claim:

1. Write out the basic description or information you need to give about your subject:

2. Do a **three column log** for your topic

Criteria	Possible Evidence	Possible Judgment
a.		
b.		
c.		

3. Reread the shaping strategies in Chapter 8. Which one of the strategies described there might work for your topic? Explain.

<u>Readers Fill Out:</u>

1. Read the description/information given on the previous page. What additional information do you need? What additional information might the writer's audience need? Explain.

Reader #1

Reader #2

2. Examine the criteria in the three column log. What additional criteria might be appropriate? What additional evidence might the writer give? Where might the writer find additional evidence? Explain.

Reader #1

Reader #2

Writer: When you have read the responses on this sheet, discuss your essay with your group. Ask your group members questions about their responses. For the final five minutes, consider which workshop advice makes sense to you. Write, in your journal, your plans for this essay.

Arguing/Problem Solving Essay Workshop -- Courtesy of Dawn Cyr

Writer _____   Reader _____

Instructions: The writer should read his or her paper aloud to a partner. The reader/listener should not interrupt until the writer is finished. Then, together, fill out the workshop sheet, rereading the essay draft as necessary. Discuss the responses you put on the sheet. You have 20 minutes to complete each paper.

1. Describe the intended audience.

2. What is the overall claim of the paper?

3. Write out the thesis statement.

   Is the thesis stated clearly? Does it avoid being vague or wishy-washy?

   Is this thesis arguable or debatable? Why or why not?

4. List the main reasons supporting the writer's claim:

   a.

   b.

   c.

   If you were the audience, would these reasons convince you? Why or why not?

5. List any opposing arguments the writer develops:

   a.

   b.

   c.

   Suggest at least one additional con argument the writer should address.

6.   What argument has the <u>best</u> supporting evidence, statistics, personal examples, observed detail, quotations from authorities, and so forth? What kind of evidence does the writer use?

7. What argument does <u>not</u> have sufficient supporting evidence? Together, think of <u>evidence</u> the writer could use, or <u>sources</u> the writer could use for supporting evidence.   Write suggestions for evidence or possible sources here:

8. Together, the reader and writer should draw up a <u>revision plan</u> for this essay, listing in order the three or four things the writer still needs to do:

    a.

    b.

    c.

Collaborative Writing Groups

Collaborative writing groups are popular with composition teachers because they teach an important real-life skill: Working with other people to produce a co-authored written document. In business, people regularly work together to produce plans and reports for a company. In engineering, research and development teams are the rule. Scientists with different areas of expertise work together on a project report that is collaboratively researched and written. In the humanities and social sciences, investigators sometimes work collaboratively on academic projects.

The Problem Solving chapter of <u>The Prentice Hall Guide</u> illustrates a sample of a collaboratively written essay. Three students, Kristy Busch, Steve Krause, and Keith Wright collaboratively wrote an essay that analyzes the parking problem on their campus and offers a solution. The prewriting materials and drafts illustrate one possible procedure for collaborative writing.

Most teachers agree that collaborative writing is effective for certain purposes and types of papers. It is probably more useful for investigating, problem-solving, and arguing papers than it is for the more personal remembering essay. It allows students as a group to gather substantial amounts of information, and the group dynamics promote critical and creative thinking about possible solutions to a problem or possible pro and con arguments.

Three possible drawbacks to collaborative writing are problems with time, organization, and evaluation. Collaborative writing takes more time than a conventional essay. Since students need to meet several times at various stages during the writing process, two weeks is a bare minimum. Three weeks is optimum.

In addition, collaborative writing requires special planning and organization from both students and teachers. Teachers need to schedule time for both in-class and out-of-class meetings. The collaborative groups must each design a writing plan, and the teacher needs time to oversee and advise the groups to avoid the myriad problems that can occur. A conference with each group to review their progress is essential.

Finally, teachers need to think carefully, beforehand, about responding to and evaluating collaborative writing projects. One scheme is to assign a defined percentage of the final grade at several different points during the writing process. For example, the group's plans for their project are worth 10%; research materials (photocopies of sources and interview/survey notes) are worth 10%; each student's individual draft, based on the pooled resource materials, is worth 40%; and the collaboratively written final document worth 40%. Teachers may wish to add other items to include in the grading scheme: abstract for the project, revision plans, conference grade, in-class discovery drafts, research log, and so forth. The teacher should present the evaluating scheme to the class up front, for comment and modification, early in the project.

Collaborative Learning Groups

Teachers should remember that collaborative groups can be especially effective even when the groups are not producing any written document. The situations below are just some of the uses for collaborative learning groups.

• Use collaborative learning groups for annotation of essays or texts. Students should annotate individually first and then collate their responses in a small group.

• Use learning groups for collaborative reading and response. Students can respond to the Questions for Writing and Discussion at the end of each essay, or they can focus on a question they agree is important.

• Use learning groups to respond to and revise your evaluation procedures for essays. Students should help negotiate the criteria that you use to evaluate their essays and they use during workshops to respond to each other's drafts in class.

• Use learning groups to gather information for class discussion or presentation. Especially for long writing projects such as an arguing essay or a research paper, divide the class into groups to give 10 minute oral reports on some phase of their papers: finding journals in the library; evaluating sources; avoiding plagiarism; using the government documents section of the library; editing for particular points in grammar, punctuation, or usage.

Critical Reading and Writing

Numerous research studies have established the clear connection between reading and writing skills, so writing teachers should include critical reading-and-writing activities throughout the writing process. The basic premise of current theories of reading is simply that reading processes are similar to writing processes. In both activities, readers and writers know the rhetorical situation, have expectations and make guesses, collect information, shape thoughts, revise perceptions, and relate ideas as they actively construct meaning. Reading is not a spectator sport. It requires active engagement of the text, both individually and collectively. The capsules below, which explain key assumptions about reading processes, are followed by some classroom activities that illustrate how to put those ideas into practice.

• Reading is not a one-way or "conduit" process through which a single meaning from a text is transmitted from the text to the reader. It is active, requiring the reader's participation in constructing meaning, and it is transactional, suggesting that the text and the reader act on each other, producing a unique meaning or experience based both on what the text says and what the reader brings to the reading activity.

• In the composition classroom, reading should be liberated from the "Read and Then Write" pattern that teachers traditionally follow. The old reading paradigm is dominated by the "Read this essay and then write your own essay" assignment which treats both reading and writing as self-contained, non-recursive, non-interactive processes. The new paradigm uses writing and speaking and collaboration <u>before</u> and <u>during</u> as well as after the reading activity.

• Reading is a process of making meaning that parallels the writing process: It is active and transactional; it is recursive; it is social and collaborative; and it is rhetorical, requiring plans and guesses about audiences, author's intentions, and writing situations. Composing (in both reading and writing) is a process through which the student learns by actively engaging and shaping language in order to construct meaning.

• Social, collaborative activities are as important in reading as they are in writing. How does the reader know what meaning he or she has constructed until he or she tries to explain it to others? Readers learn what is important in their reading by noting and reacting to the meaning found by other readers. Collaborative activities construct meaning just as surely as private readings.

• Reading needs to be critical (active, analytical, and contextual), but it need not <u>begin</u> with analysis any more than writing should begin with product-oriented, reader-based writing. Just as writing often begins with schema-priming journal activities and expressive writing, reading needs to begin by participating in and enjoying the text as a reader. Readers should be shown how to move from "reading like a reader" to "reading with a writer's eye."

• The "metacognitive" activities, or activities in which students explain what they are learning about their writing (reviewing their process, articulating and evaluating plans, and writing postscripts) work especially well in the reading process. Students should be encouraged to prewrite about the subjects of text that they are going to read. They should articulate their expectations of texts, describe how they are reacting or how they reacted at key points in the text, and review how their perceptions of texts changed during discussions and rereading. Writing about what they are learning from reading is a key part of the reading process.

• Finally, students need to <u>connect</u> their reading and writing experiences. Teachers should help writers apply what they learn from reading a specific text to the writer's own assignment and drafts. Without continual movement between reading and writing, students will discuss essays in class and then go home and write their essays without transferring what they learned during their reading to their own writing.

Below are some classroom activities which will help you connect reading and writing.

1.   Try <u>prereading journal entries</u>, especially for those unusual, difficult, or controversial texts. Possible prewriting journal assignments for essays in <u>The PH Guide</u> are as follows. In each case, the purpose is to set student's schema, to orient them to the writer's context, and to allow them to decide what they think about a topic <u>before</u> they are thrown into the writer's world.

Alice Walker, "Beauty: When the Other Dancer is the Self"

Describe a traumatic incident from your childhood. Explain what happened and how you coped with it years later.

Jonathan Kozol, "The Homeless and their Children"

Choose two of the following activities: renting an apartment, grocery shopping for dinner, buying an appliance, commuting to work, or seeing a doctor about an illness. Now explain how you would do these activities if you were illiterate and could not read signs, labels, forms, or instructions.

Edward Abbey, "The Damnation of a Canyon"

In the past, radical ecologists have made the news by spiking trees, pouring sand in bulldozers' gas tanks, and sabotaging logging operations in order to save forests and wildlife. In your opinion, how far should ecologists go in order to save the environment? If their activities disrupt business, should they refrain? If their activities cost Americans their jobs or break laws, do their ends justify the means?

Write your own prereading journal entries for other essays. The key is to assign the prereading journal entry several days before you make the essay assignment so that you have time to discuss their responses in class before assigning the essay.

2. Show students how to respond as readers to the essays they read. Actually, most students habitually practice reader-response: They are likely to respond primarily to content, they react quickly--and negatively--to long winded or boring essays, to complex sentence structures, and to difficult vocabulary. The point is to have students acknowledge and articulate how they respond so that their responses can become a basis for discussing audience reactions and, eventually, revision strategies.

A typical reader-response activity would be to discuss and model how to respond as a reader, and then have one group of students in a collaborative activity focus on their responses as readers. For example, divide the class into 5 groups to work on the questions that follow each essay. Assign groups 1-4 the first four questions for writing and discussion. (Group 1 does

Question #1, Group 2 does Question #2, and so forth.) Ask the fifth group to note their own responses as readers. This group should work individually for 3 minutes and then collate or list their responses. The reader-response group's reactions will often show whether the rhetorical features (which the other groups are analyzing) are working for a particular audience.

3. Reading with a writer's eye is an especially effective critical reading strategy. Many of the Questions for Writing and Discussion that follow each essay ask students to look for those rhetorical features that help writers understand their own writing. In addition, though, try the following activities:

Before discussing an essay, ask students to articulate the problems they are having with their current drafts. Write those problems on the chalkboard. Then ask students, either individually or in groups, to reread the assigned essay, looking for places in the essay that might show how to solve the problems listed at the board.

Have students reread an assigned essay, looking for evidence that shows how the writer wrote the essay--how he or she gathered evidence, focused the essay, and organized the ideas. This strategy works well for many of the essays in the text, but especially the observing essays by Kingsolver and White, the investigating essays by Koenenn and Kozol, the explaining essays by Iyer and Talbot, the evaluating essays by Rapping and Cowley, and the problem solving essays by Tannen and Postman.

4. Annotation of texts is a critical reading strategy that students have rarely practiced. Because high schools sometimes frown on students who write in their texts, they often think it is wrong to write in the margins. (Often, students need to be persuaded that they will still be able to resell their books even if they have written in them.) First, you will need to model how to write questions and reactions in the margins of essays. Demonstrate, on an overhead, comments that you make as you read. Some students will be familiar with yellow highlighting, but they rarely write out comments, reactions, or their own ideas in the margin. Early in the course, as part of your reading assignment, demonstrate on an overhead how you write comments in the margin. Then ask your students to write their individual reactions to the content, organization, style, or some other feature of the essay that you assign.

5. Try collaborative text annotation to improve your students' critical reading skills. Too often, teachers design reading assignments and activities that have no collaborative or social dimension. Several teaching tips in the margins of the second edition of The Prentice Hall Guide suggest specific activities, but the basic strategy is to ask students to annotate an essay in the margin for particular features that you are discussing: focus, intros, coherence, showing vs. telling, or style features. Then, have students in groups of 3 or 4 collate their annotations on a photocopy of the essay (you provide each group with a photocopy). After the group annotates for 10 minutes, the group reporter then explains to the rest of the class what their group discovered, using their notes as reference. Students then hand in the photocopies, so you can monitor their critical reading progress.

An effective alternative is to have students collate their responses on a transparency copy of the essay and then have students show their responses on an overhead projector. Remember, though, that each group will need one special marking pen that works on transparencies.

6. Connecting reading activities to the student's own writing is crucial to effective critical reading in the composition class. The point is not to discuss essays as though they were art masterpieces in the Louvre. When students finish some critical reading activity, ask them to pull out their drafts and notes and apply strategies that the class has discussed (types of lead-ins, shaping strategies, audience cues, paragraph hooks, showing details, or elements of style or voice) to their own essays.

Another critical reading angle is to take a problem solving approach to your discussion of professional and student essays: What problems did this writer face and how did he or she solve them? Which of those solutions might work for their own essays?

Apply the same critical reading procedures, questions, and strategies that the class has used to read professional essays to the workshops that students have on each other's essays. If you use the same questions for student drafts that you use for professional essays, the connection between reading and writing will be clearer to your students.

Write-to-Learn Activities

A write-to-learn activity occurs when students use informal writing to assist them in thinking about some text, discussion, or piece of writing. Write-to-learn activities are writer-based, informal, and brief. Although many prewriting and revision exercises for essays are actually write-to-learn activities, teachers usually reserve the write-to-learn label for short journal entries designed to elicit informal reaction to a class discussion, a group activity, an assignment in the text. Since they promote articulation of expectation and reaction as well as reflection and synthesis, they can be excellent pump-priming or review activities. To keep the emphasis on discovery and learning, most teachers do not collect or grade them.

The virtues of write-to-learn activities can hardly be overstated. They allow <u>every</u> student to respond actively to a discussion question, rather than just the few students a teacher calls on. They provide for <u>varied learning styles</u> by allowing teachers to reach students who need time to pause and reflect before they can contribute to a class discussion. Some students are much more confident about entering a discussion if they have a response written in front of them. They encourage <u>metacognitive</u> activities, where students explain in writing what they are learning. They permit the teacher to get <u>immediate feedback</u> to a particular discussion issue or question rather than guess how many students understand the topic under discussion. Most important, they draw on inherent <u>powers of writing</u> to help students recall, reflect, and learn.

Write-to-learn activities, like the ones listed below, can be used at any point during reading, writing, or discussion to promote active learning. Write-to-learn activities are not a separate category of teaching methods, however. Many of the ideas suggested below also appear in <u>The Prentice Hall Guide</u> as collaborative activities or critical reading strategies.

1. Write about reading assignments.

• Many teachers like to review reading assignments in <u>The Prentice Hall Guide</u> to make sure that students comprehend the material. A short write-to-learn activity over one or two topics in the assigned reading enables teachers (and students) to see which points need to be explained in greater depth.

• Prepare your students for a discussion session on an essay by having them write for 2-3 minutes on one key question. The resulting discussion will move more quickly and have greater depth since students have time to collect their thoughts in writing.

• During a discussion of assigned essays, asking your students to write their reactions <u>before</u> you begin the discussion encourages students with minority opinions to express their views. Often students are hesitant to voice offbeat, minority, or "stupid" opinions after the "majority" opinion assumes authority.

• In the middle of a heated discussion about a controversial topic, call a "Time Out" and have everyone write down his or her position. First have everyone write out the main point of discussion or controversy and then have them explain their own position on this issue. The "Time Out" writing gives <u>everyone</u> a chance to articulate his or her own position.

• Prereading journal assignments on professional or student essays are, in fact, write-to-learn strategies. See suggestions for possible prereading journal topics in the previous section on Critical Reading and Writing.

2. Write about their plans for essays.

• In their journals, have students frequently write their current plans for their next steps in their writing process. If they are collecting, have them write what sources they plan to use next. If they are shaping, have them actually test two or three possible shapes (comparison, chronological order, causal analysis) to see which will work best. If they are beginning a revision, have them make a list of the 2 or 3 most important things they still need to do.

3. Write about what they are learning from their writing process.

• Exploit the metacognitive dimensions of write-to-learn activities by asking students to reflect in their journals on what they have <u>learned</u> so far in the writing process. What do they <u>think</u> the purpose of the assignment is? What have they learned during group work? What have they learned by writing an essay? What have they learned by <u>revising</u> an essay? The "Postscript on the Writing Process" in each chapter is just one of those possibilities.

4. Write about class discussions.

• During a discussion, even experienced teachers are rarely sure whether students are "getting" important points. Again and again, I've heard myself-- and other teachers--ask the class, "OK, do you understand what I mean by <u>show</u>?" Invariably that question is followed by silence. "All right, who doesn't understand what I'm talking about?" Silence. "Does anyone have any questions?" Again, silence. If the idea is important, or if you believe that the point is not getting across, stop and have students write in their journals for just a minute or two, explaining the point under discussion. Then ask volunteers to read their answers. When you hear their responses, you'll know who still has questions or what points need more discussion.

5. Write responses to the instructor's comments on essays.

• One effective write-to-learn assignment is to ask students to respond, in the margins of their essays, to the comments and questions you write when you return their drafts or essays. Re-collect their essays with their responses. Their short responses enable you to see which of your comments are communicating, which are raising their hackles, and which had no effect. (Encourage students to address individual marginal and summary comments rather than the overall grade.)

Designing Writing Assignments

The assignments in <u>The Prentice Hall Guide</u> focus on a purpose or aim, but are open-ended to encourage students to discover topics that create maximum potential for learning. However, specific writing assignments can be effective, too. Specific assignments growing out of a knowledge base created by shared course readings usually generate class conversations that spill over into the students' writing. Content-based topics can also help inexperienced writers succeed by providing them with ideas, information, and context. Finally, a reading-based assignment can be easier for teachers and peer readers to respond to, coach, and evaluate because most of the students respond to the same content and cope with similar collecting and shaping problems.

Many teachers prefer to mix open-ended and specific writing assignments. Often teachers use open assignments for autobiographical essays, investigative reports, exploratory essays, and research papers but design specific assignments for explaining, evaluating, or problem-solving essays. As you design writing assignments, keep the following tips in mind.

• If possible, use assignments that have been tested. You can give assignments other teachers have tested and revised, you can pre-test assignment questions on a small group of students, and you can write the answer to the question yourself, to see how you would actually respond to the question.

• Create <u>real purposes and audiences</u> for questions. Write a scenario for your assignment: What is the writer's purpose in writing and the reader's purpose in requiring or reading the piece of writing? Who might have to write this assignment? Who would be the probable audience? How would the writer go about writing this assignment? How might the readers evaluate the writing?

• As you phrase your assignment, choose <u>key words</u> with care. Avoid overly general directives, such as "discuss" or "comment on." Don't use words such as "define," "compare," or "classify" that restrict students to only one developmental strategy (unless you are focusing on an exercise). Instead, use key words related to the chapter <u>purposes</u>, such as "explain," "evaluate," or "argue."

• Establish <u>criteria for evaluating the writing</u> when you make the assignment (see model assignment sheet on following pages). Then have the class give you input on these criteria and, as necessary, revise them as students work on the assignment. Finally, use these criteria when you discuss the professional essays and when you design workshop questions on rough and revised drafts. Planning your grading criteria carefully may be the single most important thing you do as a writing teacher. Not only will it save you unnecessary grief over grading hassles, but it will give students a clear idea of the standards they are trying to achieve.

• Make sure the assignment is appropriate for students with a range of interests and writing abilities. If appropriate, give students a <u>choice</u> of related topics with similar purposes, but perhaps different subjects or audiences.

• Give writers sufficient time, training, and support for the writing assignment. The writing and learning process can be short-circuited without sufficient time. If assignments are or appear to be too difficult for the allotted time, writers' frustrations may undermine the whole process.

For additional suggestions and advice, see Lindemann's chapter, "Making and Evaluating Writing Assignments."

When you make an assignment, give your students as much information up front as possible. Do NOT give assignments orally without backup information on an assignment sheet. Do not merely write the assignment on the board, either. Writing a lengthy assignment on the board is a waste of class time. Instead, write out all the important information about your assignment on a sheet to ditto or photocopy. Each student should have a copy of the assignment to refer to throughout the writing process. On the following page is a sample of an assignment sheet; revise the format as necessary for your particular class.

Evaluating Essay Assignment
E101, sec. 19. Ms. Jackson

<u>The Assignment</u>:

Write an evaluation of a campus or community service or organization. The purpose of this assignment is to evaluate the strengths and weaknesses of the organization or service.   Possible audiences for this essay include a prospective member of this organization or user of this service, an administrator of the service, or a funding agency for the organization.

First, you must use (or have used) the service. In addition, you must do some research for this essay. You must observe the organization or service in operation and you must interview at least one representative from this organization and at least one user of the service . You may also use a survey to collect responses from other members or users and you may use any written sources, including pamphlets and library sources. Be sure to cite your sources accurately in the text of your essay and on a Works Cited page. Copies of interviews, survey results, written sources, and pamphlets MUST be turned in with your final draft. Essay length is approximately 3-5 pages. Final draft should be typed, double spaced. Essay is due Class #14.

<u>Essay Schedule and Deadlines</u>:
Mon. Sept 20: Assignment given in class. Prewriting.

Wed. Sept 22:   Read Chapter 8 and assigned essays; Do two journal
                entries from #1, #7, #8, as well as the "Freewriting"
                exercise.
Fri. Sept 24:   Assign Chapter 6, sections on interviews, surveys, and
                written sources; Choose subject, gather information,
                & set up interviews; Annotate sample student essay.

Mon. Sept 27: No class. Do draft, bring notes to Conference.

Wed. Sept 29: Bring rough draft to class for workshop.

Fri. Oct 1:   Bring revised draft and all collecting notes and
        photocopies to class for workshop.

Mon. Oct 4:   Final draft of Evaluating Essay due. Hand in all notes,
                 photocopies, results of surveys, rough drafts,
                 workshop sheets, and prewriting in pocket folder.

Grading for Evaluating Essay:
1. Attendance and satisfactory participation
   at scheduled conference   . . . . .   10 pts./%
2. Rough draft done and attendance on
   Wed., Sept 29   . . . . .   20 pts./%
3. Final draft, evaluated on the following criteria:
   a. Clear purpose; overall claim stated;
      addresses audience; Effective introduction
   b. Accurate description of organization or service
   c. Criteria clearly stated and appropriate for audience
   d. Judgment clearly stated for each criterion
      (Must note some weaknesses as well as strengths)
   e. Sufficient evidence for each criterion/judgment
      (Must have at least two interviews.)
   f. Organization, coherence, paragraph transitions
      clear
   g. Style clear; few distracting typos or errors
      Works Cited sheet; photocopies of written sources

   The above seven criteria are weighted equally
      and total   . . . .   70 pts./%
                                        _____
                         Total   100 pts.

Note: These deadlines are firm. If you miss the conference, you lose 10
points or 10% of the essay grade. If you don't have your rough draft or miss
the rough draft workshop, you lose 20 points or 20% of the grade. If your
final paper is late one day, you lose 10 points or 10% of the grade. If the final
paper is more than one day late, it will not be accepted. If you know
beforehand that you must miss a class or if you are ill, let me know before
you miss a class.

Responding to and Evaluating Student Writing

Responding to and evaluating writing are part of the same process, but the terms "responding to" and "evaluating" warrant careful distinction. First, not all response needs to be or should be evaluative, nor should it lead immediately to a grade. Some response is descriptive. Teachers (and peer readers) should learn to label features, such as thesis, paragraphs, specific examples, transition devices, and so on. Some response is personal and reactive, imitating the response of a reader: "When I read this paragraph it reminded me of _____ incident in my own life." Or, "This incident made me feel angry" (or happy, amused, depressed, and so forth). Evaluation, on the other hand, consists of those comments that explain or justify a value--most commonly, a grade. Most comments written in the margin and at the end of an essay tend to become evaluative simply because they are given in the context of a grade.

As teachers think about how to respond to and evaluate writing, they should ask the following four questions:

1. Exactly <u>when</u> and how frequently during the writing process should teachers respond or evaluate?
2. <u>How much</u> response is useful? Can students usefully process all the comments they receive on one essay?
3. <u>From whom</u> should students receive response or evaluation--from peers, from the teacher, from outside readers?
4. Finally, <u>what form</u> should that response or evaluation take? Should it be oral, in conference or small groups? Should it be written? Should it be on set response or evaluation forms or should it be informal, in the margins? Should it be expressed quantitatively, with points for specific areas, or should it focus mainly on major strength or weakness?

The following sections on responding to student writing and evaluating student writing will help you decide when you should respond and when you should evaluate, and what methods and strategies you might use. From the variety of approaches illustrated here, choose those strategies most appropriate for your class.

Responding to Student Writing

Responding to student writing is an ongoing process, not a single act. Like the process of revision, response begins immediately after students start working on their topics. Teachers and peers should, as potential members of the writer's audience, respond to possible topics for essays, to appropriate collecting and shaping tactics, and to a writer's plans for composing as well as to a writer's rough and revised drafts. The actual written comments on a student's essay or intervention comments on a student's draft should be only a small part of the responses writers receive in a composition class. The following sections discuss three kinds of response activities: responding during class activities, responding during conferences, and responding to written drafts.

The point of listing all these kinds of responses is partly to give teachers some variety of response activities, but also to wean teachers away from responding only in a red-pen mode, only on final drafts, and only when they are giving grades. Giving grades and writing careful marginal and summary comments are necessary, but not on all writing assignments. Teachers need to avoid turning themselves into "composition slaves" who think they can respond only by writing comments on endless papers, weekend after weekend.

Responding During Class

Below are just a few of the possible response activities that can occur during the writing process:

- Writers discuss their topics in small groups and students respond.

- Writers read aloud from their drafts, and the class members listen and respond.

- Students write tentative thesis sentences on the board, and the class and the teacher respond.

- Teachers respond orally to students' questions in class and during peer workshops.

• Students interview each other about topic ideas, about their plans for an essay, or about their revision plans.

• Writers annotate their own drafts, describing or labeling key features (leads, thesis sentences, showing detail, key images, transition devices) of their own writing. Their rereading of their own drafts constitutes a response.

• Teachers conference with students, both during class and outside of class, responding to writers notes, plans, and drafts.

• Peer workshop groups respond to each other's writing, sometimes in a reader-response mode, sometimes in a criteria-based mode.

All of these activities indicate that responding to student writing continues throughout the writing process. It is not limited to--and should not be limited to--written comments justifying a grade on the final draft.

Responding During Conferences

Most teachers use both in-class and out-of-class conferences. In-class conferences tend to be brief and spontaneous, but timely response in class is often crucial to keeping a student's writing process on track. Conferences in your office (or in a student lounge, cafeteria, or writing center) are longer and provide more time to answer questions, review drafts and discuss revision plans.

In-class responses occur usually while students are in small groups, workshopping each other's ideas, plans, or drafts. Teachers should announce that during workshops, students should raise their hand and ask questions about the papers they are reading or, more importantly, about the advice they are receiving from their peers. Even if students are not asking questions, teachers should circulate, checking on progress and answering questions. During the 10 or 15 minutes available during a workshop, teachers can usually answer several questions and/or confer for 3-4 minutes with a particular student with a problem.

Conferences scheduled outside class give students and teachers more time to discuss their writing, but unless the teacher carefully plans these sessions, they can quickly become time-consuming and emotionally draining. The tips below will help you organize your conferences efficiently and effectively.

• Remember that you can schedule conferences to support a <u>variety</u> of different activities. Most teachers ask students to bring written drafts to a conference, but conferences can focus on a variety of other goals. The first three types of conferences described below are about the student and his or her writing. If a student wishes to discuss a specific grade, it is wise to ask the student to schedule a specific conference focusing on their grade. Teachers should not allow students to shift the focus of a writing conference to a harangue about their grades.

1. At the beginning of the year, some teachers ask students to stop by for a brief getting-to-know-you conference. The conference is short (5 minutes), relaxed, and informal. Some teachers like to take notes, briefly profiling their students. They ask about the student's major, academic background, special interests, experience in writing, or even attitude toward writing. Since

attitude and motivation are crucial to a student's success, a conference early in the semester sets up a personal relationship and a positive, constructive tone for the whole term.

2. For longer and more complex papers, a short (5-8 minute) conference early in the writing process, over possible topics, sources of information, and basic writing plans, is extremely helpful. To avoid having students wander in and converse aimlessly about their topic, require that they have completed some specified amount of prewriting <u>before</u> the conference.

3. Most conferences focus on a student's rough or revised draft. Practice varies widely here, but teachers have usually read and responded to a written draft, at least briefly, before the conference takes place. During the conference, students should take an active role: They should review what they have written, indicate what advice they have received in class, and explain what they plan to do next. The teacher's role is to respond and give advice.

4. Finally, individual students occasionally request conferences about their grades. Teachers should honor those requests and treat the student as professionally as possible. Teachers may explain their grading practice, offer to review the essay, and even offer to have a supervisor review a specific essay. Students with official grade complaints should be asked to see the Director of Composition. During these conferences, keeping a professional tone is extremely important. Teachers should say, "I'm happy to have someone else look at this paper. I've been as objective as I can in evaluating your paper. I've followed the criteria we agreed upon in class. But if you think the grade is not fair, then we need to have some outside feedback." Teachers should always treat grades not as something they <u>give</u> but as a value the writing <u>earns</u>.

• When you schedule conferences, always pass a sign-up sheet around the class and then leave it posted on your office door. <u>In addition, many teachers hand out a conference prewriting sheet to ensure that students have reviewed their writing progress and have specific questions that they wish to ask.</u> Revise the models below to fit your own particular conference plan. The first is a conference sheet focusing on gathering evidence; the second worksheet assumes that students already have a draft that has received some peer and/or teacher response. If students have completed these worksheets, your chances for a successful, productive conference will rise dramatically.

• Finally, when the conference begins, pay attention to the kinds of questions you ask. You want to keep a delicate balance between <u>asking questions</u> and providing <u>actual instruction</u> where necessary. Phrased another way, you want to <u>intervene</u>, give suggestions, and teach, but you don't want to <u>appropriate</u> the student's writing. Begin the conference with questions. When students' responses suggest that they want your help, try to get them to do the actual writing and revising. Keep the pen out of your hand as much as possible, but encourage <u>the student</u> to write as much as possible.

Questions that will get the ball rolling are the following:

- "What did you like best about this paper? Show me the parts you liked best. Why are they effective?"
- "What are the things that still need work in your essay? Why do they need work? Can you fix them by doing what made your good passages strong?"
- "What was the best piece of advice you got during workshop? Why?"
- "What was the worst piece of advice you got? Why?"
- "What questions did you have for me about your draft?"
- "What point that we covered in class could we review together?"
- "What's your plan for revising this essay?"

Students should leave a revision conference with feedback that will help them revise. Perhaps the most important thing they should have at the end of a conference is a plan of action. Make sure students know the next two or three specific things they intend to do next.

On the following pages are sample handouts of a Goals and Expectations sheet to hand out and discuss with your class, a sample Topic Proposal sheet, and a Conference Prewriting sheet.

<u>For additional advice about conferences, see the articles by Madigan and Newkirk in the Background Readings in Part III.</u>

Goals and Expectations for Writing Conferences

What's the Goal?

One of the defining characteristics of experienced writers is their ability to identify major strengths and weaknesses in their own writing--a skill that comes through practice. The writing conference provides one way of practicing that skill. During a conference, you will discuss what you think is effective and ineffective in your writing, especially in terms of global issues such as audience, purpose, focus, development, and coherence. The conference goal is to help you become a more <u>independent</u>, self-evaluative reader--and reviser--of your own writing.

What's the Teacher's Role?

To make you a more independent writer, I will help you see the skills that you already possess. The role I play in the conference is unlike some of the other roles I play because I will not be the source of information, and I will not be formally "grading" you. In the conference, I will be like a <u>coach</u>, a person who encourages you to do your best--but don't expect me to direct the conference or actually revise your essay for you. Mostly, I will be a sounding board, a reader who will give you honest responses to your questions.

What's the Student's Role?

It is your responsibility to make the conference valuable. That means that you should come to the conference with ideas or a draft and with <u>specific</u> <u>questions</u> related to global issues. You should leave the conference with a <u>plan</u> to improve your draft. In the writing conference, you will actively set the agenda. You will decide what we discuss, and you will be expected to help identify the major strengths and weaknesses. Be prepared to explore ways of solving the problems you identify.

To facilitate our discussion of your ideas or drafts, you should bring any notes, research materials, drafts, and class texts to the conference. In addition, bring any materials assigned for this conference, such as your Conference Prewriting Sheet or your Topic Proposal. In addition, bring some paper so you can make notes about your revision plans.

My conference will be at _____ (time) on _____ (date) in _____ (Bldg)

(Courtesy of Jon Leydens)

Formal Topic Proposal: Arguing/Problem-Solving Essay

--Courtesy of Anne Norris

Name _____

Section _____

Conference Day and Time _____

My Claim is:

The major arguments FOR my claim or solution are:

The major arguments AGAINST my claim or solution are:

I have IN MY POSSESSION photocopies of the following library sources: (List by author, title and call number.)

I have IN MY POSSESSION the following notes from field sources, including interviews, surveys, or data:

Additionally, I plan to do the following investigative research:

My three major questions about gathering information for this topic and writing my essay are:

1.

2.

3.

Conference Prewriting Sheet

Name _____

Conference Day and Time _____

1. Topic for my essay:

2. Intended purpose and audience for essay:

3. Brief list or outline for your current draft:

4. According to feedback I've received in class, the strengths and problems in the draft are as follows:

Strengths   Areas Still Needing Work
_____

5. According to the instructor's comments, the strengths and problems in the draft are as follows:

Strengths   Areas Still Needing Work
_____

6. Based on this feedback, here is my plan for revising this essay:
(List **specific** steps you intend to take and **specific** paragraphs
 you intend to revise.)
a.
b.
c.
Three questions I want to ask the instructor are as follows:

a.   b.   c.

Responding to Written Drafts

When teachers respond to written drafts, they should use several kinds of response, depending on the student, the assignment, the writer's purpose and audience, and the writer's own process.

• First, teachers should respond to the writer's <u>purpose and audience</u>: "If you hope to persuade this audience, use another example about underage drinking that might appeal to them." "Your audience for such a narrative essay expects you to describe scenes using sensory detail, to give dialogue between characters, and to focus on some main idea."

• Second, teachers should also <u>respond as readers</u> to the ideas and content. If you are reading an early draft of an essay and giving intervention suggestions rather than comments supporting a grade, explain how you felt or how you reacted as you read: "When I read this paragraph, it reminded me of my own experiences." "When I finished the third paragraph, I wanted to ask you this question." "After reading your introduction, I thought your point was X, but when I finished your paper, you seemed to be saying Y. Which is your main point?"

• Third, teachers should relate their suggestions to the student's <u>writing process</u>: "Since this paper needs more specific examples and showing details, try another collecting strategy as you revise." "Draft two other lead-ins for this essay and then test them out on your workshop group. See which one they like best." Don't miss an opportunity to send students back into the writing and revising process.

• A non-threatening but valuable kind of response is simply to <u>describe</u> or <u>label</u> the main features of the essay you are reading--and then ask students if they recognized or intended those features: "The last paragraph of your essay focuses on your third point, thus ending your essay without a conclusion. Was that your intention?" "I see that you're using a five-paragraph format, complete with a topic sentence for each paragraph. Why did you choose this format?"

• Teachers should occasionally ask <u>questions</u> and make <u>suggestions</u>: "Is this always true?" "Does this contradict what you said above?" "Try combining this sentence with the previous one." "Read this sentence aloud and see if you can express this point more concisely. Hint: Read the section on vague words on pp. _____ in your handbook."

• Many comments on a draft may be <u>evaluative</u>: "This paragraph lacks coherence. It has a unity problem because you discuss two topics: cigarette addiction <u>and</u> alcohol abuse." "In paragraph three, you simply assert that alcohol should be banned at football games, but you give no reasons or evidence." Such evaluative comments should relate to standards or criteria for a particular paper that the class has repeatedly reviewed and discussed.

• Finally, a teacher's responses should also consider the <u>writer's own perceptions</u> about the essay's strengths and weaknesses. If a student writes in his or her Postscript that the essay's weakness is its lack of sensory details, but its strength is its focus and coherence, then teachers should respond to that perception. There's no sense writing a long comment about weak development if the writer already knows that the paper has insufficient support. On the other hand, if the writer thinks his or her coherence is strong and it is really weak, a teacher needs to help the writer see that problem.

<u>For additional suggestions about responding to student writing, see the articles by Donald Daiker, and Jeffrey Sommers in the Background Readings in Part III</u>

Evaluating Student Writing

Responding to student writing, in itself, may or may not be evaluative. Response becomes evaluation, however, when comments--oral or written-- occur in the context of a judgment or grade. Teachers use a wide variety of evaluation schemes, from portfolio grading (where often grades are postponed until near the end of the course) to traditional grades for each major writing assignment. Some teachers believe that traditional grading schemes are appropriate and realistic since they reflect the kinds of evaluation students will receive in other academic classes. Some teachers modify traditional grading by giving "As," "Bs," and "Cs" but giving "Us (Unsatisfactory) and requiring revisions of any "D" or "F" papers. Still others avoid grades until the last possible moment, believing that receiving grades (especially low grades) interferes with a student's self-esteem, learning, and freedom.

The comments and advice in this section assume that you will be making judgments and giving grades at some point during the course, and that when you do, your criteria should be as up front and as objective as possible. More importantly, criteria should be established and implemented as a community. The more students help articulate criteria and apply them as readers, the more sense standards and grades make.

In Teaching Expository Writing, William Irmscher suggests a starting point for discussing how to assign grades:

A--Demonstrates unusual competence
B--Demonstrates competence
C--Suggests competence
D--Suggests incompetence
F--Demonstrates incompetence

Now, we must figure out what we mean by these labels. What does "competence" mean? Are there any external standards for competence, or must we define competence in the context of the class or even in the context of a single writing situation? What does "unusual" mean--How much above competence must a writer rise in order to receive an "A"? At this point, most teachers begin describing specific features of prose, hoping to define the criteria more clearly. One teacher used the following handout to help explain grades to her students:

Grading Criteria

An "A" Essay:

<u>Rhetorical Stance</u>: Writing has excellent balance of voice, subject, purpose, and sense of audience in writing.

<u>Focus and Development</u>: Has sharp focus on a main idea that clearly relates to purpose. Ideas are original, logical, thought-provoking. Supporting examples, showing details, and data are rich and relevant to the main idea. Connections between idea and example are clearly made.

<u>Organization</u>: Introduction captures reader's interest, and the writing develops clearly, smoothly, and logically from main point. Coherence or smooth flow sustained with transitions, paragraph hooks, and audience cues. The reader's expectations are set and then clearly met. Individual paragraphs have clear focus, unity, and coherence.

<u>Style</u>: Sentences reveal and sustain appropriate voice and tone. Good sentence variety. Sentences are clear, concise, and easily read by intended audience. Diction is precise and avoids wordiness and inappropriate jargon. Punctuation, usage, spelling, and mechanics have no distracting errors.

A "B" Essay:

<u>Rhetorical Stance</u>: Writing has good balance of voice, subject, purpose, and sense of audience in writing.

<u>Focus and Development</u>: Focuses on a main idea that clearly relates to purpose. Ideas are clear and logical. Supporting examples, showing details, and data are ample and relevant to the main idea. Connections made between ideas and examples.

<u>Organization</u>: Introduction captures reader's interest, and the writing develops clearly from the main point. Coherence or smooth flow sustained with transitions, paragraph hooks, and audience cues. The reader's expectations are set and then met. Individual paragraphs have basic focus, unity, and coherence.

<u>Style</u>: Sentences have appropriate voice and tone. Good sentence variety. Sentences are clear and easily read by intended audience. Diction avoids wordiness and inappropriate jargon. Punctuation, usage, spelling, and mechanics have few distracting errors.

A "C" Essay:

<u>Rhetorical Stance</u>: Writing has rhetorical purpose, but may have some problems balancing voice, subject, purpose, and sense of audience.

Focus and Development: Main idea is evident, but focus may be fuzzy or not relate clearly to purpose. Ideas are clear. Supporting examples, showing details, and data may be thin in spots or not clearly relevant to the main idea.
Organization: Introduction sets main idea, and the writing develops from the main point. Coherence or smoothness of ideas may have some rough spots. Individual paragraphs usually have basic focus, unity, and coherence.
Style: Sentences are clear and easily read by intended audience but writing may lack voice.   Diction may have occasional wordiness or inappropriate jargon.   Punctuation, usage, spelling, and mechanics may have some distracting errors, but meaning is still clear.

A "D" Essay
Rhetorical Stance: Writing lacks rhetorical purpose.
Focus and Development: Main idea or focus is not clear or not clearly related to purpose. Supporting examples, showing details, and data may be thin or missing altogether, or not relevant to the main idea.
Organization: Introduction may set wrong expectations. Writing often makes several unconnected main points.   Coherence often rough; Individual paragraphs may lack basic focus, unity, and coherence.
Style: Sentences may be confusing to intended audience. Diction frequently wordy or unclear. Punctuation, usage, spelling, and mechanics often have distracting errors that obscure meaning.
Note: A "D" essay usually does not have problems in all of the above areas. It may have good focus and development, but stylistic problems severely interfere with meaning. Or it may be clearly written but consist only of assertions and generalizations without evidence.

An "F" Essay
An "F" essay has severe problems in rhetorical stance or focus/development or organization or style. Essay does not communicate successfully with audience or meet minimal expectations. Often essay is a writer's early draft that shows little or no collecting, shaping, or revising.

As you consider how to use or revise this model for your own class, keep a few points in mind.

1. You may wish to balance comments that describe the writing ("paragraphs have unity and coherence") with comments that describe the intended reader's reaction ("Readers finish with a sense of excitement about the subject and a desire to reread the essay.")

2. Avoid sentences that describe the "A" writer rather than the "A" essay. If you say,"The 'A' writer has striking insights and a fluid style," you'll reinforce the notion that some people are "naturally" "A" writers and others are "born" "C" writers.

3. Avoid using the word "ideas" or even "content" in your description of grade levels. Students are quick to assume that if they get a "C" it's because "the teacher doesn't like my ideas." Using words such as "focus," "development," "support," or "showing detail" conveys the proper message that you are looking for clarity and quality of development, not for particular ideas, beliefs, or positions.

4. Often teachers overload their grading criteria with impressionistic phrases: "highly imaginative," "artful and pleasing transitions," or "fine and imaginative insights." You need some evaluative language, but try to avoid phrases that are difficult to pin down. Strive to be careful and descriptive in your explanations of criteria.

5. Be sure the language of your criteria, your discussion of the criteria, and your actual grading practice indicate that you are not looking for papers that take a particular social, sexual, political, or ecological stance. Avoid those "hidden agendas" in your grading. In a composition class, your task is to facilitate open discussion and debate. Grading for a particular viewpoint or stance is the surest way to stifle discussion and learning in your class.

Holistic Scoring Guides. As an alternative, grading criteria may be based on holistic scoring guides. You may describe the highest grade and then note typical deficiencies in lower range essays. As the sample sheet below indicates, the "A" description sets the standard, and the lower grades are described by noting the deficiencies in one or more of the criteria.

Grading Criteria

In this class, we are working on improving your writing in four major areas: Focus, Development, Organization, and Style. Although the description following each criteria will change slightly as we write different types of papers (Remembering, Explaining, Arguing, Interpreting literature), the basic criteria remain the same.

"A" essays satisfy the following criteria:

a. Focus--These essays have a clearly identifiable main idea, thesis, or claim. The writer's purposes are appropriate for the writing situation. Promises made to the reader early in the essay are kept. Expectations for the reader are set and then met. Ideas, examples, and reasons developed in the body of the paper are clearly related to the main focus.

b. Development--These essays have ample supporting evidence: sensory details, specific examples, statistics, quotations, or other data. The writer's assertions are immediately followed by supporting evidence. The writer shows rather than just tells. Appropriate research (personal experience, interviews, surveys, library sources) supports the writer's main idea, thesis, or claim. The writer shows how or why evidence is relevant to main idea or claim.

c. Organization--The ideas and paragraphs proceed in some logical and apparent sequence or pattern. The writer uses sufficient audience cues to let the reader know what has been discussed, what is being discussed, or what will be discussed. Attention-getting titles and leads, essay maps, summary and forecasting statements, paragraph hooks, transition words and phrases, and effective conclusions guide the reader from beginning to end.

d. Style--These papers have appropriate voice and tone as well as effective sentences and word choice. The style is appropriate for the purpose and audience. In addition, these papers avoid problems in usage, grammar, punctuation, mechanics, and spelling that interfere with the writer's ideas or distract from the audience's pleasure in reading.

"B" essays are deficient in <u>one</u> of the four criteria:

a. Focus--These essays have a clearly identifiable main idea, thesis, or claim. Promises made to the reader are fulfilled. Deficiencies in focus may exist, but the overall purpose is still clear.

b. Development--These essays have good supporting evidence. Typically, support may be thin or deficient in spots, but relevant evidence supports assertions or general statements.

c. Organization--The ideas and paragraphs proceed in some logical and apparent sequence or pattern. Occasional deficiencies in audience cues may exist, but the overall shape is clear to the reader.

d. Style--Typically, these papers communicate clearly, but the voice may not be as clear, or a few deficiencies in sentence structure, word choice, grammar, or punctuation exist.

"C" essays are deficient in two of the four criteria:

a. Focus--These essays have a clearly identifiable main idea, thesis, or claim. Often, though, these essays shift the focus at some point in the essay.

b. Development--Typically, these essays do have some supporting evidence, but some evidence is not relevant or some assertions or general statements are left unsupported.

c. Organization--Often, an overall pattern or sequence may exist, but the writer has made little effort to guide the reader through the major ideas.

d. Style--Sometimes these papers have a lackluster "Engfish" style, appearing to be written mechanically to fulfill an assignment rather than directed to a specific audience. Distracting sentence errors may interfere with communication.

"D" essays are deficient in three of the four criteria or have one major flaw that seriously disrupts communication:

"F" essays have few redeeming qualities. Typically, they are little more than rough drafts that do not meet the requirements of the writing situation, or they have major flaws that prevent communication.

<u>Analytic Scales</u>. Some grading sheets are based on an analytical scale, and have the virtue of converting judgments into points on a scale. Typically, teachers use a 1-5 or a 1-10 scale. This sheet has less discussion of the criteria, and so needs to be modeled with one or two sample papers to illustrate the range of scores. One of the virtues of this grading scale is its easy application to peer workshop grading. If teachers model how to use the scale, students can become adept at "scoring" each other's essay.

Grading Criteria and Scale

For the explaining essay, we have agreed on the following scale for the key features of the essay. During your workshop sessions, if you think we should add or revise one of the below features or think we should readjust the numbers, please note your reactions. Before the final draft of the essay is due, we will discuss this scale and revise it as necessary.

Scale
Rate each feature for its overall merit by circling the appropriate number. Total the points in each category and write the total at the bottom.

Introduction
    Catchy title and lead-in   1 2 3 4 5
    Focus on thesis   2 4 6 8 10
    Map/Preview   1 2 3 4 5
                                      20 pts. poss   _____

Support
    Specific examples, showing   4 8 12 16 20
    details, evidence from
    sources, data
    Connections between   2 4 6 8 10
    ideas & examples

                                      30 pts. poss   _____

Organization
    Transitions between paragraphs, 2 4 6 8 10
    hooks, audience cues
    Paragraph unity and coherence   2 4 6 8 10
                                      20 pts. poss   _____

Style
    Appropriate voice, tone   1 2 3 4 5
    Sentence clarity &   1 2 3 4 5
     appropriate diction
    Appropriate punctuation,   2 4 6 8 10
     usage, mechanics, sp.

                                      20 pts. poss   _____

Rhetorical Stance
    Purpose clear throughout   2   4   6   8   10
    Audience clearly addressed   2   4   6   8   10
                             20 pts. poss   _____

                      Total 100 pts. poss   _____

<u>Grades</u>

A 90-100 B 80-90   C 70-80   D 60-70   F Below 60

    <u>Cover Sheets</u>. Some teachers prefer to use grading sheets that are less analytical and less intimidating for the students. For each essay, then, the teacher agrees with the class on the general areas that are important and then designs a cover sheet with sufficient room for comment, both positive and negative. These cover sheets should be used during at least one workshop, so students have a chance to familiarize themselves with the general categories. Teachers may use these sheets for grading a final draft, but they are also effective for intervention response to a draft, for portfolio versions of an essay, or for essays that need to be revised. One of the virtues of this sheet is to remind teachers (or peer responders) that they must cite specific strengths in the essay--not just itemize weaknesses or problem areas.

Summary Sheet

Name _____
Essay _____
Date _____

	Strengths	Needed Revisions
Purpose, audience		
Focus/Thesis/Claim		
Development/Evidence		
Organization/Coherence		
Style/Mechanics		

Suggestions for revision:

Writer's plans for revision:

Marginal and Summary Comments on Essays

When teachers write responses on essays, usually they comment both in the margin and in summary comments at the end of the essay (or on a summary sheet). Marginal comments, reactions, and questions usually highlight specific strengths and weaknesses in the essay, while the summary comment reviews the essay's successes and problems overall. The marginal comments should point to specific instances that support or illustrate your summary comments.

In addition to the suggestions offered in the section on Responding to Student Writing, keep the following tips in mind.

• The first time through a stack of papers, many teachers recommend dropping the red pen, reading the papers quickly, and sorting them, holistically, into three piles: upper range, middle range, and lower range. This initial "prereading" of the essays will let you see how the class as a whole responded to the assignment.

• Write marginal comments in pencil rather than pen. If you make a mistake or change your mind upon rereading, its easier to revise your comments and suggestions.

• In your marginal and summary comments, concentrate on those aspects of writing that you have emphasized in class or that you're focusing on for that assignment. Review the criteria sheet the class helped you develop for that particular essay. Don't hold students responsible for strategies you have not yet covered in class.

• Don't forget to relate your marginal comments to the writer's purpose and the intended audience: "If your purpose is to argue for this claim, then you need to address the arguments of the opposition." "Your readers want you to state your idea as clearly as possible. They don't want to guess for two pages what your main idea is."

• Be sure to include positive comments in both the margin and in the summary comment. Writers need to know what is working so they can build on those strengths.

• Avoid writing vague comments in the margin. Don't say a sentence or paragraph is "awkward," "illogical," "vague," or "incoherent" unless you immediately explain the source of the problem. After all, if the student knew how or why a sentence was "awkward," she'd be able to fix it.

• As you mark papers, look for <u>repeated</u> problems in development, repeated grammatical errors, repeated punctuation problems, or repeated instances of wordiness, lack of detail, or awkward or non-existent transitions. Don't mark every problem or error. Note trends and patterns rather than isolated problems.

• After you've written some marginal comments but <u>before</u> you write your summary comment, reread the student's statement about purpose and audience and his or her Postscript on the Writing Process. Knowing the writer's intentions will help you assess strengths and problems. Comparing the writer's self-evaluation with your own assessment of strengths and weaknesses lets you know what and how much you need to explain.

• In your summary comment, support your evaluative comments with <u>specific</u> reference to a particular problem in the essay. If you say that an essay needs more evidence, for example, direct the writer to a specific paragraph where you have a marginal comment that highlights the problem.

• A summary comment can contain an assignment as well as an evaluation. If a student is having trouble with supporting evidence, for example, ask him or her to revise just one paragraph. If an essay has a flat lead-in, ask the student to write another lead and compare the two. If a student has problems with audience cues or paragraph hooks, ask him or her to revise just one passage.

• Remember that problems in design or execution in your students' essays may be related to problems in your assignment. Ask yourself, "Is this student doing what the assignment asked? Was the assignment clear?"

Even with all this advice, you will still have problems with certain essays that you don't know <u>what</u> to say in response. It always helps to trade essays with another teacher and say, "Read this essay and then my comments. Am I addressing the main problem here? How else might I explain it?" Often, a fresh reader can suggest an easy solution to a frustrating or baffling problem.

**Part Two: Chapter Commentary and
Answers to Questions**

Chapter 1: Writing Myths and Rituals

Some teachers like to begin with a discussion of writing rituals while others prefer to get their students writing immediately without spending much time in the first week discussing myths and rituals for writing. But whether you assign this material early, or do it later in the context of the first or second writing assignment, having students discuss their perceptions about writing and their writing rituals is valuable for several reasons.

First, even if writers are not "blocked" by the task of writing, procrastination is a tenacious opponent. Encouraging students to discuss <u>how</u> they write should enable them to see that most writers do not begin with the intimidating task of producing a final draft. Instead, they start with some form of invention or prewriting that begins the all-important momentum.

Second, a writer's attitude is crucial to the writing process. Some students may not have a positive attitude about writing or may have had negative experiences. Teachers should learn how the past performances of their students are affecting them or how an attitude about writing may be discouraging them.

Third, writers learn about their writing by observing their process and articulating their successes and problems. If teachers are going to help writers <u>during</u> rather than after the writing process, students need to learn self-diagnosis. They have to learn <u>when</u> and <u>where</u> they need help. They need to learn to say, "I think I'm having a problem here," even if they do not yet know how to solve the problem. Teachers should be coaches, but that metaphor hides a crucial difference between physical games and writing. Much of the writing game is thinking, planning, and drafting, and little of that process is visible from the sideline. Teachers need to teach students to become more aware when they have a problem and need help.

If your course begins immediately with a writing assignment, work in a discussion of myths and rituals after the first essay while students' writing processes are fresh in their minds.

Chapter 2: Purposes and Processes for Writing

A bit of background review on the purposes of writing may be helpful here. This text revises the old paradigm based on the <u>modes</u> of writing (Exposition, Description, Narration, and Argumentation--sometimes referred to as EDNA) and the traditional organizational <u>strategies</u> (definition, classification, division, process analysis, comparison/contrast, and causal analysis). The text is based, instead, on a <u>sequence of purposes for writing</u>. This scheme is derived from Kinneavy's aims for writing (see articles by Kinneavy and Secor in Part III), but is modified to provide students more practice in referential and persuasive aims. In <u>The Prentice Hall Guide for College Writers</u>, description as a mode is translated into Observing, and narration becomes Remembering. Writing from reading and writing from library and field resources is then covered in the Reading and Investigating chapters. These chapters provide practice in the three basic sources of invention: writing from observing, writing from memory, and writing from other texts. Then the chapters on Explaining, Evaluating, Problem Solving, and Arguing illustrate the major types of claims made by writers of expository/argumentative prose: claims of fact and claims of cause-and-effect (treated in the Explaining chapter), claims of value (covered in the Evaluating chapter), claims of policy (explained in the Problem Solving chapter), and multiple or combined claims (as illustrated in Chapter 10, Arguing).

The key point here is that writing assignments based on categories of <u>purpose</u> serve the writer better than categories of mode or strategy. The writer's plan or intent is the beacon that guides the writing process. Writers do revise their purpose on some occasions, but college writing assignments typically contain an embedded purpose: recall a personal experience that relates to a given class topic; report on a laboratory experiment; respond to an article; explain how a natural process works; evaluate an article, film, or community service; propose a solution to a given problem; or argue for or against a proposition.

Writing processes, like purposes for writing, are varied, shifting, and individual, but most writers agree that there are distinct dimensions such as invention, shaping, and revising that occur in most complex writing tasks. The writing process modeled by this text is a compromise between linear textbook models and recursive and multi-dimensional writing practices. Just as a writer cannot put all her ideas down at once but must sequence them in the scribal, linear form that is writing, so teachers and writers sometimes need plans to give them a sense of purpose, direction, and accomplishment. The writing process described in this chapter (and outlined in the <u>Guide to the Writing Process</u> on the inside front cover of this text) is intended to be a flexible guide, not a blueprint. The required linearity of print and the rigid placement in graphics always belies the recursiveness and downright muddiness of the actual task. Although the actual cognitive path of the writer may be confused and torturous, linear plans can help direct some writers as they wrestle to discover the language necessary for effective communication.

Finally, discussing purpose and audience in class helps students understand the important <u>rhetorical dimension</u> of writing. How to write, what to say, how much evidence to provide, how to organize, what voice or style to use--all of these are questions that have answers only in a given rhetorical situation. The sooner students see that all writing is situated or defined by a rhetorical context, the sooner they will realize that the "rules" of writing vary from one context or piece of discourse to the next. As a writing coach, your most frequent answer to a question about a given piece of writing is, "**It depends.**" Should writers use "I" in an essay? It depends on the desired degree of formality. Should writers use personal experience? Probably, but it depends on the assignment, the audience, and desired effect. Should writers avoid passive voice? Again, it depends. Writers should learn to see how the rhetorical dimensions of their writing (purpose, audience, occasion, genre) establish the "rules" of writing for that particular piece of writing.

Elizabeth Wong, "The Struggle to Be an All-American Girl"
Robert Zoellner, "I'm OK, But You're Not"

These essays are both short personal essays featuring a strong voice and memorable examples and details, but they differ in tone and content. Wong's essay is an excellent example of a remembering essay about growing up in a multicultural background, while Zoellner's essay uses personal experience and an ironic tone to take an unpopular stand in favor of smoker's rights. Often, students assume that Zoellner is simply arguing in favor of smoking, but his thesis is more accurately reflected in the title and the final paragraph: Zoellner is attacking any attitude or behavior that makes us feel self-righteous or gives us that "holier-than-thou" feeling. Because Zoellner's essay always provokes a lively discussion and response, it is a good essay to practice writing a summary/response journal entry. (See Chapter 5, Reading.)

Responses to Questions for Writing and Discussion.

1. List key words that the students used to describe each essay. Then ask students to cite particular passages that illustrate why they reacted as they did. Can they then analyze the class an "audience" for these two essays?

2. The primary purpose of the Wong essay is to express the author's ambivalent feelings. Zoellner's essay is more persuasive throughout, arguing that people should examine their own lifestyles before criticizing others. In both essays, the thesis crystalizes in the final sentence.

3. Wong's role is more reflective: She reminisces about her childhood, writes in simple sentences that capture her childhood experience, and focuses more on her own attitudes than on the reader's. Zoellner's role is more imposing; he is more of a gadfly. He is more formal in the beginning (e.g., the reference to John Barth), his sentences are more complex (e.g., the first sentence of the next-to-last paragraph), and he argues a more controversial issue. (The students' guesses about each writer's role or personality should prepare them to grasp concepts of tone, voice, and persona discussed in Chapter 4.)

4-5. These questions ask for the specific details that create each essay's sense of audience and structure. In comparison to Wong's essay, Zoellner's structure is more formal (Barth's insight, illustration, conclusion), his political references more frequent and overt, and his vocabulary more demanding of the reader.

Neil Petrie, "Athletes and Education"

Neil Petrie's essay, which appeared originally in The Chronicle of Higher Education, appeals both to teachers and students. Most teachers have felt the pressures from collegiate athletic departments to excuse students from class and help them make up missed work. And many students are aware of the preferential treatment which some athletes receive. What most students don't see, however, is how some athletes like John are themselves used by the system and, as Petrie says, discarded "after the final buzzer." Petrie's thesis makes this essay easy to discuss in class, since both regular students and athletes can begin to realize how they contribute to a system that creates a few heroes and exploits many others.

The essay works wonderfully for pre-reading and discussion activities. Have students write for 10 minutes about the virtues and abuses of college athletics before they read Petrie's essay. Follow this write-to-learn activity with a brief discussion. Then assign the essay for the following class period. During the next period, ask students to report on their responses to Petrie: Did his essay confirm their preconceptions? Did his essay change their point of view? What most surprised them about the essay?

Another fruitful angle for discussion is to ask students to discuss how the "system" of collegiate athletics is created and sustained. Even if they don't attend basketball or football games, how do they as students contribute to the status quo of the system? What kinds of resistance are likely to modify or change the system? Perhaps some students will begin offering evaluations, policy recommendations, or arguments for or against the current system. You can use that discussion to discuss the various kinds of essays (remembering, investigating/reporting, explaining, evaluating, problem-solving, arguing) that can be written on a single topic or to preview the kinds of essays that they will write during this course.

Responses to Questions for Writing and Discussion.

2. Have students discuss, preferably in small groups, the audience and purpose of the essay. Perhaps bring copies of The Chronicle of Higher Education to illustrate the magazine's audience. Petrie's subject is the student-athlete, but his audience is other educators. He appeals to this audience by describing himself as a member of academe, by citing several

examples of student athletes in his and his colleagues' classes, and by using "we" in paragraph 17. Petrie's purpose is to evaluate the collegiate athletic system (see paragraphs 1, 9, 17, and 18). He states the thesis most clearly at the end of paragraph 9. (Paragraph one explains the dilemma that sets up the thesis.)

3. Paragraphs 1-4: introduction to the dilemma and short examples; 5-8: problems in the system; 9: statement of the problem in the system (thesis); 10-16: extended example of John; 17-18: conclusion and restatement of thesis.

4,5. Asks students to project a solution from Petrie's evaluation of the problem.

Declaration of Independence

Responses to Questions for Writing and Discussion

1. This question asks students to describe the differences between the language of the version they know and the language of the rough draft.

2. The sentence "We hold these truths . . ." is a good example of an effective revision.

3. Use of the words, "dissolve" and "separation" in the first sentence, for example, makes the meaning or intent of the declaration much clearer and stronger.

4. Eliminating sexist language requires replacing "mankind" with "people" or "all people" and "men" with "people." Were we, today, advising Thomas Jefferson and the committee of five, however, we might ask them to address human rights as well as political rights.

Chapter 3: Observing

If you are teaching the Observing chapter, pay attention to three objectives. First, you are teaching <u>methods of observation</u> that should be useful for later writing and thinking. Second, you need to show students how to get beyond <u>purposeless</u> iteration of observed details in order to write descriptive prose that <u>focuses on some main idea</u> or dominant impression. They will probably begin their notes or log with unrelated details, but during the revision process, ask students to focus on a main idea by considering what they <u>discovered</u>, what they learned, what surprised them, or how the reality differed from the initial appearance. Finally, you need to think about the skills you hope students will <u>carry over into later assignments</u> in the term. The observing and describing skills will be important in nearly all of the later chapters.

First, the Observing chapter gives students advice about methods for observing their subjects, writing in their journals, and making sketches of what they see, but the most important habit they should learn is to <u>repeatedly</u> observe the person, place or thing they are focusing on. Teaching students to repeatedly observe helps students see detail; it helps them get beyond their preconceptions; and it enables them to see how their subject is changing. Most importantly, however, it begins the difficult process of teaching <u>revision</u>. Reobserving is revision.

Second, without careful guidance, students will write purposeless "so-what" essays with eight or eighty examples of sensory details, but no point, or no main idea.. Sometimes, teaching patterns for expressing the main idea will help students identify their purpose or point. Often the main idea can be expressed as a contrasting statement about discovery, surprise, or learning:

I expected to see x, but I was surprised to see y.

Other people (friends, experts, etc.) usually see x, but I saw y.

Initially, I saw x, but after repeated observations, I discovered y.

In fact, several of these patterns are worked out in the professional examples in the chapter. Mowat expects to gather data proving that wolves are decimating the caribou, but discovers another key food source for the arctic wolf. Dinesen at first sees a radiant, pulsing Iguana, but after it dies, she sees only a grey lump. During your class sessions, conferences, and workshops on the observing essay, make sure students subordinate their sensory details to their discovery or to their main idea.

Finally, think what you want your students to <u>learn</u> from writing their observing essays and to <u>carry over</u> to their next essays. Typically, I want my students to learn the difference between SHOWING and TELLING. I want to teach them how to make sensory details do the work in their writing. Without those "showing" details of color, roughness, odor, grit, and vibration, they will never engage their reader's senses and the reader's active imagination. Without the reader's engagement and active participation, communication will likely fail.

Samuel H. Scudder, "Take This Fish and Look At It"

Right from the start, students should understand that this essay is about observing, but it is not, strictly speaking, an observing essay. "Take This Fish and Look At It" is a remembering essay about methods of observation, and especially about the role observation plays in the scientific method. Like any good remembering essay, it has scene-setting, detailed description, good use of dialogue, and a clear point to the essay: "Facts are stupid things until brought into connection with some general law." Put another way, Scudder is saying that general laws enable us to see and understand what we are looking at. Or, as Frank Smith says in Understanding Reading, "What we see is related to what we are looking for, not to all possible interpretations." Scudder's essay helps us understand that "reading the world" is very much like reading texts. This essay prepares students for the methodology needed for their observing essays as well as for the active reading strategies discussed in Chapter 5, Reading.

Responses to Questions for Writing and Discussion

1. Since this chapter is about using observing to learn and communicate, ask students what observing they did of their best teachers and how those teachers taught them to observe.
2. Upon rereading Scudder's essay, students should notice that this essay is more about the *process* of observing than it is a model of observing. Still, the essay illustrates many observing techniques: writer's role—as student; sensory details—about the fish in paragraphs 7-9 and 12, about the professor (1-6, 17-21); comparisons and images—"neckless," "infectious," and "like a shadow" (7); what is not there—"those were not the days" or "dared not show any aversion" (7); noting changes—"the fish began to look loathsome" (8). This essay has many other examples of observing techniques.
3. Scudder informs us about fish; he explains how Agassiz taught his students; he persuades us that Agassiz's teaching is effective; and he entertains us by recounting his anxiety and discomfort. Scudder's primary purpose, however, is persuasive: What Scudder learned from Agassiz was of great value (29).
4. Some initial details are objective ("In ten minutes," "my specimen was dry," "I dashed fluid"). Later impressions are more subjective ("loathsome" and "ghastly"). The dominant impression is Scudder's growing anxiety and despair over his predicament.

101

Barbara Kingsolver, "High Tide in Tucson"

Kingsolver's essay not only models how the observing essay should contain vivid, sensory details that support a key idea or discovery, it also shows how writers can move from observation to reflection. In Kingsolver's essay, her "discovery" (that "even a desert has tides,") leads to her reflection about the similarities between Buster's adventures and her own life. The second half of Kingsolver's essay, beginning with paragraph 15, becomes a personal essay reflecting on the parallels between her own life and Buster's and the similarities human beings and animals. Yet Kingsolver continually points toward her main idea: "We humans have to grant the presence of some past adaptations, even in their unforgivable extremes." That focus leads to her conclusion that we should begin this new century "by renewing our membership in the Animal Kingdom.

Responses to Questions for Writing and Discussion

1. Kingsolver brings "new eyes" when she notices that Buster seemed to be dead and that he would not move for days. She reflects on the lunar cycles and then remembers information from when she was "a graduate student of animal behavior." F.A. Brown's story about the tides enables her to observe Buster in a new light and then to understand how Buster's behavior relates to her own life.

2. The early paragraphs of Kingsolver's essay are full of details of sight ("one long red talon of a leg") and sound ("tap-tap-taping like a blind man's cane"). She has images ("a pair of eyes on stalks, and a purple claw"), metaphors ("the long grasp of its ice-tong legs"), and similes ("fearless like a rock climber's dream"). She describes what is not there when she says her house "had a deficit of males" or when she notes that "Chicago has no ocean." She continually notes changes in Buster's behavior ("Buster seemed to be dead" and realizes later that Buster had "lapsed into hyperactivity."

3. Other examples of Kingsolver's use of humor are her observation that in Arizona, the nearest water source was the "munincipal sewage-treatment plant and her comparison of Buster to Cinderella's sisters "preening for the ball." Her humor in the early part of the essay allows readers to see her as a person, not just a scientist observing the behavior of whelks. Kingsolver's

essay is a "personal essay" in the true sense: the essay is about how she understands her own role in life and her connection to her animal heritage.

4. Paragraphs 15 and 16 set up the parallels between Buster's experiences and Kingsolver's life: "donning the shell" of a car, being a "refugee," moving far from her original home, getting used to being in the desert, and yet never ceasing to long in her bones for what she left behind.

5. In paragraph 19, Kingsolver poses the question, "What does it mean . . . to be an animal in human clothing?" and gives her answers: We are "creatures of inexplicable cravings," "thinking isn't everything," "we need to grant the presence of some past adaptations," and her main point that "the most shameful tradition of Western civilization is our need to deny we are animals."

Farley Mowat, "Observing Wolves"

All three professional essays in this chapter illustrate how observing essays require some narrative framework (usually a beginning and an ending) to set up and conclude the scenes of observation. As a discussion or small group exercise, have your students identify which paragraphs form the narrative or expository framework and which paragraphs constitute the actual observation. After they have discussed how Mowat shapes his essay, have them work on their own observing essays, setting up the key scene(s) and writing a conclusion.

A second topic for discussion is Mowat's observational method. While Annie Dillard is a bystander, watching as the events with the snake unfold in front of her, Mowat disturbs the environment just to see how the wolves will react--just as a child might disturb a spider web with a stick to see how the spider reacts. After students identify places where Mowat sets up his behavioral "experiments," have them look at the drafts of their own essays. Have they actively changed or altered the environment that they are observing? Should they?

Responses to Questions for Writing and Discussion

1. Use this question as a pre-reading prompt for students to answer the day you assign the essay. Discuss their preconceptions briefly in class that day and then again after students have read the essay.

2. Mowat describes his equipment and habits of observation throughout the essay, but particularly in paragraphs 1-3 and again in paragraphs 23, 29, and 32.

3. Much of the fun of Mowat's essay comes from his personality--from his sense of humor, his ingenuity, and his scientific training. Mowat's personality, however, leads him to participate in the scene while other scientists might remain as detached as possible. Ask your students to discuss whether Mowat should be an active or passive observer of wolves.

4. Mowat illustrates four of the keys to vivid and successful observation. First, he repeatedly observes the wolves, in order to learn their paths and their behavior. Second, most of his sensory detail is visual, but he refers to smells

in paragraph 2 and sounds in paragraph 5. Third, Mowat marks his own territory precisely to observe changes in the wolves' behavior. Finally, Mowat describes what is not there in paragraph 2, when he says he took no weapons of any kind, when he discovers that wolves were not nomadic roamers (paragraph 7), or when he says in paragraph 9 that he never discovered "any evidence of bickering or disagreements" between neighboring wolves.

Jennifer Macke, "Permanent Tracings"

Macke's strength in this essay is her immersion in the location which enables her to observe the tattoo parlor setting, the customers, the tattoos, and the person who actually does the tattoos. Her essay could include some additional descriptions of individual tattoos, but she does a nice job of visualizing for the reader the tattoo parlor, the customers and the proprietor. In addition, her essay also illustrates how observing and describing are important skills for later chapters. It would be easy for Ms. Macke to turn this paper into an essay investigating the tattoo parlor and/or evaluating it.

Responses to <u>Questions for Writing and Discussion</u>

1. Paragraph 1 does a good job of providing descriptive details of the sights and sounds of the office: "dark paneled walls," "color Polaroid snapshots," "gold and green davenport," "the oscillating fan," "the buzz of the needle," and "a freeze-dried turtle." All these details support the dominant impression that the office has a "decor reminiscent of the 1970s." Have students examine other paragraphs for vivid sensory details. Some readers want Macke to describe sample tattoos, such as the rose with a heart stem or one of Gasket's tattoos that the writer compares to "Picasso's brilliantly colored dreamlike images."

2. Macke could add descriptions of the various tattoos just before or immediately after the paragraphs describing the belly button tattoo of a young college female. Describing sample images used in tattoos or describing the number of colors typically used would give readers a better visual picture of Macke's work.

3. Make copies of the peer response questions printed earlier in the Observing chapter, and use those--with Macke's notes and her essay--to model how to give peer review advice. If students practice giving advice to Macke, then they will be better prepared to give each other useful and constructive feedback on their own drafts.

4. Often, it is easy for students to give each other advice about drafts but hard to revise their own essays based on peer's advice. Having students examine how the advice they would give to Macke might work for their own essays may teach them to critically revise their own essays without subjecting their papers to the criticism of peer reviewers.

Stephen White, "Empty Windows"

The observing chapter suggests that "describing what is <u>not</u> there" can shape and focus an entire essay. In "Empty Windows," White relies extensively on his imagination to contrast the tangible, broken houses in the gloomy canyon with the "sunny home" that once must have supported the "peaceful, agrarian Anasazi." Paragraphs 5-7 show White's imagination actively working to reconstruct what is not there--what he can only imagine of the lives of those ancient Indian people.

Responses to <u>Questions for Writing and Discussion</u>

3. In White's essay, paragraph 5 has sensory detail ("clicking of camera shutters," "trickling of a stream," "red adobe walls,"), a contrast between the excavated ruins and the abandoned houses, and a comparison of the excavated ruins to a modern city. Throughout the essay, White refers to the Anasazi, who are not there. He notes, in paragraph 6, the change between the ancient prosperous community and the present silence. White projects his role as a tourist who is compelled by the force of his imagination to contemplate as well as observe the empty ruins.

4. Chronological order shapes the essay overall. No paragraphs follow a spatial order, but comparison shapes paragraphs 5 and 6. The image of the gloom and gray weather also recurs frequently enough to help shape this essay.

Chapter 4: Remembering

Students love to write narrative essays, but frequently they have problems focusing on some main idea for their experiences. In teaching the remembering essay, then, focus on the process of revision. Students who are unsure of their main point may discover it during an early draft. After the first draft, students should concentrate on <u>sharpening their main focus</u> and amplifying supporting details and events and, at the same time, reducing or eliminating the less relevant details and episodes.

Just as students should learn SHOWING vs. TELLING from their observing essay, they should learn what a SPECIFIC EXAMPLE is from their remembering essay. Have students think of a specific example as compressed narrative incident, <u>set in time and space</u>. The chapter is full of such specific examples: Andrea Lee standing in "Mayakovsky Square, not far from the Tchaikovsky Concert Hall," looking at a computerized electric sign. Scott Momaday remembering her mother standing at the stove on a winter morning. Helen Keller remembering the moment that Anne Sullivan sticks her hand under water and spells "w-a-t-e-r." Alice Walker recreating the moment when her eye is stinging and the blood rises to block out her vision of the leaves of the tree. In writing their remembering essays, students should learn (and recognize that they have learned) how to write a specific example based on personal experience.

Helen Keller, "The Day Language Came Into My Life"

One way to narrow and focus the remembering essay assignment is to ask students to concentrate on just one memorable day in their life. Helen Keller's essay provides an excellent example for a short essay about just one day. Keller uses the first opening paragraphs to set up the context for that important day, describes the day in the middle paragraphs, and then concludes (see paragraphs 8 and 9) with what she learned that day and why it was important in her life. If students use Keller's essay as a model, however, remind them that they may want to use dialogue between the characters and more visual description of the scene and the key people. For obvious reasons, Keller uses details of sound and touch more than visual images. Perhaps, though, students should follow Keller's example by closing their eyes and remembering sensory details of smell, sound, and touch to supplement their visual memories.

Responses to <u>Questions for Writing and Discussion</u>

1. One of the purposes of this journal exercise is to set students' expectations and schema about "first memories." Another purpose is to teach students what a specific example is--an incident located in time and space that illustrates some idea or point.

2. Students usually recognize the archetypal patterns in Helen Keller's story: The difficult battle with a disability and the victory of the heart and mind over physical limitation.

3. The analogy in paragraph three compares a voyage at sea in a dense fog with her struggle with blindness and deafness. Keller is trying to explain a difficult concept--the notion of language acquisition--through a simpler and more tangible event.

4. Writing a list of names of things from students' lives at the board may allow students to see how names allow people to perceive relationships among the things and names. Perception of relationships allows Keller to think, to discover a "new thought."

5. Keller changes from being frustrated and destructive to being fascinated by her newly discovered world. She changes from an inward-focused, almost autistic personality, to an out-going, eager, and excited person.

6. Asking students to share their experiences with disabled or "differently abled" people should help students move beyond their stereotyped perceptions about people with differences. Their experiences should bear on the act of observing, too. What they discover about a disabled or just different person should be different than their initial expectations.

Mike Rose, "Lives on the Boundary"

If Keller's essay models a compact and focused essay about one day in our lives, Rose's' essay models a more reflective remembering essay that recreates only a few actual scenes and covers a wide range of time. Rose's essay is a good model for students for its topic and for it's reflection on the value of education, but be sure to tell your students that they should focus on just a FEW scenes from just ONE time period of their education. In only 3-5 pages, they can't cover the kind of ground Mike Rose does in this lengthy chapter.

Responses to <u>Questions for Writing and Discussion</u>

1. In his essay, Rose refers to several boundaries that he faces and must "cross." Some are physical, geographical boundaries, such as the boundaries around Ninety-first and Vermont which he "crosses" with the help of the busses. Other boundaries include the tests he takes, the vocational track he finds himself placed in, the boundaries of lack of education faced by his parents, and the boundaries faced by the voc-ed students such as Ken Harvey who says, "I just wanna be average." Rose crosses the boundaries encircling the voc-ed students, he crosses some boundaries by being a member of the track team and by being in Jack MacFarland's class; he does not cross the boundaries in mathematics and physical sciences. Rose calls his introduction to reading under MacFarland a "Baedeker to a vocabulary of ideas," an image which echoes the geographical boundaries metaphor. Finally, at the end of the essay, Rose says that his new knowledge allowed him "to act as though I were living beyond the limiting boundaries of South Vermont."

2. Rose uses detailed and vivid descriptions of the students in his voc-ed program, of his teachers, of his test-taking escapades, of Jack MacFarland, and of the hundreds of books in Jack MacFarland's apartment. Of MacFarland, for example, Rose says, "He was a beatnik who was born too late. His teeth were stained, he tucked his sorry tie in between the third and fourth buttons of his shirt, and his pants were chronically wrinkled." Paragraph 16 presents a vivid description of MacFarland's apartment: "Books were all over: stacked, piled, tossed, and crated, underlined and dog eared, well worn and new. Cigarette ashes crusted with coffee in saucers or spilled over the sides of motel ashtrays." Rose does not describe what is missing or absent, but he does give images to make his descriptions more vivid. In paragraph 4, for example, Rose says "students will float to the mark you set"; he calls vocational education a "dumping ground"; and he describes the kids

as "scuttling along at the bottom of the pond." Rose writes consistently from his own autobiographical point of view, as a voc-ed student becoming a literate reader and intellectual. The dominant idea is contained in the sustained metaphor of facing and crossing physical, personal, and intellectual boundaries.

3. Rose also effectively uses remembering techniques throughout his essay. He describes the voc-ed students well; he describes the textbooks with the plastic overlays; he describes key characters; and he describes the conflicts and changes he underwent as he crossed geographical, cultural, and intellectual boundaries. Rose could do more scene-setting, narrating specific scenes set in time in place, instead of describing typical or habitual actions. Rose also could use more actual dialogue instead of just referring to MacFarland's literary barbs or Jim Fitzsimmons' "chops." Rose uses reflection to good advantage, especially at the end of the essay.

4. Rose interweaves his narrative and reflective voices throughout the essay. For example, in paragraph 2, Rose begins by describing the tests that Mercy relied on, but he soon interjects his own reflective comment on "the current spate of reports on the schools" that criticize parents for "not involving themselves in the education of their children." Similarly, Rose begins paragraph 4 by saying, "Students will float to the mark you set," before he talks about his teachers, such as Brother Slattery, who worked hard to educate the vocational students. Much of the middle part of the essay, Rose narrates key events in his education, but he closes with a couple of paragraphs of reflection: "Let me be the first to admit that there was a good deal of adolescent passion in this embrace of the avant-garde."

Alice Walker, "Beauty: When the Other Dancer Is the Self"

Walker's essay is long and complex, but students always enjoy reading it. This essay is repeatedly cited by students as the best essay in the textbook. Perhaps because of its power and vividness, however, the essay tends to take possession of the narrative territory in students' minds. It can be so powerful that students think they must deal with large, emotional issues, and tell a ten-year story of their lives. In some ways, therefore, Keller's essay, with its more focused scope, or Richard Rodriguez' story of his childhood are better models for the short narrative piece that most students should attempt. For these reasons, then, some instructors prefer to wait until students have their own essays in draft form and then use Walker's essay to discuss ways to revise their drafts--by adding dialogue, using flashbacks, adding poetry, or switching to present tense.

Responses to <u>Questions for Writing and Discussion</u>

Note: Following discussions of this and other essays in the text, remember to <u>connect</u> what the students learn to their own writing. Have students apply the same reading skills to each other's drafts: Why is the writer sharing these experiences? What techniques for writing about memories does the writer use? What is the main point or dominant idea? What are key scenes or images? Where does dialogue help the writer retell the event?

1-2. She writes to share experiences with readers and at the same time to create a work of art for readers to experience. These questions encourage readers to use Walker's essay--both as self-expression and as literature--to probe their own experiences.

3. The blinding episode (paragraphs 8-15), for example, has many <u>sensory details</u>, is itself a <u>specific scene</u>, develops the <u>conflict</u> between Alice Walker and her brother, describes a dramatic <u>change</u> ("I watch as its . . . leaves are blotted out by the rising blood"), and ends with a <u>contrast</u> between past and present.

4. The dominant idea is her reconciliation with her blind eye and thus with the part of her personality (represented by the dream dancer) that "comes through all right."

5. Scenes: summer day in 1947; Easter Sunday, 1950; eight years old and a tomboy (1953); eight years old in school (1953); twelve years old (1957); fourteen years old (1959); a woman interviewer (1983); talking to Jimmy (unidentified year); thirty-three years old in the desert (1978); and twenty-seven years old with her baby daughter (1975). She changes the chronological order because she realizes in 1983 that she has already made her peace. She then remembers three episodes (with Jimmy, in the desert in 1978, and with her daughter in 1975) that helped her make her peace. The dream dance occurs last also because it most dramatically represents her reconciliation.

6. For an effective workshop, assign small groups one episode each and have them locate images of sight and blindness. Throughout, images of seeing and not seeing, imagining, and understanding are intermixed, leading to the dream dance (ironically to Stevie Wonder's song).

7. The italicized sentences at the beginning or end of episodes reveal her thoughts, as she writes in the present about past events. Walker continually uses the contrasts between past and present to set up her dominant idea.

Todd Petry, "The Wind Catcher"

Petry's essay provides an excellent model of a remembering essay that grows out of looking at a familiar object. Other objects that may stimulate memories for students are old photographs, childhood books, toys, a pet, or even a house they used to live in. Some instructors have even asked students to bring one object from their homes or from their rooms that reminds them about something in their past. The ensuing brief "show and tell" discussion can be an excellent invention exercise for every student.

Responses to Questions for Writing and Discussion

1. The "twisted off balance" appearance reminds him of the time when he threw the hat in the face of an irate mother cow, and the missing hat band reminds him, briefly, of the brush at Pray Mesa.

2. Some other titles: The Rode Hard Hat, The Cow Manure Special, The Old Cow Catcher, The Dilapidated Resistol, My Favorite Hat, General Custer's Hat, Old Hat. List titles--good ones and silly ones--at the board and ask the

class to explain which is most effective and why. Choosing an appropriate title helps both readers and writers focus on the dominant idea, key images, and tone in a piece of writing.

3. The main idea is captured most explicitly in the final sentence in paragraph five.

Julie Bovard, "The Red Chevy"

Although Julie Bovard does remember and describe the day of her rape, her essay focuses more remembering and recalling the short and long term psychological and emotional effects of her rape. As if to help distance herself from the traumatic event, she discusses statistics about rape, details about the courtroom proceedings, and facts about "typical" responses to rape. She describes herself both from a personal point of view and from the point of view of a rape counselor. She states that her fear that the rapist would return was "normal," that her inability to face unfamiliar situations was a "classic" symptom, and that the question, "why me?" really has no answer. Despite this distance, however, Bovard returns to her own personal story at the end to declare that although she was a victim or rape, she is not a victim any longer.

Responses to <u>Questions for Writing and Discussion</u>

1. Ask students to respond to these questions in a journal entry or, if your students agree, in an electronic discussion forum.

2. Bovard wants her readers to know—even to feel—the emotional effects of rape. She is giving information about who rapists are, who their victims are, and what the emotional effects are, but her goal is to convince her readers that the after effects of rape include "physical repercussions," but also have an "enormous psychological and emotional impact."

3. Bovard uses several of the techniques for writing a remembering essay. Although she does not describe the physical features of her rapist, she describes the cuts and bruises he inflicts and the emotional effect of his cologne on the day of the courtroom hearing. She focuses on specific times and places—particularly the car, the place of the rape, and the day of the courtroom hearing. She describes changes, contrasts, or conflicts when she remembers the "event" as she describes it, and especially when she describes the effect of actually seeing her attacker again in the courtroom. Bovard draws connections between the past and present most clearly when she describes how her therapy and counseling enabled her to understand that the rape was not her fault. Finally, the focus throughout the essay is clearly on the psychological and emotional effects of the rape.

4. Bovard uses research to gather statistics about rape, about rapists and their victims, and about the "normal" feelings and experiences of rape victims.

Bovard uses her research as part of her strategy of gaining control of herself and her situation—a sense of control that makes possible and leads to her final emphatic statement: "I was a victim of rape, but through years of counseling and support *I am not a victim any longer*."

5. Bovard's title, "The Red Chevy," is a label but it does not make us curious or hint at the content or the thesis of the essay. Would another title be more effective? Have your students brainstrom a list of possible titles. Which of these titles reflect her purpose most accurately while maintaining the tone that she creates in her essay. After students do this exercise, ask them to go back and look at the drafts of their own essays. What other titles for their own essays might they consider?

Chapter 5: Reading

The reading chapter enables students to spend more time learning active reading strategies (prereading, text annotation, collaborative annotation, summaries) and practicing responding to written texts. In previous editions of **The Prentice Hall Guide**, reading and summarizing texts was treated only briefly in the Investigating chapter and in the teaching tips and suggestions. As our composition program--and others around the country--began to spend more time teaching critical reading, however, we found ourselves designing materials to supplement the Investigating chapter's treatment of reading, paraphrasing, and summarizing.

This new chapter allows teachers to introduce very basic psycholinguistic theories of reading, to discuss critical reading processes, and to teach short summary and response essays that introduce students to text-based writing. During several years of experimentation, we used the summary-response format as an impromptu placement examination, as an exit examination, as journal assignments to prepare students for class discussions, and as short assignments to help students learn to read critically and evaluate sources for the longer argumentative and research essays. Both teachers and students reported that practicing summarizing and responding early in the course helped students with their later assignments, made their longer research projects easier, and prepared them for writing assignments in their other courses.

For writing courses where teachers are using thematic groups of essays in a reader, the Reading chapter also enables teachers to incorporate outside readings early in the course. Students can read several essays and write a short (two page) summary and response prior to class discussions. As every teacher knows, class discussions are much more lively and fruitful when students have already read, summarized, and responded to the assigned essays.

Nicholas Lemann, "Atlas Shrugs"

Nicholas Lemann's review essay summarizes and comments on several "texts." After giving background on the history of geography, he reviews an exhibition at the New York Public Library featuring maps of the American West. Lemann then comments on the critical cartography movement, as illustrated particularly by J. B. Harley's *The New Nature of Maps* and Susan Schulten's *The Geographical Imagination in America, 1880-1950*. Lemann's purpose is to review these texts but also to introduce his reader to the notion of "critical cartography." Lemann wants us to understand these authors' argument that maps are polemic—they are always social constructions that make cultural and political arguments.

Responses to <u>Questions for Writing and Discussion</u>

1. Asking students to inventory maps in their possession is just a first step in getting them to read texts as maps. For your discussion of this essay, you may wish to bring Harley's and Schulten's books to class to show your students kinds of older maps that these authors are discussing.

2. Most of the information in paragraphs 1-8 helps orient readers to the history and background of "critical cartography," but the concepts and vocabulary may be difficult for your students. Ask them to point to passages that are easy to understand versus those that are more difficult. Do your students think Lemann has given them enough information? Has he given enough or too much summary? Should he make his explanations clearer for them as readers? During this discussion, be sure to require them to point out specific passages and sentences that are clear or are too difficult.

3. The "texts" that Lemann discusses include the exhibition at the New York Public Library, the two books by Harley and Schulten, the maps of Frederick Von Egloffstein, Rand McNally's *Elementary Geography*, and *National Geographic*. Ask your students whether they need more summary of each text or whether some of these texts might be removed from his essay to give his review a clearer focus.

4. Use Lemann's comments in paragraph 17 as a starting point to discuss the main point of the essay—and thus the basic argument of critical cartography. A good many students will almost certainly believe that maps *are* just a set of directions for getting from point A to point B.

David Quammen, "Animal Rights and Beyond"

Although David Quammen is writing for a popular audience--the readers of Outside magazine--his subject and style is fairly representative of academic essays that students might read in their other classes. Quammen's essay itself is a critical review of books by two animal rights philosophers--Peter Singer and Tom Regan--and Quammen deals seriously with the "important and tricky" philosophical notions raised by these philosophers about how human beings should treat the animals who share our planet. Thus, Quammen's essay is a good model for the kind of critical review--or summary-response essay--that students will write in this chapter. And since the issues are timely and controversial, Quammen's essay can also be used as the subject for students own summary-response essays. (See, for example, the essay by Paula Fisher at the end of this chapter.)

Responses to <u>Questions for Writing and Discussion</u>

1. Question 1 asks students to "draw the line" between those species who deserve protected status or special rights and those who do not. Students may either draw a line and argue that lichen are inherently different from cats, or they may--perhaps wisely--refuse to draw the line, following Quammen's argument that everything that has life deserves special consideration. Whichever response they choose, however, this answer will help them articulate their own beliefs and thus be able to respond more fully to Quammen's essay.

2. Quammen's summary of the books by Singer and Regan is contained in paragraphs 4-14. In these paragraphs, Quammen uses most of the features of a good summary. He mentions both authors and both titles. He occasionally quotes directly from both authors. He regularly uses author "tags" such as "Peter Singer declares," "Singer admits," and "According to Regan" to continually remind the reader that he is summarizing these authors' ideas rather than giving his own reactions. Most readers would agree that Quammen is trying to be fair and objective in his summary of their ideas.

3. Quammen does not spend much time analyzing the rhetorical effectiveness of either book, but he does at least grant that both men are "applying the methods of systematic philosophy" to this important question. Thus,

Quammen suggests that he has no complaint with their rhetorical or philosophical method. Quammen spends most of his response agreeing and disagreeing with both authors. He commends them for "fighting a good fight" and for calling attention to animal abuses. Then, however, Quammen argues that their ideas reveal a "breathtaking smugness and myopia." Although some of Quammen's response might be called reflective, the majority focuses on Quammen's disagreement with their philosophical positions.

4. Quammen's outline is as follows:

    I. Intro: Paragraphs 1-2
    II. Review of early philosophers' views: Paragraph 3
    III. Summary and review of Singer and Regan: Paragraphs 4-14
        Singer: Paragraphs 5-9
        Regan: Paragraphs 10-14
    IV. Quammen's responses: Paragraphs 15-18
        Positive responses: Paragraph 15
        Negative responses: Paragraphs 16-18

Have the class identify the signals that help them identify each section.

5. Students probably will laugh at the thought that some readers think Quammen actually has a sense of humor, but there is some humor in paragraphs 2, 5, 7, 8, and 11.

6. The various texts represented in this chapter--Singer's and Regan's books, Quammen's essay, and Paula Fisher's response create a conversation that students should join. The more they read, the more clearly they should understand and be able to articulate their own position.

Paula Fisher, "Drawing the Line"

When students read Paula Fisher's essay, they may wonder why she should be writing a summary-response essay to an essay by David Quammen that is itself already a summary-response essay. The answer is, of course, that she is just engaging in a conversation about animal rights that has been going on for several centuries. Much academic writing is, in fact, part of a continuing conversation about a topic that is examined, revised, reconsidered, and repositioned in light of new evidence, different contexts, or changing beliefs. In writing her own summary-response essay, Paula Fisher merely adds her own voice and experience to the accumulated knowledge or changing ideas. When students write their own summary-response essays, they will also be engaging in a conversation that started long before they "discovered" the topic and will continue long after they have added their own voice and experience. (For another example of the summary-response or "conversation" essay, see "Who Should Take Charge?" by student writer Eui Young Hwang in Chapter Nine, Problem-Solving.)

Responses to Questions for Writing and Discussion

1. A key problem in writing an effective summary is to represent the most important ideas in an essay without paraphrasing all the ideas or giving unnecessary details from the essay. Ask students if Fisher's summary is too brief. If so, what should she include that she now omits? A key problem in a response is to relate all of the responses to one clear thesis. Does Fisher establish a thesis and relate her other responses to it? (Her thesis is most clearly stated in the final sentence, but her response might be clearer if this thesis were stated more explicitly at the beginning of paragraph 2.)

2. Fisher uses references to Quammen's text to support her agreement in paragraphs 2 and 3. She uses ideas from outside texts (uncited) when she refers to the LD-50 test in paragraph 3. She refers to her own experience in paragraph 5. Her most effective evidence occurs in paragraphs 3 and 4, where she refers to cruel experiments and anti-animal rights texts. Her personal experience in paragraph 5 could, however, be much more specific. Which specific practices are cruel and unnecessary and which ones are justifiable? What specific experiences did she have growing up on a cattle

ranch that would illustrate the difference between cruel practices that should be changed and those which are not cruel? What incidents might illustrate where farmers' rights should take precedence over animal rights?

3. A comparison of Fisher's double-entry log and her essay suggests that Fisher might use more of the information from her summary description on the left-hand side (more ideas from Singer and Regan; more of Quammen's positive and negative reactions) and more of her personal experience from the right-hand side (humane society, animal testing, grad students, medical testing, farming).

Jennifer Koester and Sonja H. Browe, "Two Responses to Deborah Tannen"

Before discussing these two student essays, be sure to have students read Deborah Tannen's essay in Chapter 7, Explaining, and write their own notes for a summary and response. Then they can read and discuss these two essays in light of their own summaries and responses.

Students should note that both Koester's and Browe's responses focus on a rhetorical analysis of the effectiveness of the text. Be sure to discuss other kinds of legitimate responses to these texts: relating Tannen's ideas to other gender based learning studies, recalling personal experience to support responses, and/or interpreting the significance or relevance of the Tannen's essay.

Responses to <u>Questions for Writing and Discussion</u>

1. Be sure to have students do this question before they read Koester's or Browe's responses.

2. Koester's summary focuses on three differences of classroom style between men and women that she finds in Tannen's essay, while Browe notices those differences but also describes Tannen's classroom experiment. Most students will argue that Browe's summary more accurately represents Tannen's article.

3. Both Koester and Browe concentrate on analyzing the effectiveness of the text. Be sure to have students brainstorm ways in which readers might agree/disagree with Tannen's text, or offer an interpretation or reflection supported by personal experience.

4. Koester focuses on Tannen's use of qualifications, on her effective use of evidence, and on her use of a parallel comparison/contrast format. Koester does ignore some of the unsupported assertions that Browe finds.

5. Browe finds that Tannen's essay "lacks credibility and is unfocused" (paragraph 2). Browe develops the lack of credibility claim in paragraphs 3-6 and explains how the article is unfocused in paragraphs 7 and 8.

6. Have the class members discuss which of their personal experiences might fit in Koester's or Browe's essays.

Chapter 6: Investigating

The purpose of an investigative essay is to **inform** readers about a fairly narrow aspect of a subject. An investigative essay usually answers a question or set of questions that readers might have (or questions that the writer generates for the reader) about the subject. Curiosity drives the writer of the investigative essay; curiosity about the answers to the writer's questions holds the reader's interest.

It is important to notice that investigating essays (i.e., essays whose purpose is to **report** about a subject or **inform** a reader) are similar to explaining essays, but the investigative essay has several unique characteristics:

First, the investigative essay is journalistic in spirit. The writer may appear in the essay as a person curious about the facts and dedicated to uncovering some facts or information that may surprise the reader (and the writer). It can be narrative and written in the first person, describing the chronological steps in the writer's search for answers. Always, however, a report assumes that the writer is getting ideas and information primarily from some <u>outside</u> source. An explaining essay, by contrast, may originate, at least in part, from the writer's own prior knowledge or expertise about the subject.

Second, in the spirit of the journalistic reporter, the writer of an investigative essay focuses on objectively representing the facts, ideas, and information from his or her sources. The writer is not "making it up" or giving his or her own information. In Chapter 5, Reading, the summary is actually a "report" on the main ideas from a text; the response, then, is the writer's explanation, analysis, or interpretation. In the summary, the writer is **reporting**; in the response, the writer is **explaining** or even **arguing**.

Third, investigative essays clearly show their dependence upon sources. Typically, these sources include both written texts and field resources (interview, surveys, and observations). Explaining essays obviously may use sources, but they may also rely on the writer's knowledge and expertise. The writer of an investigative essay says, "Here's what my sources say about this issue" while the writer of an explaining essay says, "Here's what I know or have learned about the issue."

One of the purposes of the investigating chapter is to familiarize students with an additional source of ideas. The observing and remembering chapters focus on writer-based information; the reading chapter focuses on text-based information, and the investigating chapter focuses on library-based and field-based sources of information. Most experienced teachers know that they cannot teach all the necessary library and field research skills in a single "research paper" at the end of the semester. Instead, these research skills must, like any other complex cognitive skill, be taught a bit at a time with frequent repetitions. The object of the writing in this chapter is to familiarize students with research strategies early in the term and then give them ample opportunity, in subsequent assignments, for practice.

From this chapter, students should learn how to conduct an interview, design a survey, find a few sources in the library, write a summary (if they did not already write a summary-response essay in Chapter 5), and incorporate their research into an essay. Obviously, with this many goals, teachers should not expect polished or lengthy investigative essays. But students can begin to learn these skills. As part of your assignment, have students do the following as they write their investigative essays: Complete an orientation tour in the library and find (and photocopy) one source. Practice writing a summary of their source in class. Practice interviewing each other in class, and then interview a person who is knowledgeable about their chosen topic. Design (and get small group feedback on) a short survey that they might use in their essay.

As you design your assignment, then, don't require a paper with more than two or three written sources. Ask students to use either an interview or a survey, to keep things simple. Have students focus their investigation on just a few key questions they need to answer for their audience.

Finally, as you teach this chapter, consider assigning it in conjunction with another chapter. For example, just as you might assign the observing chapter with the evaluating chapter, so the investigating chapter and the explaining chapter work well together. Or consider assigning a short investigative essay just before the problem solving essay. The investigative essay would report on a particular problem and the current "solutions" being applied to that problem. After reading the problem-solving chapter, then, students could argue for one particular solution for the problem they have identified and investigated.

Connie Koenenn, "Plotting a Net Gain"

Koenenn's essay nicely models for students how to use a variety of investigating sources. She uses personal interview, copies of a radio interview, material from Turkle's books, and personal observation. Be sure to have students notice this variety of source material as they read her essay and make plans for their own essays. Be sure that students notice how they are combining their reading skills from Chapter 5 and their observing skills from Chapter 3 as they investigate their subjects. Caution them, too, that investigating essays do not themselves argue for or against any position or interpretation. As Koenenn does, students should report their findings in an objective manner.

Responses to <u>Questions for Writing and Discussion</u>

1. The following sentences give answers to the second part of Connie Koenenn's investigating question: "What does Sherry Turkle think about the Internet?" Paragraph 1: "MIT sociologist Sherry Turkle looks at the Internet and sees a transformation in the way we view ourselves." Paragraph 2: "We can easily move through multiple identities . . . and we can embrace--or be trapped by--cyberspace as a way of life." Paragraph 5: "Her theory--that the computer isn't a tool but that it is giving you access to parts of yourself that you didn't have before--is revolutionary." Paragraph 9: "People can experience other aspects of themselves online."

2. Ask students to use this question as a write-to-learn entry during class. Some students will remember personal bits of information about Sherry Turkle, some will remember biographical details, and some will remember her comments about computers and the internet. The article intermixes information from all three areas. Then ask students if they have questions about Turkle that Connie Koenenn does not answer or if they want more information about Turkle than Koenenn provides. Analyzing their responses to Koenenn's article will prepare students to give constructive responses on their peer's drafts.

3. Koenenn uses a variety of sources as she constructs her essay. She begins by citing information from <u>Newsweek</u> and <u>Wired</u> magazines (paragraphs 4 and 5). Then she cites sentences taken from Michael Jackson's talk show (paragraphs 7 and 8). Beginning in paragraph 9, she uses information and

quotations taken from a personal interview. In paragraph 11, Koenenn cites ideas taken from Turkle's book, <u>Life on the Screen</u>, and she mentions two other works written by Turkle. Other biographical information may come from Koenenn's interview or from outside biographical sources. Having students reconstruct the sources for an investigating article enables them to see what kinds of sources are available or necessary for their own essays.

Jeremiah Creedon, "Life After Oil"

Writing in *Utne* magazine, Jeremiah Creedon summarizes the main ideas from an article in *Prospect* magazine by David Fleming. Creedon puts Fleming's comments in the context of the controversy over the potential drilling in the Artic National Wildlife Refuge and the debate over global warming and then adds other ideas from authors Thomas Gold and new age thinker Terence McKenna. In contrast to the more sophisticated article from *The New Yorker* on critical geography by Nicholas Lemann, Creedon's essay is shorter, easier, and less rigorous in its analysis.

Responses to <u>Questions for Writing and Discussion</u>

1. Use Creedon's essay to teach students basic interviewing skills. In addition, after students have interviewed each other, they will be better critical readers of Creedon's essay.

2. Creedon gets his readers attention not only with the title but with the opening sentence of his first paragraph: "Long after the oil age has burned itself out, the future will assign a date to when the flame first wavered." Creedon also provides good background information by answering several "W" questions. What: the Big Rollover; Who: the United States; When: approximately 2020; and Why: "There aren't more big discoveries to make."

3. In his investigating essay, Creedon focuses on two key questions: When will the Big Rollover happen and what effect will it have? Creedon addresses the first question initially in paragraph two, and addresses the effects it will have throughout the rest of the essay.

4. Creedon uses "author tags" to identify Fleming throughout the middle part of the essay. In paragraphs 5-9, for example, Creedon uses the following phrases to remind the reader that he is drawing on Fleming's ideas: "Fleming says," "Fleming warns," "adds Fleming," "Fleming laments," and "Fleming believes." Remind your students that attributing information to your sources is essential for good investigating and research.

5. Analyze this paragraph in class to show your students how to find clues about analyzing audience. The first sentence in this passage evokes the image of Americans (and readers of <u>Utne</u> magazine) as cooperative, willing to pitch in during an energy crisis. With the phrase, "barreled into the White

House," the third sentence hints at the political bias of the magazine—and the assumption by the editors that <u>Utne</u> magazine readers are suspicious of Republican politics and the effects of Reaganomics. The sixth sentence, however, says that the "Texas oilmen" currently in the White House are not any more likely to solve environmental problems. In this sentence and the concluding sentences of the paragraph, the editors clearly suggest that environmental concerns are more important than political affiliation and that, once again, Americans will need to pull together and begin to solve problems that politicians are afraid to face.

6.   If your students have not visited café.utne, have them go to this site and see the wide range of responses to Creedon's article (or, if these responses are no longer available, responses to another current topic in <u>Utne</u>. Encourage them to read a current article, print out several responses, and/or respond to a current topic that catches their interest.

Jonathan Kozol, "The Homeless and Their Children"

While Saltzman's essay uses many specific examples of actual people, Kozol focuses primarily on one key person. In addition, Kozol's essay uses the narrative skills students practiced in their remembering essays as well as the observing skills necessary for writing an investigative report. Too often, students will assume that investigating essays begin and end in the library, with perhaps one outside interview. Kozol reverses this pattern. He demonstrates how in-depth observation (a single case study)--combined with just a bit of background information from the library--can become the focus of an investigative essay.

Kozol's essay also forces students to think about the nature of objectivity in investigative reporting. Is true objectivity possible? Is it desirable? Can an objective report, in fact, be persuasive? (See question #2, below, for a discussion of Kozol's "distancing" techniques.)

Responses to <u>Questions for Writing and Discussion</u>

1. An informative essay should not argue overtly for one belief or another, but it may contain bits of information that "surprise" the reader. That surprise (contrasting with our uninformed expectations) often leads to the main idea in an investigative essay.

2. Kozol is amazingly objective and detached throughout the essay. His "distancing" techniques help him (and the reader) remain unemotional: In the first sentence of paragraph 4, for example, Kozol says that lead poisoning is "Laura's first concern" (suggesting that it is <u>Laura's</u> concern, not his as a reporter or ours as a reader). The beginning of paragraph 5 also shows Kozol remaining unemotional and keeping his distance: "Laura has one other urgent matter on her hands. It appears that she has failed to answer a request. . . ." The matter is "on her hands," and Kozol adds even more distance by saying that "it <u>appears</u> that she has failed to answer a request." Kozol also uses understatement to provide distance: "The timing is bad; it's a weekend."
   Kozol shows some sympathy in phrases such as "Laura . . . is so fragile that I find it hard to start a conversation" (paragraph 2), "she knows enough about the dangers of lead to grasp the <u>darker implications</u> of this information" (paragraph 3), "There are no table lamps to soften the fluorescent glare, no books, no decorations" (paragraph 6), or "Before I go, we stand beside the

window. Blowing snow hits the panes and blurs the dirt" (paragraph 38). By themselves, these passages seem fairly objective, but in the pathetic and emotional context, these phrases carry significant emotional weight.

Kozol does not editorialize about the plight of the poor or about necessary reforms in the welfare system. His extreme restraint, in fact, prompts the reader to become angry at Laura's predicament and at the welfare system that locks her in her poverty.

3. Laura's illiteracy causes her as many problems as her poverty--it keeps her from improving her condition. She cannot read the letters from the hospital. When she complains to the hotel management, she cannot do it in writing, so her voice has no power. She cannot read requests for information from the welfare office. She may pass on her illiteracy to her children because her apartment has no books. She has to use pictures to shop at the grocery store. She cannot read the instructions for her medicine. She cannot read the letters from the hotel management. She can't read the eviction or adoption papers. She cannot read the welfare papers that give evidence that she is searching for a better place to live.

4. In addition to the interviews with Laura, Kozol has interviewed Kim, one of the residents of the Martinique. He relays information from a report published by the Community Service Society of New York. Kozol gets information from another resident at the Martinique about laundry costs. Kozol investigates the sprinkler system in the hotel and discovers that the fire-alarm system is "inoperable."

5. According to Kozol, the welfare system provides Laura with the money to pay her rent, although Laura has to go and get it. She is eligible for benefits, consisting of $173 restaurant allowance and $200 in food stamps. However, the welfare system occasionally drops her from the rolls, a practice called "churning." Students should discuss what practical or feasible changes in the welfare system might improve Laura's situation.

Lauren Strain, "The Hollywood Indian"

As with most investigative essays, Lauren Strain's curiosity drives her investigation. She states her investigative questions early in her essay. She wants to know how accurate Hollywood's portrayal of American Indians is, which Native American actors have helped portray their people accurately, and how history has contributed to changing stereotypes. Strain uses her personal experience, her research, an interview, and an informal survey to gather information.

Responses to <u>Questions for Writing and Discussion</u>

1, 2. For questions one and two, asking students to do a brief journal entry or post their responses on an electronic forum will help them share ideas about Hollywood and stereotypes of Native Americans.

3. Strain could more smoothly integrate her findings from her interview and her survey. For example, Strain might use a quotation from her interview in paragraph 2 and she could include her survey results in paragraph 19. If you have students work on this question, they will be less likely to tack on their interview and survey findings as Strain has done.

3. Encourage students to use their discussion of Strain's essay to branch out to other media images of minorities. Are their racist or sexist images in other contemporary films, in advertising, or in the media? Might one of those topics be a subject that students might want to investigate?

Bridgid Stone, "My Friend Michelle, An Alcoholic"

Bridgid Stone uses many of Kozol's strategies as she tackles an emotional topic for her investigative essay. The fact that Michelle is Bridgid's friend makes a distanced or objective stance more difficult. Sometimes Stone relies on conversation to carry the informational load. At other times, she interweaves statistics and background information to distance herself. The result, however, is a report nicely grounded in Michelle's own lifestyle.

Responses to <u>Questions for Writing and Discussion</u>

1. Stone's opening paragraph clearly sets the tone for the entire essay: "Five million teenagers are problem drinkers, according to <u>Group</u> magazine's article, 'Sex, Drugs, and Alcohol.' One of these five million teenagers is my friend, Michelle." Stone narrates this investigative report in the first person, present tense ("We head back to the dorm . . ."), but the focus is usually on Michelle, not the narrator. Stone does permit herself a few editorial comments to color her report ("I wish the other twenty-seven percent could be here now"), and she does rebuke Michelle ("Michelle, you don't even go to class"), but usually Stone maintains her reporter's stance. Be sure students see how Stone re-establishes her distance at the end of the essay.

2. Stone's audience is anyone interested in alcoholism, in teenage alcoholism, and teenage alcoholism on college campuses. A college newspaper or publication would be an excellent publication source for her essay.

3. Ask students to react to Stone's interweaving and balance of personal narrative and statistics. This balance may be exactly right for a college newspaper, but would it work for the topic and the tentative audience for the students' own essays?

4. Stone uses the present tense to describe most of Michelle's actions, but she does switch to past tense to relate Michelle's statements ("Michelle was partially correct, though, when she stated, 'Everybody else drinks'"), when she concludes her essay ("I moved out of the dorm . . .") and when she reports Michelle's final comment ("'It wasn't that bad,' she told me.")

5. If your students have read Kozol, they should notice that Stone uses some of the same strategies: describing key scenes, quoting a relevant statistic, using actual conversation to dramatize the predicament, and keeping as much distance as possible.

Chapter 7: Explaining

As in other chapters of this textbook, have students begin the assignment with journal entries to practice their writing. If you assign three journal entries that require, in turn, process analysis, definition, and causal analysis, you can discuss how each of these strategies might help them with their assignment. Some teachers then have the assignment require combinations of strategies, including cause and effect, in order to teach more sophisticated, critical thinking. (If some of your students can fulfill your assignment with a simple process analysis while others are doing definition and causal analysis, you'll have wide variations in level of difficulty.)

An explaining assignment with an academic or cross curricular focus works especially well for this assignment. Students might explain some facet of a prospective major or profession. They might explain some idea or concept from another course they are taking. For this assignment, students can write to other members of their composition class. Other possible topics for cross curricular assignments are suggested by the sample questions in the Appendix on <u>Writing Under Pressure</u>.

For the explaining assignment, be sure your grading criteria are set and clearly explained. (See the section on Evaluating Student Writing in this manual.) All explaining essays should have a clear <u>purpose</u>, appropriately address the <u>audience</u>, focus on a <u>thesis or main idea</u>, <u>develop and support</u> the central ideas with evidence, <u>organize</u> major ideas in a clear sequence and pattern, and be written in a clear <u>style</u> with few distracting errors. By this point in the course, students should be familiar with these basic criteria and should use them in their peer workshops.

For classes with a shared knowledge or content base, the explaining essay works well in tandem with one of the earlier chapters. Teachers can successfully combine the Observing and Explaining chapters or the Reading and the Explaining chapters in a four or five week unit. In the first two weeks, for example, students can practice their critical reading, summarizing, and responding skills on the essays or texts selected as the focus for the unit. Then they can focus on defining a key idea or explaining a cause and effect relationship to other members of their class (or to a specific audience such as the readers of a certain magazine).

Margaret Talbot, "Les Tres Riches Heures de Martha Stewart"

Martha Stewart may be an expert in cooking and gardening and the arts of domesticity, but Margaret Talbot is a writer whose learning and sophistication and wit easily overmatch her subject. Talbot has researched the history of home economics, so that she can set Martha Stewart against a tradition of cooking and domesticity. Talbot knows also about the history of feminism and can explain how Martha Stewart belongs—and doesn't belong—in that tradition. Most importantly, Talbot knows how to present her explanations in a classically organized explaining essay: lead-in comparison with Julia Child, focus on her thesis ("What does the cult of Martha mean? Or . . . what have we done . . . to deserve her?"), crafted topic sentences, copious and telling examples, sophisticated sentences and vocabulary, and biting wit that completes her analysis and satire. Talbot's essay tests the reading powers of our students, but the essay amply rewards close attention and extended discussion.

Responses to <u>Questions for Writing and Discussion</u>

1. This question is a pre-reading or perhaps a pre-discussion activity that encourages students explain what their own dream home might be—as preview or counterpoint to Martha Stewart's dream house.

2. Julia Child and Martha Stewart are similar in that they both are sophisticated chefs, they both have books and TV shows, and they both have many admirers. The primary differences are that Julia Child—in contrast to Martha Stewart—is "anti-snob," is "messy and forgiving," and is interested in the taste as well as the appearance of food. Martha Stewart's ambition and empire far exceed the business accomplishments of Julia Child. Margaret Talbot leads with this comparison because, among other things, she wants to show how obsessive and perfectionist Martha Stewart appears by comparison.

3. What the cult of Martha means, according to Talbot, is that "there is no corner of your domestic life that cannot be beautified or improved under careful tutelage, none that should not be colonized by the rhetoric and the discipline of quality control." The "discipline of quality control" is the key to understanding what we need if we are to become a "Martha adept."

Talbot's examples of the homemade pumpkin soup, the little bamboo brushes, the terracotta pot, and the forty-nine "essential" gardening tools illustrate the kind of discipline and quality control required for the Martha adept.

4. Talbot says that working women are attracted to Martha Stewart because they feel "estranged" from home, they are seeking a "lost tradition," and they are seeking to apply the professionalism and excellence they exhibit at work to the domestic chores at home. If some of your students admire Martha Stewart, ask them what makes her appealing.

5. Talbot suggests that although it is "tempting" to see Martha as a "symptom of anti-feminist backlash," she is too much a businesswoman and too "prickly" to fit the traditional model of the June Cleaver housewife. As Talbot says, Martha Stewart is not really interested in husbands or children, and is "not remotely interested in the messy contingencies of family life." As for the class issues, Talbot makes it clear that "class consciousness" is a major reason for the success of Martha Stewart. The cost of all of the Martha home improvements is prohibitive—or as Talbot says, "If you have to ask [how much something costs], maybe you're not a Martha kind of person at all."

6. At the end of the essay, Talbot is arguing that Martha is really selling a kind of domestic conformity that requires no individual creativity or taste. If homemakers merely follow a script, then they are not, Talbot suggests, "really living at all."

7. Additional places where Talbot satirizes Martha Stewart include paragraphs 7 and 8 where Talbot satirizes Martha's pumpkin soup, her bamboo brushes, and her forty-nine essential gardening tools; paragraph 9 where Talbot makes fun of the vocabulary of "shelter" magazines; paragraph 13 where she pokes fun of the "It's a good thing" mantra; paragraph 16 where Talbot suggests that Martha uses children as "accessories," much like "Parisian women deploy little dogs"; and paragraph 20 where she ridicules Martha's "husbandless hauteur." Have your students find other examples. Do they think these jabs are amusing? Do they think they are accurate or fair?

Pico Iyer, "The Global Village Finally Arrives"

Novelist Thomas Wolfe, author of <u>Look Homeward Angel</u>, believed that "we can't go home again." What he meant was similar to what Heraclitus, a Greek philosopher meant when he said, "You cannot step twice into the same river." The accelerating rate of cultural and technological change in our lives is the subject of Pico Iyer's essay on our Global Village. It is as though we live in a river of cultural changes—we do not need to go to Europe or Asia or Africa to have artifacts from those cultures wash over us. The cultures of the world are becoming interconnected as never before. Or as Pico Iyer explains, "As fast as the world comes to America, America goes round the world." The result is that "a common multiculturalism links us all."

Pico Iyer is writing an essay of definition, an essay explaining "what" the Global Village is today. Although his approach is narrative and informal, he analyzes a variety of cultural artifacts: language, food, clothes, music, transportation, technology, literature, business, and religion. He occasionally uses phrases such as "The global village is defined . . ." but his goal is not to analyze each element rigorously but to describe the flow of culture around us.

Responses to <u>Questions for Writing and Discussion</u>

1. Since Iyer's purpose is to show us how we are interconnected in the global village, having your students reconstruct this list of over 30 countries, 30 cities and 10 languages should help them see the kinds of evidence Iyer brings to support his essay defining the global village. This question makes a great group activity. Have one group make a list of countries, one a list of cities, and one a list of languages. Give a fourth group a world map, and have them start locating each city and country. The point of this activity is to make manifest the extensive evidence Iyer brings to his explaining essay.

2. Even more than in other essays in this book, Iyer's vocabulary itself supports and helps reveal his thesis. Ask students to explain how his vocabulary and thesis are connected. This may lead to a discussion of the dynamic and evolving nature of the English language.

3. Several sentences that point to the thesis of Iyer's article include the last two sentences of paragraph one (the essay is about identity and location and how those concepts are related in a multinational world); the second

138

sentence in paragraph two ("the whole planet . . . is going global"); the first two sentences of paragraph 3 (" a common multiculturalism links us all"); the final sentence of paragraph 5 ("As fast as the world comes to America, America goes round the world"); and the first sentence of paragraph 10 ("Nonetheless, whether we like it or not, the "transnational" future is upon us"). Your students may list other possible sentences that also suggest the thesis of this essay.

4. It may be useful to discuss how metaphors of our nationality shape our thinking. The older "melting pot" idea suggested that European cultures added flavor and spice to a "stew" and that individual cultural identities were thus lost in the gumbo. The metaphor of the "mosaic" suggests that individual cultures retain their identities, but each gives off its own light and image which adds to the overall picture. Other metaphors that Iyer uses suggest other fluid and dynamic relationships. In paragraph 2, Iyer says that "all the world's a rainbow coalition." In that same paragraph, he says that the world is "hyphenated." In paragraph 4, Iyer says that "souls are mingling," again suggesting a more fluid sense of identity. (To reinforce this idea, have students recall Elizabeth Wong's essay, which suggests that her identity is both American and Chinese.) In paragraph 10, Iyer refers to "the cadences of world music," suggesting an image of each culture contributing to the overall melody.

5. Iyer suggests some potential dangers in paragraph 9, when he seems to foresee the continuing struggles in the Balkans—struggles that will continue to occur in a post-national world. Also, he points out that the gap between the haves and the have nots, between the "fast" and the "slow" worlds, shows that technological progress is not necessarily a democratic process. The fact that capital is now global has created horrific working conditions in the many industries. Finally, Iyer suggests in paragraph 7 that values travel at the speed of fax. Sometimes that seems good, as when westerners help Asians fight for more human rights; some of it is bad, as when America exports guns, divorces, and media violence to other cultures.

Deborah Tannen, "How Male and Female Students Use Language Differently"

Tannen's essay makes for an interesting in-class discussion for a variety of reasons. First, the topic of gender differences in conversational styles always provokes spirited discussions. Second, Tannen's application to the college classroom encourages students to see their own classes as an experimental laboratory for observing gender differences. Do the tendencies and preferences she describes operate in their own class discussions? Third, students can examine the extent to which Tannen's own style and organization illustrate gender differences. Students might compare the logical organization of Elmer-DeWitt's essay, for example, with the more informal and conversational patterns in Tannen's essay. The focus of Tannen's essay changes slightly as she explores this topic, she writes in a conversational style, she uses anecdotal evidence, and she relies on a very small sample group to suggest her perceptions rather than try to scientifically "prove" all her points (also see Sonja Browe's critique of Tannen's essay in Chapter 5, Reading).

Responses to Questions for Writing and Discussion

1. Encourage students to describe their own experiences with gender-based differences in class discussions. You might ask students to write their observations before discussing them in class, and then ask students to consider whether writing their observations or discussing them aloud in the class was easier or more satisfying.

2. Some possible statements and restatements of Tannen's focus or thesis are found in paragraph 1 ("reevaluating my teaching strategies"); paragraph 2 ("how different regional, ethnic, and class backgrounds, as well as age and gender, result in different ways of using language to communicate"); paragraph 4 ("These patterns have stunning implications for classroom interaction"); paragraph 9 ("These different teaching styles must make our classrooms wildly different places and hospitable to different students"); or even the final sentence of the essay, in paragraph 24: "realizing that one monolithic classroom participation structure is not equal opportunity is itself a powerful motivation to find more diverse methods to serve diverse students. . . ." Tannen's style is to modify and revise her focus as she works through

her essay. She definitely does not use a top-down or thesis-support form for her explaining essay.

3. Tannen defines conversational differences between men and women in paragraph 3 and defines "ritual opposition" in paragraph 5. She uses process to show these contrasts in paragraphs 7 and 8 and again in paragraph 12. But Tannen's dominant mode is causal analysis. Throughout the essay, Tannen shows how differences in gender and culture result in different classroom dynamics. She also explains the reverse--how different classroom teaching styles affect students differently.

4. Tannen uses evidence from her own studies; she cites various researchers in paragraphs 3, 5, and 6; she uses anecdotal examples from her colleagues in paragraphs 10 and 11; and she uses personal experience in paragraph 8 as well as in paragraphs 15-19. Have students list--at the board or in small groups--the kinds of evidence they discover.

5. You might begin this discussion of gender differences by polling students to see who liked this essay or thought that it was well written. Do more women than men think that this essay is well written? Such an informal poll is a good place to begin a discussion of perceptions about gender differences or gender preferences. Are traditional standards of writing--for example, those promoted in this textbook--gender biased? Do readers have common expectations and needs regardless of gender?

Christine Bishop, "English Only"

When students write argumentative essays, often they rush to judgment and argue that one side is right and the other is wrong—without doing sufficient reading and exploring to see the many complex sides to a single issue. To help encourage students to look disinterestedly at the arguments on both sides (or in some cases, all sides) of an argument, Ms. Bishop's instructor, Susan Weaver, decided to have her students write their argumentative essays in two stages. First they would write an exploratory essay whose purpose was merely to explain the key arguments surrounding a controversial issue. Then, the second assignment would be to choose a position from the ongoing debate, and argue for that position. Ms. Bishop's essay, reprinted here, responds to that first assignment. Her purpose here is to explain the arguments on both sides in a clear and balanced manner.

Responses to <u>Questions for Writing and Discussion</u>

1. Reviewing the first and revised drafts helps reveal the exploratory dimension of this essay. Bishop has a topic that interests her, and that she has an opinion on, but she uses her research and her first draft to set down arguments from both sides of this controversy. She reorganizes—and improves—the essay by devoting the first half of the revised version of the essay to the arguments of the English-only proponents and the second half of the essay to those who oppose English only.

2. Bishop devotes paragraphs 3 and 4 to the arguments favoring English-only legislation; Bishop uses paragraphs 5 and 6 to explain the arguments of those opposing English-only legislation. Paragraph 7 looks at the possible middle ground in the argument, and paragraph 8 examines possible effects of current English-only legislation. Bishop does balance arguments from both sides, but proponents of one side or the other may argue that she ignores some important issues. In paragraph 3, for example, Bishop does counter the argument that Hayakawa gives when she says, "Of course, Hayakawa's analogy with Quebec and India may be difficult to support. . . ." Ask whether students think Bishop is possibly taking sides when she makes this comment. Similarly, in paragraph 7, Bishop critiques Hayakawa's statistics. Ask students whether such analysis is appropriate in an essay whose purpose is merely to explain the arguments on both sides. (Within the guidelines of the teacher's specific assignment, these bits of analysis were considered appropriate.)

3. Bishop does define some of the key terms and issues. In paragraph 1, she explains the jist of Arizona's English-only law, but she does not fully explain what consequences that wording has in terms of education or government. Also, will her readers assume that "bilingualism" (see paragraph 3.) is a movement that is antithetical to the notion that immigrants should learn English? Finally, should she define for her readers words such as "xenophobic"?

4. As a group exercise, have students review the peer response guidelines for this chapter and then use them to practice giving peer response to Bishop. After students practice on the rough draft of Bishop's essay, they will be better prepared to give helpful and constructive advice to each other.

5. If you like to do a "daily" or short journal writing exercise at the beginning of class, try this assignment: Have students assume they are Pico Iyer and write a response to Bishop, to Hayakawa, or to Rodriguez. Their responses will make an excellent lead-in to a discussion of Bishop's essay and the whole topic of English-only and/or bilingualism.

Nancie Brosseau, "Anorexia Nervosa"

Brosseau's essay has been a perennial favorite of students for several reasons. The topic appeals to everyone, but especially to women who have felt the pressures of society to be as thin as possible. Brosseau's style is vivid, tactile, and compact. Her explanations of causes and effect are crystal clear--even unforgettable. And her clear thesis, essay map, and two part organization clearly illustrate a workable expository model.

Responses to <u>Questions for Writing and Discussion</u>

2. Thesis and map occur together in the final sentence of paragraph one. Map is "both physically and emotionally." Paragraphs 2 and 3 focus on the physical aspects; paragraphs 4, 5, and 6 deal with emotional problems. Within the second section, Brosseau also "maps out" or previews three emotional problems in sentence two of paragraph 4: self-deception, lying [to others], and depression. These topics are developed, in order, in paragraphs 4, 5, and 6.

3. Paragraph 4 makes a clear transition from physical to emotional health. The opening sentence in paragraph 5, however, might begin, "In addition to deceiving myself, I also began to deceive my parents" to relate the two kinds of lying. In paragraph 6, Brosseau might connect her lying with her depression by beginning the paragraph, "the more I lied to myself and my family, the more depressed I became." Have students in your class, working singly or in small groups revise transitions to make them clearer. Since Brosseau's essay is such a clear example of organization, be sure to follow this class discussion with a short workshop on the students' own drafts.

4. Brosseau <u>defines</u> "anorexia nervosa" at the end of paragraph 1, but throughout the essay continues to describe and thus define this "self-mutilating disease." In paragraph 2, for example, the disease is the cause, and the paragraph lists effects: disintegrating organs, cold hands and feet, loss of hair, eroded enamel on her teeth, and broken bones.
The overall <u>process</u> is also clear in the essay. Her gymnastic exercises lead to initial desire to lose weight; the lack of food leads to physical debilitation; her fear of becoming obese leads to her lying; and finally, her physical and emotional symptoms become so debilitating that she consults a doctor and a psychologist in order to overcome the condition.

Chapter 8: Evaluating

Since evaluating essays range from the fairly mechanical <u>Consumer Reports</u>' evaluations of products to the more sophisticated film reviews, many teachers have students write the simpler evaluations as journal entries or in-class essay practice and then give a more specific and academic assignment for the essay. Whatever approach you use, be sure to give students sufficient practice writing <u>three-column logs</u>, both for essays they read as well as the essays they are writing. The three column logs reinforce essential writing skills: criteria (focus), judgment, and supporting evidence.

During the discussion of the evaluative essay, however, be sure to explain how criteria depend upon the writing situation and the audience. An automobile evaluation in <u>Consumer Reports</u>, for example, is not the same as one in <u>Road and Track</u>. A film review in <u>The New Yorker</u> will have different criteria--as well as different points of focus--than a review in the local newspaper. Be sure to have students work in small groups or as a class selecting, reviewing, and modifying their criteria based on their intended audience. Determining criteria requires group critical thinking, negotiation, and consensus-making.

Requiring some field and library research with the evaluating assignment is also an excellent idea. Students can continue to practice their reading, summarizing, interviewing, surveying, and researching skills for almost any evaluating topic.

Kathyrn Hughes and Ben Rogers, "Prime Time Art?"

Kathyrn Hughes and Ben Rogers conduct their debate about the artistic status of ER through a set of letters reprinted in Utne magazine. Because they are both British, they bring an interesting perspective to American television programs. First, they both use British writers (George Eliot and Charles Dickens) as artistic standards for comparison. In addition, the focus of their conversation (Is ER art?) is a different question than most American viewers might ask. I suspect few of our students ever ask whether any of the television programs they watch meet the standards of art. In a post-modern world, the very question may be inappropriate. But American viewers do have standards, and they prefer some programs to others. Getting our students to articulate what their preferences are, and what standards they are using for comparison is a useful goal for a discussion of this exchange.

In addition to discussing definitions of art, criteria, judgments, and evidence, be sure to use this essay to illustrate the possible **genres** than evaluation may take. Evaluation may take the form of an article in Consumer Reports, a film review in a local newspaper, a full-length academic article such as "First-Born, Later-Born," or even an exchange through letters or on an email discussion forum. Encourage your students to think imaginatively about the genre, intended audience, and publication medium as they write their own evaluations.

Responses to Questions for Writing and Discussion

1. In a class discussion or on an electronic forum, encourage students to brainstorm a list of possible criteria that they might use in evaluating a television program or other popular culture text or artifact. Selecting criteria that are meaningful to both the writer and the intended audience is a crucial part of writing an evaluation.

2. Ben does not have a single sentence or phrase that defines what he means by "art," but he suggests several possible attributes or criteria for art. First, it should "sweep up" the viewer, take us out of ourselves, and put us in contact with a "heightened reality." In addition, it can move from "farce to romance," from "pathos to high drama." It may have allusions to other works of art, it may be "clever," it may be old-fashioned, and it may promote progressive causes. For evidence, Ben refers to particular episodes (the Quentin Tarantino episode, for example); to characters such

as Romano, Jerry, Dr. Anspaugh and Nurse Hathaway; to other works of popular culture such as Tarantino's <u>Reservoir Dogs</u>; and to novels by George Eliot, Charles Dickens, Tom Wolfe, and artists such as Charlie Chaplin, Fernand Leger, and Diego Rivera.

3. In contrast to Ben, Kathyrn says that art must extend and explore the limits of its own genre. In addition, she includes as criteria the notions that art should not use stereotypes and should avoid idealized characters. For Kathyrn, art should "refuse to give up its meaning without a fight" and have the "power to make up the world in a new way." For evidence, she refers to Dickens and George Eliot and then cites other television series such as <u>Hill Street Blues</u> and <u>L.A. Law</u>. She also refers to specific episodes of <u>ER</u> and specific characters such as Kerry Weaver, Peter Benton, and Mark Greene.

4. Ask your students to start with the second letter and find passages or phrases where Kathyrn or Ben pick up on some definition, example, or phrase and respond to a point made in the previous letter. For example, Kathyrn begins her first letter by saying that she shares his "disbelieving rapture" that television could ever be this good. She also responds to Ben's comment about the Reservoir Dogs allusion and to Ben's comments about Eliot and Dickens. Students need to see that arguments are not constructed in a vacuum, but consist of responses to points already made about the subject being evaluated. In this sense, their "argument" is a debate or a conversation, in which each person listens to the other, and responds to specific points made in the previous letter. Even if students are not writing an epistolary argument, they still need to respond specifically to alternate or opposing points of view.

5. Be sure to ask your students how the authors' points of view are different from their own. For example, do your students automatically compare television series with works by famous British novelists such as Dickens and Eliot? Do they think of <u>Ally McBeal</u> as containing "small, whiny stories?" Does ER have more power for British viewers because it is "different" and "American?"

Goeffrey Cowley, "First Born, Later Born"

Students should see that book and film reviews are still variants of the same summary-response pattern they practiced in Chapter 5, Reading. The major difference between the basic summary-response and the book review is that the description is usually woven throughout the review rather than relegated to a separate opening section (as it is in a restaurant review). These differences are largely due to readers' expectations. Readers of a restaurant review want to know, primarily, whether they should go to the restaurant or not. Readers of a book review, however, expect to find more of the flavor of the book. They want to know what kind of book it is, and they want to know what it is about. Often, readers of fiction reviews have already read the novel, so they want to compare their reactions with the reviewer's reactions. Because of these readers' expectations, book reviews usually have interwoven and extended descriptions of key features of the book.

At the same time, students should be cautioned that book reviews should not merely review the main ideas or, in the case of fiction, retell the plot. As an example of a review of a non-fiction work, Cowley does an excellent job of balancing his summary of Sulloway's ideas, reacting to his ideas, and citing critics who disagree with Sulloway's conclusions.

Finally, be sure to take advantage of the popularity of this topic by doing a write-to-learn exercise the day you assign Cowley's essay. For example, have students write five minutes on the following questions: "How is your personality different from those of your brothers or sisters? Do you think that some of those differences relate to birth order--to who was the oldest, middle, or youngest child in your family? Explain." After students write for five minutes, spend a few minutes discussing their responses. The resulting discussion will set them up for an active reading of Cowley's essay.

Responses to Questions for Writing and Discussion

1. Geoffrey Cowley, as writer of this review, states his claim (which is evaluating Sulloway's research and his book) in paragraph 3 when he says, "It's an audacious claim . . . and not one that social scientists will flock to embrace. Birth-order research, for all its intuitive appeal, has a reputation for flakiness." Cowley restates that claim in paragraph 13 when he says, "Sulloway's findings are sure to strike a chord with lay readers, but social scientists may not appreciate his chutzpah."

Sulloway's claim is stated at the end of paragraph 2: "Sulloway makes a compelling case that firstborns, whatever their age, sex, class or nationality, specialize in defending the status quo while later-borns specialize in toppling it." (Cowley's claim is also suggested when he says, "Sulloway makes a compelling case [italics mine]." Clearly, Cowley's evaluation of Sulloways book is, overall, a positive one.

2. Cowley finds much to praise about Sulloway's book. Cowley says that Sulloway's research is "compelling," "audacious," and "ingenious." He cites Sarah Hrdy (this is the correct spelling of her name!) who calls Sulloway's research "monumental" and John Tooby who believes Sulloway's research does reveal the "larger patterns." However, Cowley also admits that the subject is "flaky" and cites several of Sulloway's critics: Joseph Rodgers, Cecile Ernst, and Jules Angst (paragraph 3); Ernst Mayr (paragraph 11); Steven Peterson (paragraph 13); and Toni Falbo (paragraph 14). Although Cowley's overall evaluation is positive, he does an excellent job of presenting both sides of this controversy. Be sure students see that good evaluations must include criticism as well as praise. An evaluation that is unqualified praise will look like an advertisement rather than a critical appraisal.☐

3. Cowley's essay might be outlined as follows:

    I. Introduction and statement of thesis   (paragraphs 1-2)
    II. Background, statement of Cowley's thesis,
        and statement of Sulloway's thesis   (paragraphs 3-4)
    III. Summary of Sulloway's argument   (paragraphs 5-10)
    IV. Evaluation and response to
        Sulloway's argument   (paragraphs 11-14)
    V. Conclusion   (paragraph 15)

(If students have written a summary-response essay earlier in the semester, be sure to connect the organizational pattern to that essay. Cowley's review essay clearly follows an Introduction/Summary/Response/Conclusion pattern.)

Cowley uses an historical example for his lead-in in paragraph one. Most readers would find this example effective. Spend some time in class having students identify the kinds of signals, transitional phrases, and paragraph hooks that Cowley uses to connect one paragraph with the next.

Perhaps have students work in groups on this part of the question, putting their results at the board for class discussion. Whenever possible, follow this activity by having students work on paragraph transitions in their own essays.

4. With copies the campus or local newspaper at hand, have students work in groups to figure out a revision plan for adapting Cowley's review for that local paper and audience. If students practice writing out a revision plan for someone else's essay (i.e., Cowley's essay), they will find it easier to design and follow their own revision plans.

Elayne Rapping, "Watching the Eyewitless News"

Media topics often make great topics for evaluating essays. The strengths of Rapping's essay are her energetic style and her focus on a subject that most students have direct experience with. The weakness of her essay is that she models for students giving opinions and judgments without sufficient supporting evidence. Having students work carefully through discussion questions 2 and 3 will help them see where she needs to provide more specific evidence to back up her opinions. Although Rapping is a cultural critic, she sounds in this essay more like a writer of cultural editorials: she has done her research in this topic but in this particular column, she doesn't marshall the evidence necessary to make a good evaluative argument.

Responses to <u>Questions for Writing and Discussion</u>

1. Having students write out their reader-response reactions in a write-to-learn entry is an excellent way to get a discussion going on Rapping's essay. Because her subject (the media) is a popular one and because she is clearly opinionated in an unconventional way, her essay makes for a lively discussion of the media issues.

2. Some criteria that Rapping uses in her essay include the following: News should meet its constitutional responsibility to provide information that serves the public interest (paragraph 3). News should respect its audience's intelligence and diversity (paragraph 4). News should not be driven solely by markets or ratings (paragraph 5). News should not be driven by generic, cookie-cutter formulas (paragraph 6). News should represent American life, not some Disney World stereotype (paragraph 7). Beginning with paragraph 8, Rapping gives examples from local news programs to give evidence to support her judgment that local news programs ("Eyewitless News") do not meet these criteria. Paragraph 8 provides good material for making a three-column log:

Criterion	Evidence	Judgment
News should be driven public's need to know, not by ratings.	If it bleeds, it leads. Programs show endless procession of fires, shootouts, etc., in order, to boost ratings.	Local news is driven by ratings, not by public's need to know.

151

Have students work in groups, collaborating on their three-column logs, and then write their versions at the board. As the evaluating chapter explains, a three-column log is especially useful as a prewriting strategy to help organize their own evaluating essays.

3. Rapping does have some evidence that local news programs do not meet the high standards the public should have for its news. She mentions the rule that "if it bleeds, it leads," and most local news watchers have seen the relentless procession of local mayhem and bloodshed. She says (in paragraph 11) that "National news items typically take up less than two minutes of a half-hour segment." If Rapping has the actual data to support that statement, then that evidence, too, is compelling. She accuses local news programs of being "obsessed" with "man-on-the-street" interviews, and most viewers have seen the kinds of cliched responses she ridicules-- although Rapping does not cite any statistics or specific examples. She also claims that the two longest segments, the weather and sports, are not what the public needs. In fact, that claim may be debatable. In paragraph 17, Rapping says that the researchers (undocumented) say that people want "comfort, reassurance, and a community." (The evidence in this paragraph, in fact, seems to suggest that a strong sense of community would, indeed, be a highly desirable thing.) In paragraph 20, Rapping automatically assumes that all newscasts belong in the category of "tabloid television," a category panned by sociologist Joshua Gamson. Rapping's claim, that the purpose of local news is to provide a "utopian fantasy," is itself a plausible and entertaining thesis, and she charges, in the final paragraph that because the local news "pretends" to be "real and true," the programs are much more troubling than soap operas and other trash TV.

Rapping's evaluative essay is most interesting in its statements of criteria and in its judgments; however, it is weakest in its supporting evidence. She gives almost no first-hand, specific evidence from a specific news program, or from a study of weekly or monthly trends of a specific or group of specific news programs. Because Rapping's supporting evidence is scanty, invite your students to do their own logs of time spent on various segments in their own local news programs. Do their local news programs provide data that confirm Rapping's judgments, or do those data suggest other, alternative conclusions? Question 4 will give students a rough methodology for collecting data for their own assessment of Rapping's' thesis, and it could provide for their own essays on the local TV news.

Linda Meininger, "Borrowers Can Be Choosy"

Meininger's essay is an example of a successful evaluative assignment: Evaluate a campus organization or a community service. At a time when writing courses--and writing assignments across the curriculum--sometimes include an outreach or community service component, this investigative/evaluative assignment models for students how to investigate service organizations and evaluate the service they provide to the campus or community. An additional benefit to such an assignment is that students become more aware about audience expectations: the evaluations can be published locally and even the service organization could receive a copy of the evaluation. Often these assignments can proceed--or be a part of--liaisons between writing classes and community organizations where students actually assist the organization with its own writing projects.

Responses to Questions for Writing and Discussion

1. Have students work in groups, using the Peer Response guidelines to critique Meininger's final draft. A comparison with the rough draft shows that she improved the essay's clarity of focus, organization, and quality of support.

2. Meininger sets forth her criteria in paragraph 2. Then she devotes a paragraph or several paragraphs to each of her four criteria. Students working individually or in small groups should be able to write out a three-column log for Meininger's essay and then record their findings at the board.

3. Meininger puts one of her stronger criteria (the friendliness and cooperation of the ILL staff) in the final position, introducing it with the clause, "Perhaps the strongest feature of the ILL service was the willingness of the staff to help patrons. . . ." She puts the criteria with the most negative results (timely arrival) in the middle. Clearly, her purpose is to highlight the strengths of the ILL rather than to expose the ILL for their untimely delays. Ask students whether Meininger should be more critical of the ILL--given that the delays are a crucial shortcoming. After all, Meininger couldn't even test the service for her paper because the materials would not arrive in time.

4. Ask students to critique the questionnaire in small groups. Which questions proved most useful to Meininger? Which questions should be revised or omitted? What additional questions might she ask? If time permits, have students review their own survey drafts immediately following this discussion.

Kent Y'Blood, "The Big Chill"

Although students often want to write reviews of current films, encouraging them to choose classic films or films that are released in video copies solves several problems. First, having a video copy enables students to get the basic information (actor, director, key scenes, and basic plot) through repeated viewings of the film. Also, if students choose older films, they are likely to select a film they have seen earlier. The more times they have watched a film, the more likely they are to write a critical, in-depth review.

Responses to <u>Questions for Writing and Discussion</u>

2. Y'Blood obviously knows this film very well. In order to get the names of all the actors, characters, and songs, he read several reviews. In addition, he knows key scenes fairly well; it's probable that he saw the film several times before or as he wrote this review. Reconstructing the process should let students know that writing a film review requires quite a bit of work collecting information and evidence. (Note that film reviews, as a genre, tend to use more unsupported assertions than evaluations of commercial products. Y'Blood says, "When [the characters] do talk, the chat is brilliant," but he gives no supporting evidence. Reviewing a videotape of this film, however, Y'Blood could at least get one supporting example of this "brilliant chat.")

Chapter 9: Problem Solving

The Problem Solving chapter works straightforwardly, with few surprises for the teacher or student. As in other essays, knowing the intended audience will help the writer decide how much he or she needs to explain the problem and how specific the alternative solutions and feasibility considerations need to be.   As indicated in the chapter (and in the section on Collaborative Learning and Writing Activities in this manual), problem-solving essays can adapt easily to collaborative writing efforts.

As is the case with other chapters, the problem-solving chapter works well as part of a double assignment. Teachers may wish to have students write an investigative topic proposal as the first part of their problem solving essay. Topic proposals can include an investigation and definition of a problem, a list of possible solutions, and photocopies or notes from several library and field resources. After the teacher reviews or conferences with the student on the investigative topic proposal, the student drafts the problem-solving essay.

Another chapter combination that works well is to have students write an evaluative topic proposal as part of their problem-solving assignment. Students would identify a problem and several solutions. Then they would choose one possible solution and formally evaluate it, based on criteria they establish and relevant evidence they find in their library and field resources.

Regardless of the assignment or chapter combinations, make sure that students are aware that they will be using <u>all</u> the skills from their previous writing assignments as they collect materials, shape their ideas, and draft the essay.   They should use their observing, remembering, reading, and researching skills as they look for ways to focus their essay and find relevant evidence. They will definitely use skills from their explaining essay, since they will need to use definitions of key terms or consider cause--effect relationships as they make and defend their proposals. And, as already mentioned, they will need to evaluate the strengths and weaknesses of the alternative proposals. Reviewing where they have been in the course will help them see where they are going.

Wendell Berry, "Solving for Pattern"

Berry's essay is partly about solving agricultural problems, but it is primarily a critique of the problem-solving process itself. It is valuable for students to read because it shows them how to be critical of easy solutions or solutions that do not consider the overall health of the system. The biological, ecological, or health analogies are a means to vividly demonstrate to students that solutions need to be tested rigorously for long-term as well as short-term negative and positive effects throughout the whole system.

Additionally, Berry's essay is valuable because it uses the critical language of (1) cause and effect analysis, (2) evaluation using criteria and evidence, and (3) problem solving. Often we use a textbook's peer review sheets, or encourage classes to design and draft essay criteria appropriate for a particular assignment, but Berry's essay, itself, may be the best peer review sheet for students' own problem-solving essay drafts. After students have a topic proposal or a draft, have them read Berry's essay and consider--singly and then in groups--whether or how their own essays (or their peer's essay) meet Berry's goals of solving for the harmony, health, and quality of the whole system.

Responses to <u>Questions for Writing and Discussion</u>

1. As suggested in the above note, Berry's essay is an excellent guide for critiquing any proposal.

2. Berry explains three kinds of solutions: bad solutions that cause new problems, bad solutions that worsen the original problem, and good solutions that consider the harmony, health, and quality of the whole system.

3. Use this question as a brief write-to-learn exercise to encourage students to apply Berry's system to a variety of problems. Does his "whole system" or "ecological" approach apply to all possible problems? When might it not work?

4. Finding audience cues makes an excellent small group activity. Give one group a transparency copy of one page of the essay. Ask them to identify and label all the coherence devices they find. Then one group member can put the

transparency on an overhead and explain their findings to the class. (If possible, be sure to follow this activity by having students revise their own drafts to improve coherence.)

5. Drawing analogies is a highly effective explaining or arguing strategy. Ask students to critique Berry's analogy. Do his organic analogies work in the case of agricultural problems? What kinds of problems might not be appropriate for organic analogies?

6. Have students use Berry's essay to read, understand, and critique the essays by Postman and Estrich. To what extent do both of those writers keep in mind the overall harmony, health, and quality of the system? Which essay does the better job of considering the overall health of the system?

Deborah Tannen, "The Argument Culture"

Although Tannen's essay follows the problem-solving format, the content of this essay makes it is appropriate for Chapter 10, Arguing. Make sure students read this essay before they write their arguing essays so that they can avoid a pro-con argument if that is appropriate for their subject and audience.

In this essay, Tannen focuses particularly on how language and metaphor influence how we perceive any subject. As a linguist, she is following Robin Lakoff's study of metaphor and language: the words we choose and the underlying metaphors affect perception, understanding, and our whole notion of reality. So it is not surprising to hear Tannen, following Lakoff, say, "the language of extremes actually shapes, and misshapes, the way we think about things." Tannen suggests we need metaphors other than sports and war, and one of those metaphors is "dialogue." It is unfortunate, however, that even the word "dialogue" suggests just two participants. Ask students what other words and metaphors might fit her argument. Perhaps the words "interchange" or "conversation" might fit her thesis better.

Responses to <u>Questions for Writing and Discussion</u>

1. Encourage students to try this journal or electronic forum entry either before or after they read Tannen's essay.

2. Tannen most clearly states the problems caused by the argument culture in paragraphs 6-17, and again in the bulleted items in paragraph 18. The problems with the argument culture, according to Tannen, are that people assume that there are only two sides, that the war metaphor imbedded in the argument culture negatively affects our perception of reality, that the argument culture encourages criticism, and that technology tends to isolate people in a bubble. In addition, in the bulleted list, Tannen notes that the argument culture encourages us to distort the facts, to waste valuable time, to limit our thinking, and to encourage lying. Although Tannen's solution—to look at all sides—is simplistic, it is clearly a step in the right direction. Keeping the option open of examining three or four "sides" or points of view may avoid the knee-jerk "fight" metaphors that currently pervade our thinking.

3. Tannen might take her own advice when it comes to looking at "all sides" of this debate which she frames in the last paragraph as a struggle between just two sides—the argument culture and the dialogue culture. Also, Tannen says in the last paragraph that we could add imagination, and intellectual interchange to our "arsenal," but she uses that metaphor tongue-in-cheek. On the other hand, Tannen does avoid suggesting that this debate should be a fight or a struggle. She avoids absolutes and she makes suggestions rather than arguing. For example, in paragraph 20 she says, "Perhaps it is time to re-examine the assumption that audiences always prefer a fight." Her use of the word "perhaps" and her suggestion that we "re-examine the assumption" are tactics used by people in a dialogue or conversation rather than people in a debate.

4. Tannen writes this essay, for the most part, in an informal style intended for general audiences. She appeals to this audience by talking about relations between spouses, about popular topics in the news, about automobile accidents, "road rage," and email. But she also includes touches of a more academic style. Tannen cites three different research studies conducted on this subject: a study of the holocaust denial phenomenon by Emory University professor Deborah Lipstadt, a study on the influence of metaphor by psychologists Elizabeth Loftus and John Palmer, and a study on cultural perception by anthropologist Mary Catherine Bateson. Ask your students whether they found Tannen's essay accessible—perhaps in comparison to the previous essay by Wendell Berry or the following essay by Neil Postman.

5. The notion that language and especially metaphor affect our perceptions of reality is a core assumption of Tannen's essay. She introduces this notion in paragraph 4 and then returns to this idea in paragraphs 9, 18, and 22. One important example she gives is from the study by Loftus and Palmer that shows how language affects perception and distorts reality. Although Tannen still frames her argument in terms of an either-or choice between the argument culture and the dialogue culture, she does not imbed images of fighting, sports, or war in her own argument.

Neil Postman, "Virtual Students, Digital Classrooms"

Postman's essay extends the conversation on computers and the Internet raised in other essays in this text, such as Elmer-DeWitt's "Welcome to Cyberspace," Koenenn's "Plotting a Net Gain," and Cowan's "How the Web Works." Because most students have experience with computers in their education, begin your discussion of this essay with a write-to-learn exercise. Have students write for five minutes on the following questions: "Cite three or four examples where you used computers in your formal education or for your own education at home. Has the influence of computers been positive or negative? Have you learned things you would not have learned through regular class activities or through books? Explain." Have students discuss their responses for 10 minutes before you assign them Postman's essay to read.

Responses to <u>Questions for Writing and Discussion</u>

1. If you didn't use the exercise above, try using question 1 as a prereading journal entry. This question works best if you have students freewrite in response to this question for five minutes during the class period that you assign Postman's essay. Following the students' five minutes of freewriting, have them share and discuss their responses. This activity will make students much more active and critical readers of Postman's essay. As an alternative, if your students have already read the essay, use this activity as an introduction to a discussion of Postman's essay.

2. Some possible thesis sentences for Postman's essay are the first and third sentences of paragraph 7 and the first sentence of paragraph 10. Students may also offer other suggestions, but the first sentence of paragraph 10 is the most complete statement of Postman's thesis. You may wish to have students discuss why Postman's thesis comes so late in the essay, at paragraph 10. Would his thesis be more effective if placed earlier in the essay, as John Diebold does in his essay?

3. Postman critiques the technological optimists throughout his essay. In paragraph 5, he responds to Diane Ravitch's naive vision of a technological future by reasoning that Little Eva and Young John are probably not children from the planet Earth. In paragraph 7, he responds to this optimistic vision by

pointing out that new technologies are Faustian bargains. In paragraphs 8 and 11, he critiques the notion that the computer is crucial in our information age by pointing out that we are already overwhelmed by information and by suggesting that schools need to teach children to see how computer technologies use us. Finally, in paragraphs 13 and 14, Postman responds to the idea that computers will democratize education by reasoning that computers may actually work against socialization and that, historically, technologies have always produced winners and losers.

4. Most of Postman's essay is a critique of other educational reformers' visions and proposals, but he does offer proposals of his own. First, from the opening paragraphs, Postman argues that we should not make a god of computer technology. Postman invites the reader to remember that all technologies are Faustian bargains that bring some people progress and neglect other people. Postman wants students to ask questions and critique technology, not just use it (or be used by it) without critical questioning. Second, Postman believes that schools will still be necessary in the next century because their primary mission is socializing and civilizing children. Finally, Postman proposes that schools will continue to help solve social problems if we keep competent people as teachers for students.

5. Postman develops his motif of the god of technology throughout the essay, through his references to gods, faith, belief, and religion. These images occur in paragraphs 1-4, 6-7, 11, 13-14, and 18. Since some paragraphs contain several religious references, ask students to share the references they find.

Kristy Busch, Steve Krause, and Keith Wright, "No Parking"

This essay provides a good model for a collaboratively written essay. In any collaboratively written project, students should all be interested in the topic (rather than assigned to write on it), they should agree on who does the research, who writes what, when it is due, and who does the revision. They need to have one or two mid-project meetings with the instructor to discuss their topic proposal and their progress on the project. Finally, the instructor and the writers should negotiate an equitable method of evaluating the project. Student evaluations of peer group members should be part of the instructor's evaluation of the project.

Responses to <u>Questions for Writing and Discussion</u>

1. Additional interview questions: What plans do you already have to relieve the overcrowded parking situation? What are your long range plans? What systems have other universities adopted to solve their parking problems? Are you in favor of banning cars for freshmen, for example? What surveys about the parking problem have you already done? Suggestions for the survey: Gather more information about respondents (Do you live on or off campus? What is your status--student, grad student, faculty, staff, other). Ask respondents about their responses to possible solutions, such as a shuttle, parking garage, or rezoning.
2. The specific example added to the revised version is more effective, but any typical or frustrating experience about parking would be effective. Students may also practice other lead-in types: statistics, quotation from authority, description of an ideal situation, worse-case scenario for the future if nothing is changed.
3. The authors revised their plan to follow the "Alternatives Pattern" given in the shaping section of this chapter. The revised outline is an improvement because it allows the writers to end with the "most cost-effective" and "most immediately effective" solution.
4. The essay is addressed to administrators who have the potential to change parking strategies and to students who might influence those administrators. Westfall would appreciate the fact that the writers had interviewed him and had come up with more practical alternatives than a parking garage. But the authors' essay would have more impact if they sent a copy to the appropriate faculty committee, with copies to the president of the university and to the parking director.

Eui Young Hwang, "Who Should Take Charge?"

The Hwang essay is an excellent example of a "conversation" paper. In this case, the reading ("Black Asian Conflict: Where Do We Begin?") serves more as a prompt than as the focus for a summary-response essay (see Chapter 5, Reading). However, writing a summary-response is excellent practice for writing an essay that uses other texts as references or as starting points for the student's own essay. In this case, as Hwang notes in his first paragraph, "the authors fail to specify how to implement their solutions." Hwang writes his own problem-solving essay to address this shortcoming. In his essay, however, Hwang keeps the "conversation" with the authors going by referring occasionally to the ideas in the original article.

Responses to <u>Questions for Writing and Discussion</u>

1. As in the summary-response essays, students' responses to the <u>Ms</u>. conversation will demonstrate a range of possibilities for response.
2. Hwang keeps the conversation going by referring to Alexander and Lyu-Volckhausen in paragraphs 1-4.
3. Hwang's three solutions are to involve the Korean media, the Korean-American churches, and the Korean-American business organizations. Ask students to explain which of his solutions they find most persuasive or potentially least effective.
4. None of Hwang's solutions are likely to make the problem worse or cause additional negative effects. Hwang's solutions are likely to improve the overall harmony of the system, but students might argue that the problems are not as easily solved as Hwang suggests--or they might suggest other political, economic, or educational solutions that Hwang does not consider.
5. Hwang tries to answer objections in each of his body paragraphs. In paragraph 2, Hwang says, "Many Koreans are, however, too busy to attend any educational programs." He then explains that media makes cultural education more accessible. In paragraph 3, Hwang says, "One may argue that churches are too limited. . . ." He then counters that argument. Finally in paragraph 4, Hwang considers the possibility that some Koreans will want to use their own money as they see fit. Hwang does try to anticipate and answer possible objections.

Chapter 10: Arguing

It is useful to distinguish between persuasion, which may employ any available means to convince or move an audience, and argumentation, which emphasizes logical reasoning and a fair countering of opposing positions. Most writing courses focus on argumentation because it is a widely-accepted form of academic discourse.

At the heart of this chapter is a division of argument into types of claims. The types of argument are determined by four kinds of claims: claims of fact, claims about cause and effect, claims of value, and claims of policy. (For a careful definition and explanation of the theory behind these types of claims, see Marie Secor, "Modes of Thinking, Modes of Argument" in Part III of this book.)

Recently, teachers have encouraged students to use Rogerian strategies for argument for sensitive arguments where antagonistic argumentative styles are inappropriate. Rogerian argumentation or negotiation fits well in this textbook because it contains elements of personal narration and problem-solving as well as argument. Invite your students to test their arguments to see whether Rogerian strategies might be appropriate.

Many teachers require students to use sources for their argument essay, but students should be encouraged to use personal experience and field resources as well as library sources. Teaching tips in the Arguing chapter and the Research chapter suggest ways that teachers can insure that writers have a personal connection to the topic so that they don't write voiceless, canned "research" essays. In addition, because arguing essays are complex and time consuming, many teachers encourage students to write on a topic they have explored in an essay written earlier in the term. Argument essays usually require more expertise than students can usually acquire in just a three or four week assignment period.

Cathleen A. Cleaver, "The Internet: A Clear and Present Danger?"

Cathleen Cleaver's essay on the Internet contrasts with the more optimistic view championed by Sherry Turkle (see Connie Koenenn's essay, "Plotting a Net Gain," in Chapter 6). Although Turkle admits that there is a "darker side" of cyberspace, she celebrates the connective powers of e-mail and the Internet. Cleaver's essay, while backing away from the claim that the Internet represents a "Clear and Present Danger," nevertheless focuses on the dangers of the Internet if it remains unregulated.

   The three most important rhetorical strengths of Cleaver's essay are her sharp focus, her vivid and detailed description of the problem, and her anticipation and response to opposing positions. First, Cleaver clearly identifies her thesis, the focus of her argument: "Thus, instead of defending this rather apocalyptic view of the Internet, I'll attempt to explain why some . . . regulation . . . is necessary." Cleaver then proceeds to narrow this focus further by focusing primarily on the effects of pornography on children. Second, Cleaver spends paragraphs 10-16, nearly a third of her essay, graphically describing the problem that she proposes to solve with regulatory laws. Finally, Cleaver does a good job of modeling for students how to anticipate and respond to opposing positions. Since these three rhetorical skills (narrowing a thesis, describing the problem, and responding to opposing arguments) are essential for an effective argumentative essay, Cleaver's essay makes an excellent choice for students' reading and response.

Responses to Questions for Writing and Discussion

1. Doing this prereading exercise will generate a lively discussion about students' Internet experiences and prepare them for a more active and critical reading of Cleaver's essay.

2. Cleaver begins with examples of copyright violation, consumer fraud, child pornography, antitrust law violation, and a pedophile's attempt at sexual assault. Only two of these examples deal with child pornography because Cleaver wants to place her argument about regulating child pornography in the context of the larger arguments about regulation of Internet activities. The examples are effective as lead-ins to her argument because they represent some realistic ways in which an unregulated internet may exploit its users.

3. Since Cleaver is addressing an audience in a debate environment, she does a good job of representing opposing arguments and then arguing against them. First, Cleaver addresses the opponents who say that restriction is up to the parents (paragraph 17). Along with this argument, she responds to people who say that software filters can protect children. Next, she responds to the argument that "the laws just cannot apply in this new medium (paragraph 18). Then she raises the argument about enforcement (paragraph 19). Finally she responds to the notion that regulations will hinder the development of Internet technology (paragraph 21). She sums up these objections in paragraph 22 when she says that "it's an illusion to claim social or moral neutrality in the application of technology."

4. Cleaver appeals to reason at several points in her essay, but especially in paragraph 10 where she cites statistics to support her analysis of the severity of the problem, in paragraph 17 when she responds to the arguments about parents and filtering software, in paragraph 18, when she cites historical examples, and in paragraph 19 where she uses the effective analogy of a red light or a stop sign. Cleaver's conclusion—that technology must serve humanity and not vice versa—is her final rational appeal. Cleaver's appeals to character appear throughout the essay in her reasonable and rational approach to the topic, in her use of statistics, examples, and evidence, and in her defense of the rights of humanity and especially of women and children. Cleaver's appeals to emotion are most noticeable in paragraph 13, where her descriptions are graphic and shocking. But since these emotional appeals do not distort the truth of the matter, they are legitimate and effective. In conclusion, she does not rely too much on emotional appeals, although some readers may not want to know the kinds of pornography that exist on the Internet. She could give more facts and statistics, but her rational appeal is already quite strong.

5. With a little research in the library or on the internet, students can quickly find other opposing arguments. This topic makes an excellent in-class debate which can demonstrate how to discover and respond to opposing or alternative arguments in the students' own arguing essays.

Edward Abbey, "The Damnation of a Canyon"

Abbey's essay is the perfect testing ground for students to debate whether effective argument should or should not rely solely or primarily on rational appeals. Should writers also use emotional appeals in argumentative essays? When are emotional appeals excessive or inappropriate? Have students use the emotional appeals in Martin Luther King's excerpt in this chapter as a standard for comparison. This chapter states that "Argument emphasizes reason, not emotion." Have students challenge that assertion. Is it true? Should it be true? Why or why not? To what degree does Abbey effectively employ emotion to convince his readers? Where do his emotional tactics backfire and anger readers? What conclusions can students draw from a comparison of the essays by King and Abbey to guide their own essays? Should these essays offer guidance, or do students need to decide about using emotional appeals based on their own topics, their styles, and their intended audiences?

Responses to Questions for Writing and Discussion

1. (This is also a useful question to assign before students read Abbey's essay, as a prereading journal exercise.)

3. Abbey's overall claim is anticipated in the title and gradually made more explicit in paragraphs 1, 4 ("I am in a position to evaluate the transformation of the region"), 5 ("I take a dim view of dams . . . Great for machines, yes: But unfit for people"), 11 ("The difference between . . . is the difference between death and life"), 16, 21, 22 ("We can shut down the Glen Canyon power plant . . . and drain the reservoir"). Abbey's claim combines arguments about fact (accessibility), cause-and-effect analysis (before-and-after comparison), evaluation (the untamed river is better than the man-made lake), and proposal (drain the lake).

4. Abbey uses paragraphs 2-5 to establish his credentials, and he appears reasonable here. The cantankerous Abbey appears in paragraphs 12 ("the oligarchs and politicians condemned our river for purposes of their own"), 15 ("This argument appeals to . . . the wealthy, upper-middle-class American slob"), and 23 ("This will no doubt expose a drear and hideous scene . . . and sterilize the repellent mess").

5. Abbey becomes more emotional in his idyllic descriptions of the river before damnation (paragraphs 8, 9, and 12) and in his condemnation of the powerboat mentality (paragraphs 12, 14, 15, 17, and 23).

6. This question suggests an excellent collaborative writing activity. Students against Abbey's proposal can role-play the controller; students for Abbey's proposal can write to their congressperson. Or vice-versa.

Edward Koch, "Death and Justice, " "Robert Badinter, "Death Be Not Proud," and John O'Sullivan, "Death and Justice"

Students should read these three essays together in order to see how each essay brings a unique perspective to a topic most people think is just a two-sided argument. Each essay takes a slightly different stance on the topic, and even more important, each essay is written from a different time, place, and perspective. The writer and the circumstances surrounding the writing of each essay are as important as the arguments and reasons each writer brings to the topic.

Edward Koch's essay is an excellent example of a short, concise, and classically written and organized argumentative essay. Koch has a clear focus on an argumentative (policy) claim. He makes clear appeals to character, emotion, and reason. He uses a variety of kinds of supporting evidence. He presents and then counters the relevant opposing arguments. He uses a forceful but reasonable tone throughout. And he does all this in an essay that follows a clear classical structural pattern. This essay can be a virtual template for organizing a classical argumentative essay. Koch's essay is written by a former mayor of New York, written at a time of high crime rates. Robert Badinter's essay contrasts with Koch's essay in almost every possible way. He is against the death penalty, he does not depend on logic and formal argument as much as Koch, he is writing from a European point of view, and he is more dependent on emotional arguments than on logic for the force of his argument.

Finally, John O'Sullivan essay balances arguments from both sides, and is able to acknowledge that the question is difficult and may not be solvable with a single position or solution. O'Sullivan ends his essay by commenting on issues such as DNA tests and on the barbaric nature of public executions without drawing a conclusion about the overall issue of capital punishment.

Responses to <u>Questions for Writing and Discussion</u>

1. In paragraph 4, Koch directly and simply states his thesis: "I still support the death penalty." He follows that with a sentence which maps out the organization which his essay will follow: "The reasons I maintained my position can be best understood by examining the arguments most frequently heard in opposition." Several other sentences in Koch's essay restate that thesis, including this sentence from paragraph 10: "It is by exacting the

highest penalty for the taking of human life that we affirm the highest value of human life."

When Koch says in paragraph 13, "the state has rights that the private individual does not," he is making a crucial legal distinction between acting as an individual and acting as a member of a government given power through the social contract. With this distinction in place, Koch can argue that a just social execution is different from an individual murder.

2. Robert Badinter's thesis is that America should abolish the death penalty, and he states his position at the beginning of paragraph 2: "I don't believe that Americans fully understand how their use of the death penalty has profoundly degraded the country's image in the eyes of other democratic nations." The emotional appeal in this thesis is clearly connected to the fact that he helped abolish the death penalty in France.

3. John O'Sullivan is conditionally for the death penalty, but his position is stated much more subtly. For example, O'Sullivan states in paragraph 5 that the death penalty "is a sign of civilization." In paragraph 6, he suggests that many countries abolished the death penalty in spite of majority public opposition. O'Sullivan comments that what that demonstrates "is not that Europe is more civilized than the U.S. but that it is less democratic." Finally, in paragraph 12, O'Sullivan says that life without parole is not the civilized equivalent to the death penalty since murders continue to be committed in prison. But unlike either Badinter or Koch, O'Sullivan is willing to be persuaded that there are legitimate moral arguments to be made in favor of abolishing capital punishment and that we should reject public executions.

4. Koch's essay is clearly organized along classical lines, as the following outline indicates. Koch slightly modifies the order by blending his argument in a point-by-point refutation of the opposition's argument.

I. Introduction	(paragraphs 1-3)
II. Narration/Partition	(paragraph 4)
III. Refutation/Argument	(paragraphs 5-13)
IV. Conclusion	(paragraphs 14-16)

5. Robert Badinter uses some of the elements of a classical argument. He begins with an introduction, narration and partition, but he does not spend much time refuting opposing arguments. He sets forth his own arguments in paragraphs 3 through 6, and finally considers an opposing argument (the

suffering of the victims) in paragraph 7. John O'Sullivan uses the Timothy McVeigh execution as the introduction for his essay and then gives his narration in paragraphs 3 through 5, where he considers Dr. Johnson's opinion and the historical concept of civilization. He spends more time responding to (rather than refuting) opposing arguments in paragraphs 7 through 12, and his conclusion is ambiguous.

6. To answer this question, divide the class into groups and assign each group one of the essays. Ask each group to find examples of all three kinds of appeals in their assigned essay. They should discover that Koch and O'Sullivan rely on logic more than emotion, while Badinter appeals more to emotion.

7. Koch's essay is the longest, and he has the most evidence—of all kinds. For supporting evidence, Koch uses statistics, specific examples and analogies. He uses statistics in paragraphs 7, 8, and 9. He uses specific examples of criminals and crimes in paragraphs 1-3, 8, and 14. He uses the analogy of curing cancer in paragraph 6. Ask students to explain which of these kinds of evidence they find most persuasive. How do they think Koch should revise his essay to make it more effective?

Be sure to connect the kinds of evidence Koch uses to the kinds of appeals he is making. Notice that Koch's statistics tend to appeal to reason while his specific examples tend to appeal to emotion. Koch's appeal to character is contained most clearly in paragraph 4: "During my 22 years in public service, I have heard the pros and cons of capital punishment expressed with special intensity. . . .I have listened to their ideas. I have weighed their objection carefully." Remind students that they don't have to have served in public office for 22 years to make a strong appeal to character. They just need to show that they care about the subject, that they have approached the subject with thoroughness and high integrity, and that they have argued fairly and reasonably.

Ask students to review the kinds of evidence offered in Badinter and O'Sullivan and compare them to the kinds of evidence Koch uses.

8. Ask students to find particular sentences in each essay that show how the context of the essay reflects or helps determine each writer's thesis. Koch and Badinter are most influenced by their own participation in government, while O'Sullivan draws his argument from the context of the McVeigh execution but is personally less involved and thus more objective on this issue.

Crystal Sabatke, "Welfare is Still Necessary for Women and Children in the U.S."

In recent years, welfare laws have been modified to promote job training and workfare programs. In some cases, however, women with small children cannot work or cannot meet the new requirements. Crystal Sabatke selects an appropriate audience and then attempts to persuade them that welfare is still necessary in these cases—at least until these mothers can join the workforce. Her argument looks at the various categories of women who still need welfare and answers opposing arguments with statistics and surveys.

Responses to <u>Questions for Writing and Discussion</u>

1. Sabatke represents her audience in paragraph 2 where she refers to "many government officials" and "law makers" in paragraph 2 and in the opposing arguments she describes at the beginning of paragraphs 3 and 4. Sabatke might address the assumptions that her audience has (see her prewriting materials) and critique those assumptions as well.

2. Asking students to review the peer review comments made by Bev and Amy is an excellent way to model how to give constructive advice. If students can see that some of their comments could be more specific—without hurting the writer's feelings—they will feel more comfortable giving specific and constructive advice.

3. Paragraphs 2, 3, and 4 each respond to one possible opposing argument. Ask students individually or in groups to critique Sabatke's responses to these arguments. What other arguments might Sabatke respond to?

4. In her prewriting materials, Sabatke said she would give some actual cases to convince her audience that welfare was still necessary. Perhaps some additional case studies would be helpful. Also, since the welfare laws are very complex, an early paragraph defining the current welfare rules and how they have been recently changed would help readers understand the current predicament some young mothers face.

Eric Boese, "Standardized Tests: Shouldn't We be Helping our Students?"

The recent controversies over standardized tests have called all kinds of "high stakes" tests into question. In an era of increased testing, teachers, students, parents and even university presidents have criticized the SAT test, the Texas TAAS test, or California's Stanford 9 test. Eric Boese appeals to parents, taxpayers, and concerned educators and suggests that the increased testing is "harming the educational process." Boese argues that we need to learn how to use these tests in a more productive manner. In addition, Boese contends that increased scores on these tests may or may not correlate with increased learning or improved critical thinking ability. One of the main problems is using the results of the tests properly to improve education, not reduce school funding or create more tests.

Responses to <u>Questions for Writing and Discussion</u>

1. Students' responses to question 1 should help them see their own personal connection to this topic and help them evaluate Boese's solutions as well.

2. Boese begins discussing the problems with the current testing instruments and procedures in paragraph 2 and continues through paragraph 11. Among the problems he cites are that the tests take up valuable class time, the test scores are misleading, the test scores are used inappropriately to determine school funding, the tests encourage teachers and students to cheat, and the tests may not accurately measure the goals of the curriculum. Boese's solutions, which begin in paragraph 11, include making corporations answer to the school boards, throwing out tests that are too difficult for a particular age group, testing the actual goals of each school's curriculum, reducing the time spent preparing just for the tests, and avoiding using test scores to determine school funding.

3. In his opening paragraphs, Boese's use of the first person plural ("Still we see so many children being held back") suggests that his audience includes parents, teachers, and anyone else concerned about quality education. In paragraph 7, Boese says that people "would rather send their children to school" at places where schools are funded well. In the next sentence he

suggests that test results can affect property values, thus appealing to property owners as well as parents. In paragraph 14, Boese appeals directly to taxpayers to vote to increase funding for schools they support and in his final sentence appeals collectively to parents, taxpayers, and concerned educators: "I urge you to consider the bright futures being dampened by an unproductive testing system and be the person who puts the needs of children first." Ask your students to suggest other sentences that Boese might include which would strengthen his identification of this audience and his appeal to them.

Chapter 11: Responding to Literature

Although this chapter is self-contained, most teachers prefer to supplement it with selected literary works of their own choosing. They have students read "The Story of an Hour" and/or "A Worn Path" and discuss these short stories in class, but they assign another short fiction work for the students to interpret. One word of caution, however. Although you may wish to bring in poems or dramatic pieces that illustrate key imagery or archetypal themes relevant to the work the class is studying, keep the focus on interpreting short fiction. Obviously, what students learn from this chapter about reading fiction will not necessarily help them with a one-act play or a poem.

Eudora Welty, "A Worn Path"

"A Worn Path" works well in class not because every student finds it exciting, but because its careful structure and evocative language repay close reading and interpretation. The story is suited to an archetypal analysis of the quest or journey motifs as well as the death-rebirth imagery. As part of the discussion, you may wish to hand out copies of Welty's essay, "Is Phoenix Jackson's Grandson Really Dead?" (see question 4).

Responses to Questions for Writing and Discussion

1. Student responses vary, but often students will finish the story feeling slightly dissatisfied that "nothing really happens" in this story. One of the teaching virtues of this story is that it amply rewards active reading/rereading: The more students read and discuss this story, the more ideas and suggestions they find.

2. The collaboratively revised essay by Julia MacMillan and Brett MacFadden near the end of this chapter focuses on this interpretation, but this question makes an excellent in-class small group activity if students have not yet read that essay.

3. Ask students, working in groups, to generate a list (such as the one below) of the possible tests or trials of Phoenix's physical and mental courage. When they have generated a list (and recorded it at the chalkboard), they might

discuss which 12 are most important--or whether the number should be more or less than 12. (The literary parallel is to the twelve labors of Hercules.)

(1) Meeting the real or imagined "foxes, owls, beetles, jack rabbits, coons and wild animals" in paragraph 3;

(2) Climbing up the hill with seeming "chains about my feet" in paragraph 5;

(3) Disentangling herself from the thorn bush that catches her dress in paragraphs 7-9;

(4) Struggling against the sun in paragraph 10;

(5) Crossing the log over the creek in paragraphs 11-13;

(6) Creeping and crawling through the barbed wire fence in paragraph 16;

(7) Slipping past the buzzard who watches her pass in paragraphs 17-18;

(8) Winding her way through the maze in the cornfield in paragraph 21;

(9) Mastering her fear of the ghost/scarecrow in paragraphs 22-27;

(10) Fending off the black dog that "attacks" her in paragraphs 34-35;

(11) Tricking the man with the gun to get the shiny nickel and facing up to his gun in paragraphs 36-58;

(12) Getting a lady to lace up her shoe so she can go into a big building in paragraphs 62-67;

(13) Determining from the document nailed on the wall and the gold seal that she has arrived at her destination, in paragraphs 69-70;

(14) Remembering, in the doctor's office, why she has come on her journey, in paragraphs 72-87.

After discussing their lists, students should consider whether the "parallel" between Hercules and Old Phoenix adds to an appreciation or understanding of Welty's story.

4. Begin a discussion of this question by asking students to find evidence in the story that suggests that the boy might be dead (or at least no longer sick or no longer around). In paragraph 79, the nurse asks about the boy and his throat. Then she asks if he is dead. Later the nurse suggests that Phoenix has been coming for this medicine for a long time when she says, "Throat never heals, does it?" and checks her card to learn that it was perhaps 2-3 years ago. Finally, the nurse concludes with "it's an obstinate case." Based on this evidence, do students believe that the boy might be dead?

After reviewing the evidence in the story, have students reread Welty's comment. What is their reaction and interpretation on this point?

5. This question can lead to an excellent small group and/or class discussion comparing the central characters and themes of both stories. The class might begin to notice that often literary interpretations develop out of a <u>comparison</u>

between or among characters, events, myths, and stories: Comparing Old Phoenix to the Phoenix of the legend leads to one interpretation. Comparing the tests Old Phoenix faces to the labors of Hercules leads to another reading. Comparing Phoenix and Mrs. Mallard leads to another angle of interpretation.

Toni Cade Bambara, "The Lesson"

Bambara's "The Lesson" is a classic initiation story with an unmistakable political message. Students should see the connections between the "lesson" that Sylvia and her friends learn and the reading strategies discussed in Chapter 5, Reading. (An effective prereading assignment for this story is, in fact, Jack Solomon's essay, "Masters of Desire: The Culture of American Advertising," in Chapter 5.) Miss Moore provides the children with a first lesson in the semiotic analysis of F. A. O. Schwarz. Except for Sugar, Sylvia and her friends can't quite articulate the message they find in a sailboat that costs $1,195.00--but they are on the right track. As Sylvia says of her encounter, "when we get [to the store], I kinda hang back. Not that I'm scared, what's there to be afraid of, just a toy store." Sylvia should be scared, however, because as both the reader and Miss Moore know, there's much more at stake than just toys in a store.

Responses to <u>Questions for Writing and Discussion</u>

1. Students' answers to this question should help connect their own experiences with Sylvia's stubbornness and unwillingness to confront a new experience or to try to see something just at the edge of her normal vision.

2. The opening of the sentence perfectly captures Sylvia's adolescent stage: Everyone else is stupid and only she and her friends are just right. Throughout the remainder of the story, Sylvia's thoughts and actions illustrate her narrow, self-absorptive personality. If anyone can resist a "lesson," Sylvia is the person. Years of traditional schooling have taught her to sniff out and reject any educational agenda. Curiously, the first sentence does contain some distance ("Back in the days when . . .") and suggests that Sylvia is writing the story from a more mature perspective. As she narrates the story, however, Sylvia does not suggest at any point that she knows more now than she did at the time of the story.

3. Have students identify the reactions that each of these children have. Students may realize that the rest of the children act as a kind of chorus, a background against which the drama between Miss Moore, Sylvia, and Sugar is played out.

4. Miss Moore puts the children in the physical position to make some discoveries about the world in which they live. She pushes Sylvia and her

friends to learn from the trip, but she refuses to give a lecture. Like a good teacher, Miss Moore cons Sugar into articulating the day's lesson (see paragraph 50). However, Sylvia lets us know that Miss Moore has primed the pump: "Who are these people . . . What kinda work they do . . . Where we are is who we are, Miss Moore always pointin out." Ask students to describe Miss Moore's teaching strategies and grade her performance.

5. Each of these phrases contains a piece of the theme of the story. Ask students, as part of a write-to-learn exercise, to react to and interpret these lines. (What other lines from the story reverberate in a similar fashion?)

Julia MacMillan and Brett MacFadden, "A Singular Perpetuation"

Sometimes collaborative writing produces a text that is, through synthesis, greater than the sum of the two contributions. At other times, the collaboration is relatively mechanical, producing a document that has more ideas but not necessarily any greater insight. One possible discussion topic begins with having students read both drafts and then the final draft. Did these two writers learn something from each other and create a new critical vision, or did they just combine ideas without any new insight?

Responses to Questions for Writing and Discussion

1-3. Students should be able to critique MacMillan's and MacFadden's essay using criteria you and the class establish for a good interpretive essay. What is the authors' main idea, and do they persuade their readers of its plausibility? The authors have assembled some--but not all--of the evidence available from the story: What other evidence might they use? How did the interpretation change as the authors revised their essays? Why did they omit the incidents in town?

4. After students annotate MacMillan's and MacFadden's essay, have them use these guidelines for revision (or the criteria you worked with above) to review their own essay drafts.

Pat Russell, "Death: The Final Freedom"

Ask students to critique Russell's effort in his final paragraph to universalize Chopin's "The Story of an Hour." If the story is feminist, does that make it "one dimensional"? Does a more universal interpretation "open up" the story so it becomes the "struggle of all people" to balance selfishness and selflessness? Use these two viewpoints to give students the opportunity to negotiate different interpretations. Are interpretations always in conflict with each other? Must one interpretation "win" at the expense of another?

Responses to <u>Questions for Writing and Discussion</u>

1. Russell's essay was itself a reaction to a class discussion of possible feminist readings of "The Story of an Hour." In a like manner, students can use Russell's essay as a point of departure for their own interpretation.

2. The class should consider whether Russell is working with an inadequate definition of feminism. Based on his essay, how might Russell define feminism? Ask students to write out their <u>own</u> definitions and then explain how their definitions might affect or alter Russell's interpretation. Since definition of key terms is crucial in essays that interpret literature, you might follow this discussion by asking students to find a key term in their own drafts and practice writing a definition for it.

3. Russell states his thesis in the last sentence of paragraph 1, and then he restates it in the conclusion. Russell clearly has an interpretation (rather than a statement of fact) because his reading is only one of a number of possible ways of understanding the story. Class discussion should quickly reveal that his thesis is debatable.

4. Roughly speaking, Russell uses an argumentative shaping strategy for the two major paragraphs in the body of the essay. Paragraph 2 presents the evidence in favor of a feminist interpretation and paragraphs 3 and 4 show his contrasting reading.

Chapter 12: Writing a Research Paper

Unless your course has a significant block of time to devote to a research paper, assign this chapter pieces at a time, throughout the semester, rather than all in one block. There is simply too much information for students to absorb and internalize in a week or two. The best strategy is to follow your investigating assignment with bits and pieces of this chapter on several successive essay assignments. For example, you can do some of the journal exercises when students take their library tour early in the semester. You can have students practice keeping a research notebook for the investigating chapter. You can assign the sections on library sources, references, and indexes at a later point. When students are quoting from sources during their explaining or evaluating essay, you can assign the sections on documenting sources and avoiding plagiarism. Later in the semester, you can review MLA and APA documentation styles to make sure students understand the system they have chosen. Assigned and discussed and practiced bit by bit, students can become proficient at research over the course of a term. If you try to teach everything about research in just one essay, the students' frustration may boobytrap your whole plan.

Handbook: Answers to Exercises

In each case, the passages below suggest <u>one way</u> that the passage might be revised. Other revisions may also be correct or appropriate.

Exercise 2a: Revised passage eliminating inappropriate sentence fragments.

(1) Most people think that a library is as quiet as growing grass, but often it is the noisiest place on campus to study. (2) The worst time is finals week. (3) Some of the chatter is from people who come to the library just to visit: "How did you like the party Saturday night?" (4) "Did you get the notes from chemistry?" (5) The chatter goes on continually, punctuated by coughs, gasps, and giggles. (6) Just when I start to panic about my calculus examination, someone across the table tells a joke, and they all start laughing. (7) They try to cover their laughter with their hands, but the sound explodes out anyway, irritating ten other students who are trying to study. (8) Sometimes I wish the library had its own police force, to arrest those gabby, discourteous "party people." (9) I would sit there smiling as they handcuffed these party people and dragged them out of the library. (10) Ah, the sweet revenge of daydreams.

Exercise 2b: Revision of passage containing mixed constructions and faulty predication.

(1) After my sophomore year, I intend to transfer to Boston College. (2) Basically, I want to attend a school that has a city environment and a diverse population of students. (3) I want to transfer because my sister Nadine wants me to move closer to home. (4) She wants me to move closer to home. (5) Also, attending a city school will enable me to see plays, to visit museums occasionally, and to eat out at good restaurants. (6) Finally, I'd like to meet all sorts of students. (7) A good university is a place where a student can meet people from all walks of life. (8) Because Boston College has diversity, I intend to transfer.

Exercise 2c: Revision of passage containing dangling and misplaced modifiers.

(1) SP302, History of Film, is a worthwhile class to take. (2) Professor Hancock teaches the class on Tuesday night from 7:00 to 9:45 p.m. so that it coincides with dollar movie night at the campus theater. (3) Normally, a long class would be boring because of the Nod Factor. (4) However, Professor Hancock, a very energetic instructor, keeps everyone awake and entertains the students. (5) Her lecture on Citizen Kane was a particularly good example. (6) Unfortunately, the film began before she finished her lecture. (7) Rushing across the stage just as the film was beginning, she tripped on an electrical cord, causing her to lose her balance and fall. (8) She regained her composure in time to remind us that Orson Welles also wrote and performed the famous radio broadcast about the invasion of the Martians. (9) We certainly were relieved to get that important information.

Exercise 2d: Passage revised to correct faulty parallelism.

(1) Alcohol abuse is a primary cause of spectator violence at college football games. (2) On average, the police department makes between five and ten arrests at each home football game. (3) These arrests are for property destruction, public intoxication, and disorderly conduct. (4) When spectators consume too much alcohol not only do they hurt themselves, but also they act obnoxiously toward others. (5) Following a recent fight, ambulance attendants said that some drunken spectators or "Animals" actually pelted them with sod while they tried to assist an injured man. (6) The attendants tried pleading, reasoning, and shouting, but to no avail. (7) To reduce these ugly incidents and restore the enjoyment of the game, alcohol should not be sold at football games after the beginning of the second half.

Exercise 2e: Passive voice sentences changed into active voice.

1. People communicate using body movements.
2. People can interpret a nod, a gesture, or a glance in several ways.
3. A wave and a smile mean one thing, but a wave and a tear can mean something else.
4. In addition, a continual or intense stare may irritate some people.
5. A person who talks to us at very close range may also intimidate us.

Exercise 2e: Passage revised to change inappropriate passive voice to active voice.

(1) Writing on a word processor can transform the act of writing, but only if the writer has some rudimentary typing skills. (2) Unfortunately many men have a sexist hang-up about typing that inhibits their writing on a computer. (3) Traditionally, most men have felt that only females--i.e., secretaries--should type. (4) Only the macho Hemingways and Mailers of the world actually type their own novels and stories. (5) Now, however, many male business executives are caught by conflicting role-images. (6) It is socially acceptable for them to be computer literate, but it is still somehow demeaning to sit at a keyboard and practice the "female" skill of typing. (7) Thus, word processing provides one more example of how notions about sexist roles can hurt men as well as women.

Exercise 2f: Passage revised to reduce nominals and "be" verbs.

(1) As parents, we know that many young people love to ride motorcycles, motorbikes, and motorscooters. (2) Today, however, our ten-year-old kids are attracted to those off-road three-wheelers. (3) Although kids enjoy riding three-wheelers in the hills, these vehicles can cause serious injury. (4) Unfortunately, sales people do not sufficiently educate these young drivers--and their parents--about the potential dangers. (5) As a result, some activist groups oppose sales of all three-wheelers. (6) These groups want to regulate the industry in order to make riding safer for children and adults. (7) Every responsible parent should commend the efforts of these groups to reform the industry.

Exercise 2g: Passage revised to correct errors in subject-verb agreement.

(1) If you have friends or a family member who smokes, I have some suggestions to help this person quit. (2) First, if the family is supportive, try talking openly about the facts. (3) There are a few public service agencies that will provide evidence demonstrating the link between smoking and cancer. (4) Next, investigate this person's behavior: What does this person do just before he or she smokes? (5) To quit smoking, the smoker must disrupt the patterns of behavior that lead to smoking. (6) An inventory of the activities and places that cause a person to smoke provides key information. (7) For example, if the person always smokes after dinner, suggest eating snacks over a two-hour period instead of having a sit-down meal. (8) If he or she always smokes in a certain chair in the living room, change the furniture. (9) Breaking any habit is always easier if you break the entire behavior pattern. (10) Of course, each of these smokers needs to want to stop smoking.

Exercise 2h: Passage revised to eliminate any unnecessary shifts in tense.

(1) In Sophocles' play, <u>Antigone</u>, two characters are tragic figures: Antigone and Creon. (2) In the play, Antigone faces a choice of conscience. (3) Should she be loyal to her family and bury her brother, or should she be loyal to the state and obey the edict of Creon, the King of Thebes? (4) She assumes that she knows the best way to handle the situation and willfully chooses her own death. (5) Creon also faces a choice of conscience. (6) Should he punish someone who has betrayed the state, even if that person is a member of his family? (7) Like Napoleon and General Custer, Creon thinks primarily about himself and his public image. (8) In Creon's case, ego or "hubris" leads to tragic results for the people around him.

Exercise 2i/j: Passage revised to correct problems in pronoun agreement and reference.

(1) People use the term *best friend* to describe a person who has a special warmth and friendliness. (2) I still remember when Michelle Martin, one of my best friends, said that she really liked me, too. (3) I called her my best friend; we stood by each other. (4) One time at a party, I saw her talking angrily to another woman. (5) It turned out that the other woman had dated Tom, the guy Michelle was going with at the time. (6) Each of them felt cheated by her boyfriend. (7) Before I knew what was happening, they were screaming at each other. (8) When I tried to stick up for Michelle, the other woman took a swing at me, and so I swung back with my best left hook, popping the other woman in the right eye. (9) As a result, I was suspended from school for a week. (10) It just goes to show that when you have a best friend, everyone expects that you'll help her if you can.

Exercise 3a: Passage revised to make vague words and phrases more specific and vivid.

(1) When I was separated from my girlfriend, I missed her nearly every day. (2) Being alone sometimes gave me an empty feeling. (3) When I called her on the phone, we talked about the carefree times we spent together last summer at the beach, not about that fight we had about her parents. (4) Since there was no stress, we had a fun-filled, long-distance relationship. (5) I know that our relationship will improve, now that we're back together. (6) We always had difficulty talking seriously about our future. (7) Now we are more involved with each other and can talk about school, money, and even marriage. (8) For anyone who is having troubles, I recommend a temporary separation because, in the long run, the relationship will be much happier.

Exercise 3b: Passage revised to eliminate unnecessary words.

(1) One recent medical discovery is the so-called diving reflex. (2) When people fall into icy water, their circulation slows down because the water is so cold. (3) In addition, cellular metabolism slows down, conserving oxygen. (4) In a recent case, eleven-year-old Alvaro Garza disappeared underneath the ice for 45 minutes. (5) When rescuers finally pulled him from beneath the ice, he was unconscious, his body temperature was below normal, and his skin was grayish-blue. (6) Finding no pulse, the rescuers began CPR (cardiopulmonary resuscitation) immediately. (7) Within a few days, Alvaro began to recover steadily, and soon he was asking for a hamburger and French fries. (8) Although he may have some lingering effects from his ordeal, the miracle is that he survived.

Exercise 3d: Passage revised to eliminate cliches and inappropriate technical language.

(1) The television news media in America needs to be reformed. (2) Serious news has been abandoned as stations rush to entertain the viewer. (3) Trying to find an informative story on the evening news is like looking for the chicken in chicken noodle soup. (4) The station executives who program the evening news believe that the average American has the I.Q. of a city-hall pigeon. (5) As a result, viewers see in-depth stories about a sex scandal involving a local politician, but only a few seconds explaining why the stock market plunged eighty points in two hours. (6) Newscasters attempt to inject humor by telling stupid jokes that most of us heard a year ago from David Letterman rather than informing the viewer about the latest progress on arms control. (7) If station programmers actually met the public occasionally, they would recognize that they have severely underestimated their audience.

Exercise 3e: Passage revised to eliminate sexist language.

(1) People in college now are looking for that special job that will match their talents and yet bring them sufficient income. (2) Teaching is a low-paying but good career if you don't mind being one of those professors who spend their lives reading papers, getting grants, and serving on committees. (3) Secretaries or flight attendants can begin their careers with minimal training, but nurses must dedicate themselves to rigorous medical schooling. (4) In business and entertainment, women and men can work together. (5) In the entertainment field, many people dream of being a Bruce Springsteen or a Tina Turner, although most singers don't have Springsteen's talent or Turner's perseverance. (6) People in business often work their way up the ladder and become the head of the company. (7) Even staying at home and raising a family is a respectable career for either men or women, though some people simply don't have the temperament to raise children. (8) Whatever your chosen career, from letter carrier to diplomat, hard work and dedication are the keys to landing and keeping that important job.

Exercise 4b: One possible revision that corrects comma splices and fused sentences.

(1) For years, scientists have attempted to teach animals to communicate. For the most part, their efforts have failed. (2) In the 1950s, psychologists failed to teach a chimpanzee to speak. The ape was only able to grunt a few words. (3) In the 1960s, however, a chimp named Washoe learned the sign language of the deaf. (4) Washoe came to understand hundreds of words, and he used them to communicate and express original ideas. (5) As it turns out, the great apes have the capacity to learn language, but they cannot speak. (6) This research proved that humans are not the only animal capable of using language; they are, however, the most sophisticated users of language.

Exercise 4c: Passage edited to reflect conventions of comma usage.

(1) Everyone can have fun outside in the wintertime by following some common-sense rules. (2) If you are going to be outside for several hours, be sure to eat a nutritious meal before leaving. (3) On cold, damp, or windy days, wear clothes that are warm and dry. (4) To stay warm, protect yourself against moisture that builds up from the inside. (5) Most experts recommend dressing in layers. (6) The inner layer wicks moisture away from your body, the middle layer provides thermal protection, and the outer layer protects against wind or rain. (7) Curiously enough, most people tend to put on too many clothes, underestimating their body's ability to exercise comfortably, naturally, and safely in cold weather.

Exercise 4c: Passage edited to reflect conventions of punctuation.

(1) Dinosaurs, which have been extinct for millions of years, are making news again. (2) At a meeting of the Geological Society of America in November, 1987, scientists announced a startling discovery. (3) Dinosaurs that lived 80 million years ago benefited from an atmosphere that contained nearly 50 percent more oxygen than it does now. (4) Gary Landis, geochemist for the U. S. Geological Service, and Robert Berner, professor at Yale University, reached that conclusion after analyzing air bubbles trapped in bits of amber. (5) They found that the tiny air bubbles contained 32 percent oxygen, compared with 21 percent in the modern atmosphere. (6) When asked whether a decreasing oxygen supply could have caused the extinction of the dinosaurs, Berner explained, "It was a very gradual change, and most organisms easily adapt." (7) "The large, slow-moving dinosaurs probably became extinct," he said, "following some cataclysmic geological event."

Exercise 4d: Passage edited to reflect conventions of punctuation.

(1) Yo-yo dieting, the process of repeatedly losing and gaining weight, is common today. (2) Instead of changing eating habits and exercise patterns, the yo-yo dieter uses three typical strategies to lose weight: taking diet pills, drinking diet liquids, and fasting outright. (3) The yo-yo dieter, however, needs to know the truth about dieting: Diet cycles decrease the muscle-to-fat ratio in the body and decrease the body's ability to lose weight during the next dieting cycle. (4) Quick-fix diets, in other words, will lead to rapid weight losses; however, they will be followed by an even faster weight gain. (5) Ultimately, crash diets do more harm than good--the body just wasn't designed to be a yo-yo.

Exercise 4h: Passage edited to underline appropriate words and titles.

(1) Tom Wolfe, author of <u>The Right Stuff</u>, has written a novel about a Wall Street broker in his newest work, <u>The Bonfire of the Vanities</u>. (2) This novel first appeared in twenty-seven installments in <u>Rolling Stone</u> magazine. (3) Wolfe's style has always been <u>au courant</u>, and <u>Bonfire</u> is no exception. (4) This novel features New York characters who run the gamut from drug pushers to the cunning and ambitious young lions of the investment world. (5) It is not a cliche to say that this book is difficult to put down.

Exercise 4j/k: Passage edited for conventions of mechanics.

(1) The advertisement shows a skydiver floating down to earth, and the picture's caption says, "I take vitamin supplements every day, just to be on the safe side." (2) Self-styled experts, from your local pharmacist to physicians from the Mount Sinai School of Medicine in New York City, encourage the public to believe that vitamins are a cure-all. (3) There are only thirteen known vitamin deficiencies (such as scurvy, which is a vitamin C deficiency), but nearly sixty percent of the two hundred fifty-two Americans responding to our questionnaire believed in taking vitamin supplements. (4) These days, it's almost patriotic to take vitamins--even your mother says, "Don't forget to take your vitamins!" (5) During the 1980s, vitamins' popularity rose an astonishing twenty-nine percent, and revenue from vitamin sales jumped to nearly three billion. (6) Although sales are generally higher in the West, some Eastern cities such as Boston and Philadelphia have also shown dramatic increases in sales. (7) If you want to learn more about vitamins, read "The Vitamin-Pushers" in a recent issue of <u>Consumer Reports</u>.

THE COMPOSING PROCESS: AN OVERVIEW

Josephine Koster Tarvers[1]

On the surface, rhetoricians used to suppose, the composing process looked easy to explain. All we had to do was to explain how ideas got into a writer's head, and from there onto paper. But more than three decades of research into the composing process have convinced us that this process is far more complex than we initially thought. In this essay, I discuss briefly some of the major theories about the composing process, to show you not only where these theories intersect but also where they differ, and conclude with suggestions about applying these theories to your teaching.

First of all, when we speak of the "composing process," we are amalgamating a number of processes, both psychological and physical, both for discovering ideas and actually committing them to writing. Research suggests that each person's writing process is different and that it changes with the writer's age, experience, level of knowledge about the subject, and particular writing situation. It also depends on the environment a writer is working in, the culture that the writer grew up in, and the people who give that writer feedback about a particular piece of writing. So when you see a book or article like this talk about "the writing process" or "the composing process," you must begin by remembering that it is radically compressing a complex group of actions and decisions. Until the mid-1960s, few writing books or writing theorists even talked about a writing process, for writing was a product you generated, not a group of actions. But in that decade, for the first time rhetoricians began to talk about writing as an activity that has distinct stages (what we now call a stage-model theory). Most variations acknowledged some shared stages of the process: a period of gathering information and noting down ideas, one of "roughing out" those ideas, and one in which the information is reshaped and adjusted according to the writer's intentions and certain conventions of linguistic etiquette. We call these stages planning or prewriting; drafting or writing; and revising or editing. The stage-model theories, though, attempt to narrow, rather than broaden the focus of composing.

D. Gordon Rhoman and Albert O. Wlecke are credited with the first exploration of the stage-model theory. In Pre-Writing [25], they argue that a pre-assimilation of ideas occurs in the mind before writing, and that writers must learn to "picture the process" in order to imitate it consciously. They suggest techniques such as keeping journals, writing meditations, and developing analogies as ways for students to discover their messages. They also insist on the separation from and primacy of prewriting over other stages of the composing process, and that the composing process is essentially linear, views that have been assailed by later theorists.

Another noted state model theorist is Peter Elbow. In *Writing Without Teachers* [8], he promotes the technique of freewriting, which encourages writers to record ideas quickly and

---

[1] From Lynn Troyka, *Simon & Schuster Handbook for Writers*, 3/e, New York: Simon & Schuster, 1993.

continuously, without the premature editing for spelling, punctuation, and word choice that so often interrupts or destroys the writer's train of thought. One major criticism of systems like Elbow's, however, is that they privilege the initial stages of the writing process over the others. As a result, students enamored with prewriting may give scant attention to later stages, and produce less satisfactory results. Donald Murray attempts to counter this imbalance through use of a preliminary or "discovery" draft, where writers learn what other kinds of plans and explorations they might make before beginning the formal writing process.[22] But like Elbow, Murray emphasizes prewriting; revision in his scheme is the repetition of the prewriting stages of collecting, planning and developing as many times as is needed until the text is ready for editing.

As rhetoricians became more aware of the "holes" in stage-model theory, they turned more to psychology to learn how writers' minds may work. James Moffett, for instance, has based his work on the theories of Jean Piaget [2], who divided all childhood learning experiences into four stages, based on the behaviors children can learn in each stage (assimilation) and the changes they can make in those behaviors (adaptation). At each stage in Moffett's composing process[20], students are encouraged to return to the previous ones for help in planning and developing, so that their writing processes are not separate and linear but recursive, hierarchic, and spiraling, drawing on earlier knowledge to produce new kinds of writing for new audiences. In other words, they are encouraged to make cognitive plans [21].

The construction of cognitive plans is also central to the research in composing conducted by Linda Flower, John R. Hayes, and their many associates [14]. They base their conclusions on the study of "writing protocols," chronological descriptions of all the activities a writer uses in composing a text and transcripts of the writer narrating his or her decisions and choices in those activities. Flower and Hayes postulate a complex model of the composing process based on planning, translating, and reviewing texts.   Planning involves probing one's own memory, organizing that information, and making an initial plan for producing a text. In translation, the writer puts sentences on paper, leading to a draft; in review the writer improves problem areas in the draft. This process is recursive: students might plan, generate, and revise one paragraph before moving on to another, or plan the whole essay, generate a draft, and revise globally, or use some combination of these processes. Composing is goal-directed, and students use different kinds of strategic knowledge in setting these goals and evaluating how effectively they have been realized. [11]

Flower and Hayes use their model to explain how writers solve the problems of moving from the planning to generating stages by juggling, discarding, or subdividing the constraints on their writing; by drawing on routines or familiar procedures (such as the five-paragraph theme); and by readjusting their goals and hypotheses. This latter stage, revision, has recently been investigated in more detail. More than a decade ago, Nancy Sommers [27, 28] found that student writers frequently confuse revising with correcting, focusing only on "mistakes," whereas more experienced writers reconsider audience and purpose, paying attention to global issues. Sommers suggested that learning to distinguish between revising and editing in the composing process produces better student writing. Many scholars, following in Sommers's and Flower and Hayes's footsteps, have recently begun publishing their conclusions about <u>how</u> writers juggle the stages of composing, learning to move between the elements productively, to take advantage of their pauses, and to use heuristic planning strategies. [10, 24, 26]

The chief criticism of cognitive theories of the composing process is that they make writers too isolated; that is, such theories usually picture writers working alone, and ignore or downplay the social nature of writing and the writer's place in a community or communities of readers and writers. Such critics have developed a <u>social-constructionist</u> theory of the writing process, which argues that the writer, at whatever stage of a piece of writing, is working within the constraints and demands of the communities she or he belongs to. Thus, social constructionist views of the writing process are heavily influenced by the writer's purpose and audience. Richard Gebhardt [12] has suggested, in fact, that there are two large classes of composing processes, one in which the writer is relatively certain about audience, purpose, and the information these require, and one in which the writer discovers the relationship among these three elements. More recently, Maxine Hairston has proposed a three-category continuum [13] among these elements, calling the categories "message writing" needed to conduct well-understood business between writer and reader; "self-limiting writing" where the writer knows audience and purpose, and has the necessary information at hand; and "extended reflective writing," where the writer discovers information, purpose, and sometimes even the audience through the composing process.

Theorists like Kenneth Bruffee [4], Patricia Bizzell [3], and David Bartholomae [1] have expanded our knowledge of how communities influence writers; it is, in fact, safe to say that "social construction" and its paired term,"collaborative learning," are the watchwords for rhetorical theory in the early 1990s. Whether they will remain so is open to question, since evolving an understanding of the writing process is in itself an evolving process. Recently, even our notions of what defines a "community" have been called into question [19]; it's clear, then, that we still haven't pinned down the composing process, nor are we likely to in the near future.

Although no competing theories completely agree on descriptions of or labels for the composing process, most theorists agree in many respects about what is important in it:

- The composing process contains several distinct stages. Each is important, and, depending on the kind of writing, the purpose, the writer's available fund of information, and the audience, each will require different amounts of attention for any particular writing task. No one stage is intrinsically "more important" than any other. As teachers, we must help our students gain experience in handling each stage, and overcome our instincts to emphasize the stage(s) most important to us.

- Composing processes are recursive, not linear; only in the ideal world of textbooks do writers blithely choose an idea, make a neat outline, develop it, write about it, and make final cosmetic changes before presenting it to an audience. In reality, writers struggle, chew their pencils, cross out, go back, pause, reconsider, find other information, rack their brains, juggle ideas, fling

193

curses, and even start over from scratch in the process of composing a text. All of these may be positive actions in creating a text. We can help our students appreciate the recursive nature of writing by sharing our own drafts with them; when students see our corrections and stacks of paper, they are more likely to believe that such challenges face <u>all</u> writers, not just inexperienced ones.

- Writing takes many forms, depending in each case on the writer's purpose and audience. Although writers may develop certain writing habits, their composing processes will vary with every writing occasion. We need to discuss with our students how those processes may change from professor to professor or boss to boss, or from routine memo to lab report to application letter to literary analysis.

- Many techniques can stimulate the composing process; none are inherently "better" than others. Writers need to find the strategy or strategies which work best for them in each kind of writing situation they face. This means not only providing them with a repertoire of strategies to try, but also with the time to practice them.

- Before writers actually begin <u>writing</u>, they need to find subjects and gather ideas and information to write about. The time this takes will be determined by the writer's purpose, audience, and existing fund of knowledge. By varying our assignments, we can help them learn to manipulate these variables.

- The need to put ideas on paper "correctly" may inhibit writers. By drafting quickly and suspending editing until a text is nearly complete, many writers can compose more successful early drafts. Demonstrating techniques like freewriting and discovery drafts, for instance, can help students gain the courage to set aside the rules dinned in by previous teachers.

- Many inexperienced writers do not distinguish between revising and editing. Revision allows writers to test drafts against their intentions and to add, delete, and rearrange what they have produced until it suits their purpose and audience. Working together as a class and then in small groups to revise pieces of student and professional writing will help students master true revising skills.

- Editing is an act of social etiquette, in which writers decide how closely they wish their texts to conform to accepted conventions of language, and adjust those texts accordingly. Writers who choose to violate these conventions take their audience and purpose into account and accept the consequences. Asking students to react to well- and poorly-edited copies of the same texts, and to answer questions such as "Which deserves the better grade? Which writer would you hire?"

194

helps students see some of the real advantages of editing once a well-written document has been constructed.

Knowing what we do, then, about the composing process, how can we incorporate this knowledge into our teaching? We can encourage students to write frequently--and not always for grades--to make their own discoveries about the composing process. We can allow regular time in class for writing to help students develop the habit of writing. Students need to learn many different strategies to facilitate their composing. By introducing them to many planning and drafting strategies (not all at once!), we can help them become more productive writers. Questions of grammar, spelling, punctuation, and "where to start the next paragraph" often hinder students' attempts to produce texts; we can encourage them to postpone those worries and decisions until the editing stage, where they can be productively addressed. Students also need to learn to revise their papers to suit their purposes and audiences; by scheduling draft review sessions, encouraging peer editing, and holding conferences, we can direct students' attention away from "error-hunting" to more substantive questions.

Since students must also learn to write for audiences outside the classroom and in forms other than essay writing, we can provide them with practice by varying the design of our assignments. We can include other possibilities and other audiences, give students time in class not only to write, but to plan, discuss, reflect on, and generate ideas that prompt writing. We can work with our colleagues in other disciplines to provide writing across and throughout the curriculum, for many audiences and purposes. We can encourage students to practice these activities by collecting their notes and drafts along with the finished products. (Of course, the preliminary materials shouldn't be marked or graded, but we can examine them to help our students.)

And we shouldn't wait until <u>after</u> the student completes a document to offer our suggestions; rather, as Robert Zoellner has suggested [30], we need to intervene <u>during</u> the writing process, in a <u>talk-write</u> manner, so that students get maximum guidance. Zoellner uses a telling analogy: he says ski instructors don't tell novice skiers, "Ski down this slope, and I'll come back in about a week or so, look at the marks you made that still remain in the snow, and tell you what you should have done."[15] Rather, we need to be active coaches, helping writers through the process, giving them feedback, encouragement, and education. Above all, we can make our students more conscious of themselves as <u>writers</u>, people who have composing processes; teach them skills that let them work more effectively as writers; and help them realize that their texts are not merely products, but journeys--journeys of discovery, growth, and sometimes of liberation.

Annotated Bibliography of Suggested Readings

Below I list a number of works which deal, in part or totally, with the views of the writing process discussed above. This is by no means a complete bibliography, but will provide you with plenty of information and leads to follow. Abbreviations used are *CCC, College Composition and Communication; CE, College English; NCTE, National Council of Teachers of English; RTE, Research in the Teaching of English.*

1. Bartholomae, David. "Inventing the University." *When a Writer Can't Write: Research on Writer's Block and Other Writing Process Problems.* Ed. Mike Rose. NY: Guilford, 1986.

    Argues that students are often unaware of the conventions required by the academic community and must be familiarized with those if they are to succeed as writers.

2. Beard, Ruth M. *An Outline of Piaget's Developmental Psychology for Students and Teachers.* NY: NAL, 1969.

    Contains sections on the development of intelligence, on each of Piaget's four stages of cognitive growth, and on the implications of these theories for teachers.

3. Bizzell, Patricia. "Cognition, Convention, and Certainty: What We Need to Know about Writing." *PRE/TEXT* 3 (1983): 213-43.

    One of the first statements of the social-constructionist composing position, with a critique of other positions.

4. Bruffee, Kenneth. "Social Construction, Language, and the Authority of Knowledge." *CE* 48 (1986): 773-90.

    The theory and proposed practices underlying social construction.

5. Connors, Robert, and Cheryl Glenn. *The St. Martin's Guide to Teaching Writing.* 2nd ed. NY: St. Martin's, 1992.

    Overview to the profession, with an excellent chapter on the composing process and implications for your teaching.

6. Cooper, Charles R., and Lee Odell, eds. *Research on Composing: Points of Departure.* Urbana, IL: National Council of Teachers of English, 1978.

Ten essays on the composing process by well-known specialists.

7. Elbow, Peter. *Writing With Power*. New York: Oxford UP, 1981.

Emphasizes writing as a way of controlling one's world; discusses freewriting, revision, and peer editing, with many teaching suggestions.

8. _____. *Writing Without Teachers*. New York: Oxford UP, 1973.

Encourages writers to break away from traditional writing practices (such as outlining) and to use other prewriting methods (especially freewriting) to discover new information.

9. Faigley, Lester, et al. *Assessing Writers' Knowledge and Processes of Composing*. Norwood, NY: Ablex, 1985.

Surveys the cognitive backgrounds of composing and the applications of this knowledge in pedagogy and theory.

10. _____, and Stephen Witte. "Analyzing Revision." *CE 32* (1981): 400-14.

There are two kinds of revision, surface (correcting minor flaws) and text-based (addressing larger concerns). The latter must be taught to students as an integral part of composing.

11. Flower, Linda. "The Construction of Purpose in Writing and Reading." *CE* 50 (1988): 528-50.

A critique of earlier studies of writing, and of using protocols, and an elegant presentation of the Flower-Hayes theories.

12. Gebhardt, Richard C. "Initial Plans and Spontaneous Composition: Toward a Comprehensive Theory of the Writing Process." *CE* 44 (1982): 620-27.

Identifies two relatively large groups of composing processes, one in which writers handle information they already possess, and another in which they discover the information they need.

13. Hairston, Maxine. "Different Products, Different Processes." *CCC* 37 (1986): 442-52.

Identifies and give examples of the three kinds of composing, based on purpose, audience, and writer's information.

14. Hayes, John R., and Linda Flower. "Writing Research and the Writer." *American Psychologist* 41 (1986): 1106-13.

The fullest articulation of Flower and Hayes's theories to the date of publication, with full bibliography.

15. Heilker, Paul. "Public Products/Public Processes: Zoellner's Praxis and the Contemporary Composition Classroom." *Rhetoric Review* 10.2 (1992): 232-38.

Offers suggestions for incorporating talk-write pedagogy in the classroom.

16. Hume, Ann. "Research on the Composing Process." *Writing: Policies, Problems, and Possibilities*. Eds. Bruce Cronnell and Joan Michael. Los Alamitos, CA: Southwest Regional Laboratory of Educational Research and Development, 1982.

A comprehensive, detailed account of research on composing to about 1981.

17. Kantor, Kenneth. "Classroom Contexts and the Development of Writing Intuitions: An Ethnographic Case Study." *RTE* 17 (1983): 72-94.

Case study of seven high-school students in a creative writing class, focusing on the revision stage of composing.

18. Lindemann, Erika. *A Rhetoric for Writing Teachers*. New York: Oxford UP, 1982.

An overview of theories and research in the teaching of writing, with suggestions for classroom applications. A comprehensive and accessible summary for beginners and experts alike, with an extensive bibliography.

19. Lyon, Arabella. "Re-Presenting Communities: Teaching Turbulence." *Rhetoric Review* 10.2 (1992): 279-90.

Warns of the dangers in not exploring what we mean by "community" and "collaboration."

20. Moffett, James. *Teaching the Universe of Discourse*. Boston: Houghton, 1968.

A theory of discourse, drawing on students' cognitive development in producing increasingly more abstract texts. Emphasizes the relations between speaker and audience and speaker and subject.

21. _____ and Betty Jane Wagner. *Student-Centered Language Arts and Reading. K-12,* 4th ed. Portsmouth, NH: Boynton-Cook/Heinemann, 1992.

A complete language arts text based on Moffett's discourse theory.

22.   Murray, Donald M. *A Writer Teaches Writing,* 2nd ed. Boston: Houghton, 1985.

A book of advice for writers who are teachers, teachers who are writers, and nearly everyone else involved in composing. Sections on each of the stages of composing, with many teaching strategies and a full bibliography.

23. Odell, Lee, and Dixie Goswami, eds. *Writing in Nonacademic Settings.* NY: Guilford, 1985.

Fourteen essays on composing outside of the composition classroom.

24. Reither, James A. "Writing and Knowing: Toward Redefining the Writing Process." *CE* 47 (1985): 620-28.

Reminds us that the process (singular) is actually processes (plural), which are socially and culturally dependent.

25. Rohman, D. Gordon, and Albert O. Wlecke. *Pre-Writing: The Construction and Application of Models for Concept-Formation in Writing.* USOE Cooperative Research Project No. 2174. East Lansing: Michigan State University, 1964.

The writing process has three distinct stages: prewriting, writing, and revising. Prewriting has primacy; students can improve prewriting by keeping journals, writing meditations, and constructing analogies.

26. Scardamalia, Marlene, and Carl Bereiter. "Written Composition." *Handbook of Research on Teaching.* 3rd. ed. Ed. Merlin C. Wittrock. NY: Macmillan, 1985.

A thorough survey of all areas of research on writing, including the composing process.

27. Sommers, Nancy, "Responding to Student Writing." *CCC* 33 (1982): 148-56.

Students confuse revision with correction because teachers' comments usually focus on errors in editing. When teachers comment on matters revision, students learn to pay more attention to this stage of composing.

28. _____. "Revision Strategies of Student Writers and Experienced Adult Writers." *CCC* 31 (1980):378-88.

Suggests that major differences between student and experienced writers are the manner and amounts of their revisions; students make few revisions and focus on correctness, while adults are more willing to address global issues and to address the needs of their readers.

29. Warnock, John. "The Writing Process." *Research in Composition and Rhetoric*. Eds. Michael G. Moran and Ronald Lunsford. Westport, CT: Greenwood, 1984.

   A review of recent research and theory of composing.

30. Zoellner, Robert. "Talk-Write: A Behavioral Pedagogy for Composition." *CE* 30 (1969): 267-320.

   Monograph explaining and advocating this pedagogy, which has recently been "rediscovered" by the rhetorical community.

THE BASIC AIMS OF DISCOURSE

James Kinneavy[2]

INTRODUCTION

Most of us make implicit assumptions about the aims of discourse when we loosely distinguish expository writing from literature or creative writing, and, no doubt, there is some validity to the distinction. Many college composition textbooks often assume a similar distinction and address themselves to the province of expository writing. But it may be that this simple distinction is too simple and that other aims of discourse ought to be given some consideration. It is this question which I would like to investigate in this paper.

First, at least one working definition. I am concerned with complete discourse, not individual sentences or even paragraphs. It is often impossible to determine the aim of an individual sentence or paragraph without its full context. The same sentence or even paragraph in another context may have a very different aim. "Discourse" here means the full text, oral or written, delivered at a specific time and place or delivered at several instances. A discourse may be a single sentence, "Fire," screamed from a hotel window, or a joke, or a sonnet, or a three-hour talk, or a tragedy, or Toynbee's twelve volumes of *A Study of History*. Sometimes the determination of text is difficult: a conversation may trail off into another one; a novel like *Sanctuary* may pick up years later in *Requiem for a Nun;* there are trilogies in drama and novel, etc., but usually the determination of text is a fairly simple matter.

By aim of discourse is meant the effect that the discourse is oriented to achieve in the average listener or reader for whom it is intended. It is the intent as embodied in the discourse, the intent of the work, as traditional philosophy called it. Is the work intended to delight or to persuade or to inform or to demonstrate the logical proof of a position? These would be typical aims.

The determination of the basic aims of discourse and some working agreement in this area among rhetoricians would be a landmark in the field of composition. For it is to the achievement of these aims that our efforts as teachers of composition are directed.

Yet a classification of diverse aims of discourse must not be interpreted as the establishing of a set of iron-clad categories which do not overlap. Such an exercise must be looked upon as any scientific exercise—an abstraction from certain aspects of reality in order to focus attention on and carefully analyze these characteristics of some feature of reality in a scientific vacuum, as it were. The scientist who is attempting to formulate the law of gravity isolates the gravitational forces from

[2]From *College Composition and Communication*, 20 (December 1969): 297-304.

air resistance, from surface variations, from electric attraction, etc., and hopefully postulates a principle of gravity. The re-insertion into real situations--wherein wind, surface-variations, electricity, and other forces intervene come later. Similarly, an attempt to formulate the nature of information, as such, must operate in a discourse vacuum which momentarily abstracts from the fact that information can be used in propaganda or be a component of literary discourse. In actual practice such pure discourses as information devoid of persuasion, or persuasion devoid of information, or literature without some personal expression, and so forth, are almost non-existent or as rare as the laboratory concept of gravitation. But that does not destroy the validity of the classifications.

THE DETERMINATION OF THE AIMS OF DISCOURSE

Some negative and some external norms. There are some useful cautions about determination of aims made in literary theory by W. K. Wimsatt and Monroe Beardsley which can be extended to discourse theory. It is dangerous in literature (and even more in persuasion) to assume that what the author says he is trying to do is actually what the work really accomplishes. To determine the aim by author intent is to run the risk of the "intentional fallacy." A parallel danger is to assume that the reaction of a given reader is an accurate indication of purpose. This fallacy has been termed the "affective fallacy" by Wimsatt and Beardsley.[1] The stated intentions of the author and the reactions of a given reader are useful markers that can point to significant evidence in the discourse itself, as the linguist Michael Riffaterre points out;[2] for this reason they should not be disregarded. Similarly, many authors advise us to take into account the cultural conventions of the genre employed; anthropologists like Malinowski warn of the importance of the immediate historical context; McLunan emphasizes the significance of the medium used; Kenneth Burke writes a whole book on the influence of the semantic range, the grammar he calls it, of the motivational field; and even the grammatical choices offered by the language can restrict and modify the aim, as Sapir and Whorf caution us. Any of these, external to the discourse, are nonetheless weighty determinants of aim and are so many arguments against the mythical autonomy of the text.

Internal norms of aim. Among the writers who have sought to establish the aims of discourse by norms internal to the discourse there is considerable variation in the kind of norm singled out. Yet there is a surprising measure of agreement among the analysts on so fundamental an issue. In Figure 1, I have attempted to show some of these various approaches, together with the principle of division and the resulting classifications of aims of discourse. The parallel classifications of the various systems are indicated in the horizontal rows. All of the authorities whom I have analyzed could not be presented on a single page, so I have only indicated typical representatives of various approaches.

The eldest and most persistent approach in western civilization is that beginning in Plato, codified by Aristotle, continued by the medieval Arab philosophers Averroes and Avicenna, Aquinas and Albertus Magnus, and passed on to modern times by the classical tradition and some comparative philologists, like Joshua Whatmough. Aristotle and Aquinas distinguish a *scientific* use of language achieving certainty, a *dialectical* use of language operating in the area of probability, a *rhetorical or persuasive* use of language based on seeming probability and a *poetic* use of language incorporating a rigid but internal probability. The principle of division is obviously a scale of diminishing probability.

Ernst Cassirer, examining the historical sequence of Greek views on the functions of language, sees first a *mythological* view of language as a medium for expressing the aspirations of early Greek society. This partially (though not at all totally) corresponds to Aristotle's poetic function. This was followed by a period in which it was felt by the philosophers that language was admirably suited to mirror or represent the universe. This metaphysical period, as he calls it, corresponds to Aristotle's scientific use of language. The practical or *pragmatic* use of language by the sophists and rhetoricians came next. Finally, Democritus pointed to a basic and initial *interjectional* or emotive use of language--to which Aristotle has no direct parallel.[4]

In the next column of Figure 1, C. W. Morris, the semiotician, bases his aims of discourse on a behavioral analysis of how animals react to stimuli. The animal first informs itself of the features of its environment, then *evaluates* the seemingly useful features, then responds to these as *incitive* "stimuli," and finally *systematizes* his signs in order to achieve the purpose for which he engaged in this expressive activity. There is a rough approximation here to Aristotle's scientific, dialectic, and rhetorical functions. Morris' systemic has some affinity with the expressive function of the others on the chart.[5]

George Miller, a communication theorist, establishes his distinctions on the socio-psychological motives for the communications which arc revealed in the discourse. The *informative* use of language attempts to increase uniformity of fact and information in the community; the opinion use of language attempts to increase uniformity of the probable in the society; the *status change use* of language is oriented to improve one's societal position; and the *emotive* use *is* oriented to individual satisfaction in an expressive use of language. The similarities to the preceding systems arc fairly obvious.[6]

In an interesting chapter on "The Uses of Language" in *Human Knowledge, Its Scope and Limits,* Bertrand Russell takes issue with the dominant logical positivist view of a simple dichotomy of referential and emotive uses of language and distinguishes the informative, the questioning, the promotive and the emotional uses of language. These correspond quite naturally to the kinds of rhetorical sentences in the language: declarative, interrogative, imperative, and exclamatory. These image quite closely Miller's, Morris' and Aristotle's categories, though the principle of division is different in each.[7]

Hans Reichenbach, a logical positivist, in a brief introduction to his book on symbolic logic, differentiates functions of language by the faculty appealed to in the discourse. He therefore distinguishes a communicative use emphasizing thoughts to be believed by the intellect, from a promotive use directed to actions to be accomplished, from a suggestive use oriented to emotions to be aroused.[8]

Both Reichenbach and Richards take the logical positivist position as their springboard. Richards emphasizes the kind of reference found in the discourse. In his various books, Richards suggests various categories of discourse. I have followed here the distinctions to be found in *How to Read a Page* and *Principles of Literary Criticism* rather than some of his other works. Discourses exist in a continuum with decreasing referential and increasing emotive affirmations. Pure reference discourse is scientific, pure emotive discourse is poetic. Any appreciable mixture of the two is rhetoric. Further subdivisions of the mixed area (rhetoric) are generally useless.[9]

The equating of poetry with emotive discourse in Richards is a common phenomenon among these classificatory systems--a fact the figure illustrates. Sometimes poetry is subsumed under emotive, sometimes poetry is equated to the emotive (as in Richards). Sometimes there is no provision for one or the other--thus Aristotle makes no room for expressive discourse as such, though emotion is important for his concept of catharsis in poetry and in the whole second book of his *Rhetoric*.

The last column of the figure distinguishes aims by the focus on the component of the communication process which is stressed in a given discourse. At one time I thought that this principle of classification was original with me, but I later found that Karl Buhler, a German psychologist, had used it in depth in the 1930's and that Roman Jakobson, acknowledging Buhler as his source, had also used it to classify aims of discourse in the early 1960's. The beginnings of this norm can be found in Aristotle who calls science language directed to things and rhetoric language directed to persons. Alan Gardiner, the linguist, had also suggested this principle of classification in the 1950's.[10]

This principle can be seen illustrated in Figure 2. If one represents the components of the communication process as a triangle composed of an encoder (writer or speaker), a decoder (reader or listener), a signal (the linguistic product), and a reality (that part of the universe to which the linguistic product refers), then a focus on one of these tenets to produce a specific kind of discourse. Discourse dominated by subject matter (reality talked about) is called referential discourse. There are three kinds of referential discourse: exploratory, informative, and scientific. These correspond to elements in the first and second rows across Figure 1. Here, however, it seems important to distinguish the merely informative kind of writing (such as news stories in journalism, simple encyclopedia or textbook presentations) from the strictly scientific, though few authorities make the distinction. Aristotle, for example, has no theory of information, though he has one of science. And Miner has provision for informative, though he has no specific provision for the scientific. And it is equally important to distinguish a kind of discourse which asks a question (exploratory, dialectical, interrogative in some formulations) from discourse which answers it (informative) and proves the answer (scientific). Yet three of these kinds of discourse are subject-matter or reference dominated. Examples of all three are given in Figure 2. These subdistinctions of reference discourse are my own and differ somewhat from Jakobson's.

Secondly, as Buhler, Jakobson and Aristotle point out, discourse which focuses on eliciting a specific reaction from the decoder and is dominated by this request for reaction emerges as persuasion or rhetoric. In this use, the encoder may purposely disguise his own personality and purposely distort the picture of reality which language can paint in order to get the decoder to do something or believe something (as in dishonest advertising or some political propaganda). These distortions are not essential to persuasion, however. What is essential is that encoder, reality, and language itself all become instrumental to the achievement of some practical effect in the decoder. Obvious examples of such aims of discourse are given in the last column of figure 2.

Thirdly, when the language product is dominated by the clear design of the writer or speaker to discharge his emotions or achieve his own individuality or embody his personal or group aspirations in a discourse, then the discourse tends to be expressive. The expressor or encoder here dominates the communication process. Sometimes in such uses the decoder and the referential components even become negligible--as with curse words uttered in private. But often such uses carry strong subcomponents of information and persuasion, as in the *Declaration of Independence*. Some examples of such uses are given in the first column of the figure we have been analyzing.

Finally, the product or text or work itself may be the focus of the process as an object worthy of being appreciated in its own right. Such appreciation gives pleasure to the beholder. In this use of language, language calls attention to itself, to its own structures, not as references to reality or as expressions of personal aspirations or as instruments of persuasion, but as structures worthy of contemplation in their own right. Of course, reference, author personality, and persuasion may and usually are involved. But they are not rigidly relevant as primary foci. Indeed the reality may be fictional or very distorted; the author may be hidden under dramatic projections; and the persuasions involved may be quite trivial on occasion. This last use of language is called literature. It appears in such varied forms as the pun, the salacious joke, the sonnet, the novel, the TV drama, the epic, etc.

If a comparison may be drawn, it could be said that language is like a windowpane. I may throw bricks at it to vent my feelings about something; I may use a chunk of it to chase away an intruder; I may use it to mirror or explore reality; and I may use a stained-glass window to call attention to itself as an object of beauty. Windows, like language, can be used expressively, persuasively, referentially, and aesthetically.

SOME CONCLUSIONS ABOUT AIMS OF DISCOURSE:

I have not included in Figure 1 many of the other approaches to aims of discourse, most of which are fairly symmetrical to those given here. These would include the several groups interested in the functions of language at its origin (was it imitative of reality, the bow-wow theory, was it a utilitarian rhetorical tool, the yo-he-ho theory, was it an expressive emotional theory, the ah-ah, pooh-pooh theory, or did language begin in play and poetry, the ding-dong theory). These theories, like the child function theories, do parallel the four functions arrived at. Some anthropologists, like Malinowski and Doob, leave examined primitive societies and isolated the functions of language found there (they do not find a literary or play use, I might add, though Levi-Strauss did). Nor have

I mentioned the semanticists; Hayakawa's four uses of language also parallel the model sketched here. The uses of language, established by the Nebraska high school composition program and drawn heavily from the ordinary language philosophers, also closely parallel these distinctions.

The important lesson to be drawn from this almost fearful symmetry is that no composition program can afford to neglect any of these basic aims of discourse. There have been periods in the history of the teaching of composition, whether in the elementary or secondary or college level, when one or the other has been unduly prominent and others slighted or entirely neglected. The results have usually been educationally disastrous. In speech departments where persuasion was, for too long a time, too prominent, two cancerous effects have often followed: first, expository or reference discourse is assimilated into and made equivalent to persuasion and Aristotelian rhetorical proofs are extended to a discourse; secondly, even literature is reduced to persuasion, and some modern theories of oral interpretation now speak of the oral interpreter's function as one of coercing the audience into a desired emotional attitude. At the elementary and secondary school during the Deweyite progressive period, the reduction of all language to self-expression destroyed alike any objective scientific or literary norms. At the college level, in English departments during the period immediately preceding the present, the restriction of composition to expository writing and the reading of literary texts has had two equally dangerous consequences. First, the neglect of expressionism, as a reaction to progressive education, has stifled self-expression in the student, and partially, at least, is a cause of the unorthodox and extreme forms of deviant self-expression now indulged in by college students on many campuses today. Secondly, the neglect of persuasion has often caused persuasion to be assimilated and absorbed into literature in many cases. Expressionism has often been similarly absorbed so that literature has become prostituted to propaganda or the most weird forms of formless self-expression. In philosophy, with the logical positivists, interested solely in scientific statements, the ignoring of other uses of discourse has caused all of them to be lumped into the general category of nonsensical or meaningless. None of these situations is healthy. It is to the good of each of the aims of discourse to be studied in conjunction with the others.

The reason for this is to be seen in the various principles of classification used in the establishing of the aims by various writers. Scientific discourse is generally different in its logic, its level of probability, from the other aims of discourse. In fact, each aim of discourse has its own logic, its own kind of references, its own communication framework, its own patterns of organization, and its own stylistic norms. Sometimes these logics and stylistic principles even contradict each other. Overlaps certainly occur but the ultimate conflation and confusion of any of the aims of discourse with any other is pedagogically disastrous.

The study of these distinct aims of discourses is only a continuation of the basic liberal arts tradition. That tradition, coalesced into the trivium of grammar, rhetoric, and logic or dialectic, simply meant the study of literature, the study of persuasion, and the study of scientific and exploratory discourse. When the English departments presided over the dissolution of the liberal arts tradition in the early 1900's by exiling persuasion to speech departments and by exiling logic to philosophy departments, only literature (grammar) remained, and literature, as such, had never been

206

the only basis of the liberal arts. My plea is simply for a preservation of the liberal arts tradition with composition as the foundation stone.

NOTES

1. For the treatment of both fallacies, see W. K. Wimsatt and Monroe Beardsley *The Verbal Icon* (Lexington, Kentucky, 1965), pp. 3-18, 21-39.

2. "Criteria for Style Analysis," in *Essays on the Language of Literature*, eds. Seymour Chatman and Samuel R. Levin (Boston, Massachusetts, 1967), pp. 419 ff.

3. For a historical survey of this school, see J. Craig La Driere, "Rhetoric and 'Merely Verbal' Art," in *English Institute Essays, 1948,* ed. D. A. Robertson (New York, 1949), pp. 123-153.

4. See Ernst Cassirer, *An Essay on Man* (New Haven, 1944), pp. 109 ff.

5. See C. W. Morris, *Signs, Language and Behavior* (Englewood Cliffs, New Jersey, 1946), pp. 96 ff.

6. See George A. Miller, *Language and Communications* (New York, 1951), p. 253.

7. See Bertrand Russell, *Human Knowledge, Its Scope and Limits* (New York, 1948), pp. 58 ff.

8. See Hans Reichenbach, *Introduction to Symbolic Logic* (New York, 1947), pp. 17 ff.

9. See I. A. Richards *How to Read a Page* (London, 1943), p. 100; and *Principles of Literary Criticism* (London, 1925), p. 261.

10. See Roman Jakobson, "Linguistics and Poetics," in *Essays on the Language of Literature*, eds. Seymour Chapman and Samuel H. Levin (Boston, 1967). pp. 299 ff.

MODES OF THINKING, MODES OF ARGUMENT

Marie Secor[3]
The Pennsylvania State University

In *Language and Mind,* Noam Chomsky begins by asking what contribution the study of language can make to our understanding of human nature.[1] As rhetoricians dealing with the written and spoken products of our language-making faculty, we often ask a similar question- What contribution can our study of written discourse make to our understanding of human nature? And we often extend Chomsky's assumption that language reflects the structure of the mind and assume that written discourse too reveals something about the way we think, about the way we apprehend reality.

I think most of us are willing to accept the reasonableness of that assumption; certainly it underlies both ancient and contemporary discourse theory. But notice what happens to it in the following statement made by Frank D'Angelo in *A Conceptual Theory of Rhetoric:* "Thus from the existence of conceptual patterns in discourse, we infer the existence of similar patterns of thought; from the existence of conceptual patterns of thought, we can infer the existence of corresponding patterns in discourse. One of the tasks of the rhetorician is to relate the structure of thought to the structure of discourse."[2] D'Angelo sees the relationship between the mind and discourse as reversible: not only does the structure of discourse tell us something about patterns of thought, but from these patterns of thought we infer the existence of patterns of discourse. I am willing to believe that written or spoken discourse reveals a good deal about the way we think, but I am less certain we can identify conceptual patterns of thought apart from the discourse they reside in. Where do these patterns exist? Are they modes which reside "in the mind" somehow? If so, where?

I can answer these questions only by distinguishing between talking about patterns of thought or the structure of the mind and talking about understanding human nature. We still know very little about the mind. We know rather more about human nature as it is reflected in our discourse producing activities, and have for centuries. We know the kinds of discourse we produce, the ways writing affects audience and the types of appeals which operate in discourse. This understanding of human nature has been facilitated by the analytic descriptions philosophers and psychologists have developed and rhetoricians have adopted. The link between rhetoric and psychology has a long and honorable history which reaches all the way back to Aristotle, Quintilian, and Campbell; it is not a recent invention.

Argument Defined

---

[3]From *The Writer's Mind: Writing as a Mode of Thinking* Ed. Hays, et al. Urbana, Illinois, National Council on Teaching of English, 1983.

What exactly is argument's place in a theory of modes? James Britton places it on the far end of a scale with the use of language in the spectator role at one end and the use of language in the participant role on the other: "Informing people, instructing people, arguing, explaining, setting forth the pros and cons and coming to a conclusion—these are participant uses of language to get things done."[3] Chaim Perelman defines arguing as "using discourse to influence the intensity of an audience's adherence to certain theses."[4] Both of these definitions usefully see argument as a purpose, an intention which a writer or speaker directs at an audience.

It is also useful to distinguish between argument and persuasion. In his *Theory of Discourse,* Kinneavy defines persuasion as "that kind of discourse which is primarily focused on the reader and attempts to elicit from him a specific action or emotion or conviction."[5] But I would like to define persuasion as the more inclusive term, and argument as only one means by which it is accomplished. Argument is not the only means of persuasion: I can be persuaded or moved to action by a strong push, by a knife at my throat, or by a bribe. Nor is argument the only verbal means of persuasion: I can be equally persuaded or moved by written threats or bribes. But to go back to Perelman's definition, argument is the only verbal means of persuasion which attempts to gain my adherence to a position, to convince me, not just to bring about my action. If we accept this distinction, propaganda and advertising fall more often under the category of persuasion than of argument, especially when they are more interested in getting me to act than in convincing me.

As an aim, argument uses other kinds of discourse as means. To borrow Alexander Bain's classification of modes for a moment, argument might use narration to tell a relevant story, description to help an audience visualize something it might otherwise ignore, even Exposition to inform an audience unaware of certain conditions. Argument always springs from a sense of the inadequacy of a prevailing view and a sense of the intellectual, emotional, and ethical needs of its audience. Thus refutation of other positions and accommodation to a particular audience are driving forces behind, or elements in, every argument. They shape the discourse and determine its content, but they are not really the substance, the essence, of argument. To translate this theory into practical terms: when we teach argument, we need to pay attention to refutation and accommodation, but we also need to remember that argument is not essentially negative, a tearing down of what others have said, and not cynical manipulation of an audience's weaknesses or susceptibilities.

I would add one more "not" here, one more definition of what we teach when we teach argument. Argument is not formal logic. As we all learn from experience in the classroom, the ability to manipulate statements in and out of Venn diagrams and to construct syllogisms has very little to do with the ability to produce convincing arguments. Philosophers of rhetoric like Chaim Perelman and Stephen Toulmin have carefully distinguished between the logic of argument and formal logic, and Aristotle, too, carefully defines logic as a tool; syllogisms are not kinds or modes of arguments.

Similarly, the terms *induction* and *deduction,* though useful to describe variations in the arrangement of arguments (that is, whether the thesis comes at the beginning or at the end), do not really describe modes of argument or separate contrasting ways the mind operates,[6] and the exact distinction between the two is a matter of some controversy among theorists.[7]

Types of Argument

I would call the classification of arguments I am about to present a theory of types rather than a theory of modes, in order to avoid confusion with the terminology of other discourse theories. These categories describe the typical content of arguments as products of our intentions, and they give us some clues about the typical structures or arrangements of these arguments. This classification begins with the multitude of propositions or theses which can serve as subjects for arguments. We can distinguish here four main types of theses, each of which answers a different question: (1) What is this thing? (2) What caused it or what effects does it have? (3) Is it good or bad? and (4) What should we do about it? Propositions which answer these questions are, respectively, categorical propositions, causal statements, evaluations, and proposals. The thesis of any argument falls into one of these categories. The first two, which correspond to the classical topoi of definition and cause and effect, demand their own kinds of arguments with distinctive structures, while arguments for the third and fourth, evaluations and proposals, combine the other two in a variety of possible arrangements of these structures.

I will describe each type briefly. A categorical proposition is a statement which places its subject in the category of its predicate. If I wish to argue that "All art is illusion" or that "The Emperor Caligula was a spoiled brat" or that "Ballet dancers are really athletes," supporting such a statement is always a matter of showing that the subject belongs in the category of or has the attributes of the predicate. That predicate must be defined and evidence or examples given to link the subject up with it. The arguer for a categorical proposition, then, works under two constraints: the definition of the predicate must be acceptable to the audience, and the evidence or examples about the subject must be convincing and verifiable. The emphasis in the argument can be placed either on the definition or on the evidence, depending on the audience's needs.

The second type of proposition, the assertion of cause and effect, requires quite a different kind of argument because it represents a different way of thinking about reality. It is supported not so much with a definition, either assumed or explicit, but with an appeal to or an argument for agency, a basic belief about what can cause what. Just as people who speak the same language share a set of definitions, so do people in the same culture share many causal assumptions. We have a commonsense understanding, for instance, of such natural agencies as light, heat, and gravity, as well as many accepted human agencies whose operations we accept as readily as we believe in the operation of physical law. Whether or not we articulate agency (that connection between a cause and its effect) in argument depends largely on audience. For example, if we argue that a significant cause of teenage drug abuse is parental drinking and drug abuse, the agency between these two is imitation: children imitate their elders. Since most audiences will accept imitation as a motive here, we would not have to stop and argue for it. But if we claimed that wearing a plastic mouth plate can improve athletic performance, we will have to explain how, explain agency. The substance of causal arguments then will be devoted to either identifying plausible causes or showing how they produce their effects.

A third kind of argument judges; it is an evaluation, a statement like "*Jane Eyre* is a great novel." In form, an evaluation looks exactly like a categorical proposition and is argued for similarly: by identifying criteria, assumptions, or definitions of value, and applying them to the particular subject under discussion. For example, to argue for the greatness of *Jane Eyre*, I must construct a plausible definition or set of criteria for great novels which fits the evidence from the book. But evaluations deserve separate consideration because their criteria or standards can easily include good or bad consequences or effects as well as qualities; thus evaluations often require causal arguments showing that the subject does indeed produce a particular effect. To argue, for example, that it was right to bring the Shah of Iran to the U.S. for medical treatment, I might classify that decision as a humanitarian one, or I might argue that the decision was wrong by exploring its consequences in a causal argument.

The fourth and final type of proposition is the proposal, which answers the question, "What should we do?" A proposal requires a special combination of smaller arguments. We can see how that structure works if we imagine arguing for a proposal such as "Wolves should be reestablished in the forests of northern Pennsylvania." Most audiences will feel no need for action unless they are first convinced that a problem exists which needs this solution. Thus an opening categorical proposition argument might establish the existence of a situation, in this case the absence or rarity of wolves in certain areas. An audience might also need the bad consequences or ethical wrongness of this situation pointed out to it; here causal argument pointing to the overpopulation of deer or a negative evaluation might be useful. Another preliminary step might be a causal argument singling out the dominant reason for the problem. If, for example, wolves have become almost extinct because of unrestricted hunting, then a ban on hunting wolves ought to help. And once the specific proposal is disclosed, it can be supported with another series of arguments pointing out good consequences, ethical rightness, and feasibility.

I have just outlined four categories of arguments, classified according to the kind of question each asks about reality and described according to the structure and arrangement of the content. Obviously, evaluations and proposals are not separate ways of knowing but combinations of definition and causal arguments directed by different intentions. It is possible, therefore, to regroup this classification another way into two main divisions instead of four. To borrow what Richard Weaver calls a "primitive metaphysic," we can think of ourselves as knowing things either as being or becoming, either as essences or as entities altered by time. (Weaver, in fact, takes this distinction a step further and calls definition the "highest order of appeal" and cause and effect a "less exalted source of argument.")[8] I prefer to see them simply as different, complementary ways of knowing, not necessarily arranged in a hierarchy: we apprehend reality either as static or changing, as things with definitions and attributes or as things affecting others. Thus we can and do still understand discourse by describing the patterns we find in it, and we can see these patterns as descriptions of the way the mind interacts with reality, if not of the mechanism by which that interaction is accomplished.

Notes

1. Noam Chomsky. *Language and Mind*, enlarged ed. (New York: Harcourt Brace Jovanovich, 1972), 1.

2. Frank J. D'Angelo, *A Conceptual Theory of Rhetoric* (Cambridge, Mass.: Winthrop Publishers, 1975), 16.

3. James Britton, *Language and Learning* (London: Penguin Books, 1953), 22.

4. Chaim Perelman and L. Olbrechts-Tyteca, *The New Rhetoric* (Notre Dame, Ind.: University of Notre Dame Press, 1969), 66.

5. James Kinneavy, *A Theory of Discourse* (New York: W. W. Norton, 1971), 211.

6. Induction and deduction are sometimes seen as descriptions of separate mental operations as different as up and down, induction reaching a generalization from particulars and deduction affirming a particular from a generalization. The discussion of induction and the classification of four types of arguments were developed jointly with Jeanne Fahnestock. We explore both in more detail in our article, "Teaching Argument: A Theory of Types," *College Composition and Communication* 34 (February 1983): 20-30.

7. Irving M. Copi defines the two not as complementary forms of reasoning, but as reasoning toward a certain conclusion (deduction) and reasoning toward a probable conclusion (induction). *Introduction to Logic*, 5th ed. (New York: Macmillan, 1978), 23-26; also see Karl Popper, *Conjectures and Refutations: The Growth of Scientific Knowledge* (New York: Harper and Row, 1963), 46-47.

8. Richard Weaver, "Language Is Sermonic," in *Rhetoric and Composition*, ed. Richard L. Graves (Rochelle Park, NJ: Hayden Book Co. 1976), 31-32.

KNOWLEDGE AND COMPREHENSION

Frank Smith

Understanding, or *comprehension*, is the basis of reading and of learning to read. What is the point of any activity if there is no understanding? Comprehension may be regarded as relating relevant aspects of the world around us--written language in the case of reading--to the intentions, knowledge, and expectations we already have in our heads. And learning can be considered as the modification of what we already know as a consequence of our interactions with the world around us. We learn to read, and we learn through reading, by adding to what we know already. Thus, comprehension and learning are fundamentally the same, relating the new to the already known. To understand all this, we must begin by considering what it is that "we already have in our heads" that enables us to make sense of the world. We must begin by comprehending comprehension.

COGNITIVE STRUCTURE

There are several terms that can be used to refer to the knowledge we carry around in our heads all the time. I shall speak of the *prior knowledge* or *nonvisual information* stored in the brain that enables us to make sense of the *visual information* that comes through the eyes when we read. I shall examine *long-term memory*, our permanent source of understanding of the world. But the different terms do not refer to distinct areas or aspects of the brain; they are synonymous. The knowledge that we must already possess in order to understand written language (like the knowledge we need for the understanding of speech) must reside in long-term memory. And remembrance of the sense we have made of past experience is the foundation of all new understanding of language and the world. In more general contexts, this basis of understanding is also referred to by psychologists as *cognitive structure*. The term is apt because "cognitive" means "knowledge" and "structure" implies organization, and that indeed is what we have in our heads--an organization of knowledge.

Certainly, it would be simplistic to suggest that what we carry around in our heads is just "memories." The brain is not a souvenir album filled with an assortment of snapshots and tape recordings of bits of the past. At the very least we would have to say that the brain contains memories-with-a- meaning; our memories are related to everything else that we know. Cognitive structure is much more like a summary of our past experience. I do not want to remember that on 16 July I sat on a chair, and that on 17 July I sat on a chair and on 18 July I sat on a chair. I want to remember that chairs are for sitting on, a summary of my experience. We remember specific events only where they are exceptions to our summary rules or when they have some particularly dramatic or powerful or emotional significance. And even then our memories, when we "recall" them, turn out to be highly colored by our present intentions and perspectives about the world (Bartlett, 1932). Specific memories that cannot be related to our summary, to our present general understanding, will make little sense, which may be the reason we can recall so little of our childhood.

But it would also be an oversimplification to suggest that our heads are filled with an accumulation of facts and rules. The brain is not like a library where useful facts and procedures are filed away under appropriate headings for possible future reference. And certainly the human brain is not like a bank in which we save nuggets of information deposited by teachers and textbooks. Instead, the system of knowledge in our heads is organized into an intricate and internally consistent working model of the world, built up through our interactions with the world and integrated into a coherent whole. We know far more than we were ever taught.

THE THEORY OF THE WORLD IN OUR HEADS

What we have in our heads is a theory of what the world is like, a theory that is the basis of all our perceptions and understanding of the world, the root of all learning, the source of hopes and fears, motives and expectancies, reasoning and creativity. And this theory is all we have. If we can make sense of the world at all, it is by interpreting our interactions with the world in the light of our theory. The theory is our shield against bewilderment.

As I look around my world, I distinguish a multiplicity of meaningful objects that have all kinds of complicated relations to each other and to me. But neither these objects nor their interrelations are self-evident. A chair does not announce itself to me as a chair; I have to recognize it as such. Chairs are a part of my theory. I recognize a chair when my brain decides that a chair is what I am looking at. A chair does not tell me that I can sit on it, or put my coat or books or feet on it, or stand on it to reach a high shelf, or wedge it against a door that I do not wish to be opened. All this is also part of my theory. I can only make sense of the world in terms of what I know already. All of the order and complexity that I perceive in the world around me must reflect an order and complexity in my own mind. Anything I cannot relate to the theory of the world in my head will not make sense to me. I shall be bewildered.

The fact that bewilderment is an unusual state for most of us despite the complexity of our lives is a clear indication that our theory of the world in the head is very efficient. The reason we are usually not aware of the theory is that it works so well. Just as a fish takes water for granted until deprived of it, so we become aware of our dependence on the theory in our head only when it proves inadequate, and the world fails to make sense. That we can occasionally be bewildered only serves to demonstrate how efficiently our theory usually functions. When were you last bewildered by something that you heard or read? Our theory of the world seems ready even to make sense of almost everything we are likely to experience in spoken and written language--a powerful theory indeed.

And yet, when was the last time you saw a bewildered baby? Infants have theories of the world too, not as complex as those of adults, but then children have not had as much time to make their theories complex. But children's theories seem to work very well for their needs. Even the smallest children seem able most of the time to make sense of their world in their own terms; they rarely appear confused or uncertain. The first time many children run into a situation that they cannot possibly relate to anything they know already is when they arrive at school, a time when they may be consistently bewildered if they are confronted by circumstances that make no sense to them. Children are often denied credit for knowing very much. But, in fact, most of our knowledge of the world--of the kind of objects it contains and the way they can be related--and most of our knowledge of language, is in our heads before we arrive at school. At age five or six the framework is there, and the rest is mainly a matter of filling in the details.

For the remainder of this chapter I talk a little more about how this theory in the head is organized, and then discuss how it is used so that we can comprehend the world.

Comprehension is more than understanding the circumstances we are in; it is one way in which we learn. This is the reason I have put the topic of comprehension first in this book and left learning until the end. This may be the reverse of the situation that often exists in school, where children often are expected to learn in order to understand. But learning is more a result of comprehension than its cause. Learning to read is literally a matter of "understanding reading."

THE DYNAMICS OF COGNITIVE STRUCTURE

Cognitive structure, the theory of the world in our heads, may so far have seemed rather a crowded and static place, not very different in essence from a collection of facts and procedures. But the theory of the world in our heads is dynamic and not just in the sense that it is constantly being added to and changed, particularly during that lively period of intense exploration and learning we call childhood. We can do much more with the theory of the world in our heads than make sense of the world and interact with it. We can live in the theory itself, in worlds that exist only in the imagination. Within this theory we can imagine and create, testing provisional solutions to problems and examining the consequences of possible behaviors. We can explore new worlds of our own, and can be led into other worlds by writers and artists.

But the aspect of imagination with which we will be most concerned is more mundane, although at first encounter it may sound quite exotic. We can use the theory of the world in our heads to predict the future. This ability to predict is both pervasive and profound, because it is the basis of our comprehension of the world, including our understanding of spoken and written language. Reading depends on prediction.

The Pervasiveness of Prediction

Everyone predicts--including children--all the time. Our lives would be impossible, we would be reluctant even to leave our beds in the morning, if we had no expectation about what the day will bring. We would never go through a door if we had no idea of what might be on the other side. And all our expectations, our predictions, can be derived from only one source, the theory of the world in our heads.

215

We are generally unaware of our constant state of anticipation for the simple reason once again that our theory of the world works so well. Our theory is so efficient that when our predictions fail, we are surprised. We do not go through life predicting that anything might happen--indeed, that would be contrary to prediction, and in that case nothing could surprise us. the fact that something always could rhinoceros take us by surprise—like the word *rhinoceros* a few words ago—is evidence that indeed we always predict but that our predictions are usually accurate. It is always possible that we could be surprised, yet our predictions are usually so appropriate that surprise is a very rare occurrence. When was the last time you were surprised?

We drive through a town we have never visited before, and nothing we see surprises us. There is nothing surprising about the buses and cars and pedestrians in the main street; they are predictable. But we do not predict that we might see anything--we would be surprised to see camels or submarines in the main street. Not that there is anything very surprising or unpredictable about camels or submarines in themselves--we would not be surprised to see camels if we were visiting a zoo or to see submarines at a naval base. In other words, our predictions are very specific to situations. We do not predict that anything will happen, nor do we predict that something is bound to happen if it is only likely to happen (we are no more surprised by the absence of a bus than we are by the presence of one), and we predict that many things are unlikely to happen. Our predictions are remarkably accurate--and so are those of children. It is rare to see a child who is surprised.

The Need for Prediction

Why should we predict? Why not expect that anything could happen all the time, and thus free ourselves from any possibility of surprise? I can think of three reasons. The first reason is that our position in the world in which we live changes constantly, and we are usually far more concerned with what is likely to happen in the near and distant future than we are with what is actually happening right now. An important difference between a skilled driver and a learner is that the skilled driver is able to project the car into the future while the learner's mind is more closely anchored to where the car is now-- when it is usually too late to avoid accidents. The same difference tends to distinguish skilled readers from beginners, or from anyone having difficulty with a particular piece of reading. In fluent reading the eye is always ahead of the brain's decisions, checking for possible obstacles to a particular understanding. Readers concerned with the word directly in front of their nose will have trouble predicting--and they will have trouble comprehending

The second reason for prediction is that there is TOO much ambiguity in the world, too many ways of interpreting just about anything that confronts us. Unless we exclude some alternatives in advance, we are likely to be overwhelmed with possibilities. Of the many things I know about onions, I do not want to be concerned with the fact that they are dug from the ground, or that they bring my cousin George out in spots, if all I want is garnish for a hamburger. What I see is related to what I am looking for, not to all possible interpretations. Words have many meanings--table can be several kinds of verb as well as several kinds of noun—but there is only one meaning that I am concerned with, that I predict, if someone tells me to put my books on the table. All the everyday words of our language have many meanings and often several grammatical functions--*table, chair, shoe, time, walk, open, narrow*--but by predicting the range of possibilities that a word is likely to be, we are just not aware of the potential ambiguities.

The final reason for prediction is that there would otherwise be far too many alternatives from which to choose. The brain requires time to make its decisions about what the eyes are looking at, and the time that it requires depends on the number of alternatives. We take longer to decide that we are looking at the letter *A* when it could be any one of the 26 letters of the alphabet than when we know that it is a vowel or that it is either *A* or *B*. It takes much longer to identify a word in isolation compared with a word in a meaningful sentence. The fewer the alternatives confronting the eyes, the quicker the recognition. If there are too many alternatives confronting the eyes, then it is much harder to see or to comprehend.

Prediction is the core of reading. All of the schemes, scripts, and scenarios we have in our heads--our prior knowledge of places and situations, of written discourse, genres, and stories--enable us to predict when we read, and thus to comprehend, experience and enjoy what we read. Prediction brings potential meaning to texts, reducing ambiguity and eliminating in advance irrelevant alternatives. Thus, we are able to generate comprehensible experience from inert pages of print.

Prediction is not reckless guessing, nor does it involve taking chances by betting everything on the most likely outcome. We do not go through life saying "Round the next corner I shall see a bus," or "The next word I read will be *rhinoceros*." We predict by opening our minds to the probable and by disregarding the unlikely. Here is a formal definition: *Prediction is the prior elimination of unlikely alternatives.* It is a projection of possibilities. We predict to reduce our uncertainty and therefore to reduce the amount of external information that we require. Our theory of the world tells us the most probable occurrences, leaving the brain to decide among those remaining alternatives until uncertainty is reduced to zero. And we are so good at predicting only the most likely alternatives that we are rarely surprised.

Put more informally, prediction is a matter of asking specific questions. We do not ask "What is that object over there?" but "Can we put our books on it?" or whatever we want to do. We do not look at a page of print with no expectation about what we shall read next, instead we ask "What is the hero going to do?" "Where is the villain going to hide?" And "Will there be an explosion when liquid A is mixed with powder B?" And provided the answer lies within the expected range of alternatives--which it usually does if we are reading with comprehension--then we are not aware of any doubt or ambiguity. We are neither bewildered nor surprised.

PREDICTION AND COMPREHENSION RELATED

Now at last prediction and comprehension can be tied together. Prediction means asking questions, and comprehension means being able to get some of the questions answered. As we read, as we listen to someone talking, as we go through life, we are constantly asking questions, and if we are able to find answers to those questions, then we comprehend. The person who does not comprehend how to repair a radio is the one who cannot ask and find answers to such questions as "Which of these wires goes where?" at appropriate times. And the person who does not comprehend a book or newspaper article is the one who cannot find relevant questions and answers concerning the next part of the text. There is a *flow* to comprehension, with new questions constantly being generated from the answers that are sought.

Such a view of comprehension differs from the way the word is often used in school. So-called comprehension tests in school are usually given after a book has been read, and, as a consequence, are more like tests of long-term memory. (And because the effort to memorize can drastically interfere with comprehension, the test may finish up by destroying what it sets out to measure.) If I say that I comprehend a certain book, it does not make sense to give me a test and argue that I did not understand it. And a score on a test certainly would not convince me that I had really understood a book or a speaker if my feeling is that I did not.

The very notion that comprehension is relative, that it depends on the questions that an individual happens to ask, is not one that all educators find easy to accept. Some want to argue that you may not have understood a book even if you have no unanswered questions at the end. They will ask "But did you understand that the spy's failure to steal the secret plans was really a symbol of humanity's ineluctable helplessness in the face of manifest destiny?" And if you say "No, I just thought it was a jolly good story," they will tell you that you did not *really* comprehend what the story was about. But basically what they are saying is that you were not asking the kind of questions they think you should have asked.

CLOSENESS TO TEXT:
A DELINEATION OF READING PROCESSES AS THEY AFFECT COMPOSING

Lynn Quitman Troyka[4]
City University of New York

Teachers, at root, seek to help students to **become**--to gain power over their lives, have options, be fulfilled. Most people find it easier *to do* or *to be* than *to become* in our society.[1] A person can *do* something, such as design a computer program; a person can *be* something, such as a computer programmer; but for a person *to become*--to grow and evolve over a lifetime--that person must tolerate well uncertainty, change, and ambiguity.

Perhaps more than any other teachers, teachers of writing and of reading can help people *become.* Teachers of reading and of writing deal with language, with making meaning[2], with helping people make sense of their lives and the world.

To our shame, however, we who teach English have put a stumbling block in our students' way. We have condoned, by omission more than by commission, the curricular separation of reading and writing. Writing and reading are reciprocal meaning-making activities; one is diminished without orientation toward the other. Yet, most American colleges separate reading and writing courses, almost always at the developmental level and usually at the freshman level when reading for composition means looking at essays as models or for discussion of ideas. Many college teachers of writing and of literature consider reading *qua* reading an alien subject.

At the developmental level in college, the unfortunate separation between reading and writing instruction had its genesis in the fact that "remedial-reading specialists" began to join college faculty when many underprepared students had to be served. By training, usually in colleges of education rather than of liberal arts, these remedial specialists were seen as the experts in helping students catch up. Composition teachers were the novices. Thus, instead of looking for similarities in the substance of our subjects, we focused on differences in our subjects and ourselves. I am reminded of H. L. Mencken's line: "For every human problem there is a solution that is simple, neat, and wrong."

Such a perspective got me into some trouble about ten years ago when as a teacher of basic writing, I was accused of teaching reading. I was reminded that the developmental reading course was different from the developmental writing course. I was told that I had no formal training in reading, that I was going to confuse students who were enrolled in reading courses. My explanation

---

[4]From *Only Connect: Linking Reading and Writing*, ed. Thomas Newkirk. Montclair, NJ: Boynton/Cook, 1986.

was accepted after a while, and it still holds: I don't know anymore how to teach students about writing without teaching them about reading.

I need the rest of this paper to explain. For if there is any hope to lighten the weight of mass illiteracy that is crushing our nation, or to stop the perpetuation of illiteracy, we have to change our ways. Integrating reading and writing will help. Depending on how literacy is defined, America has 30 million illiterate adults (unable to read or write) or 60 million illiterate adults (including those who cannot read third-grade level materials). Too many people are closed off from *becoming*.

My discussion begins with college basic writers, though my point applies to writing at all levels. Next, to set a context for specific integrations of reading and writing instruction, I summarize psycholinguistic theories of reading and a related research project I undertook to observe readers of Braille. Finally, using my notion of "closeness to text," I describe some ways to integrate the teaching of reading and writing. I end where I began, with *becoming*.

I

Basic writers are often also very basic readers. Many read haltingly aloud. Silently, they often subvocalize, not to hear rhythm but to sound out the words laboriously. Comprehension often eludes these students because they have to concentrate on looking at each word rather than on looking through the words to make meaning.

When Phyllis (name changed) was in my basic writing class a few years ago, she was 26 years old. Like many two-year college students, she had decided to start college almost a decade after having graduated from high school. Phyllis always came to class, even in the worst of our New York winter, but she always chose a seat as far in the back of the room as possible, and she spoke up only in conference with me or in an all-female group. She was gracefully pretty, but she ignored the men who clearly noticed her.

At the beginning of the semester, when faced with written prose of any complexity, Phyllis read word by word, phrase by phrase. She often subvocalized, moving her lips to try to decipher words. When she did not know how to read a word, she would ask one of the female students or me how to call it. (Students from strongly oral traditions[3] "call" words just as all of us "call" things. For example, a word that reads "serendipity" is called "serendipity," just as something to type on is called a typewriter or a word processor.) Although Phyllis comprehended little on a first pass at new academic material, she pushed on, and she reread with determination. Look with me at two pieces of Phyllis's writing, produced eight weeks apart. As always when I publish student samples, I present Phyllis' work with her written permission. Here is Phyllis' first in-class writing, with errors as shown, composed the first day of the semester.

> The New York City Subway System can be very unreliable at times and at other times they run on schedule. This happens in other city transportations also so therefore commuters will have to compromise.

The $0.75c is very difficult for some people while for others its alright. Considering if you do not have the correct money one cannot purchase the token and without this, entering the subway is impossible.

On the other hand paying 75c for poor services is unfair to commuters who can hardly find the daily fare.

Where to begin? Teach Phyllis how to write seventy-five cents correctly? Show how to spell *commuter?* Go into an explanation of how pronoun-antecedent agreement works? No. After writing a brief comment in which I agree with her last sentence, I simply put the paper aside. Then I take my cue from the way Phyllis reads, and I begin by teaching about reading. Here is another of Phyllis's in-class writings, written just after the middle of the semester, about eight weeks after the piece above.

Rules are very important to many people. As a child, there are many rules that one had to abide by. Growing into adulthood was one way to get away from harsh rules.

My childhood days were not the best times of my life. The regulations were very harsh. Considering that I was the youngest child of my parents, one would think that I had the best of everything. Yes, I did in their eyes, but to me it was not. After reaching the age of twelve, the trouble began. My parents were so strict that I was afraid to become friends with other children. The rules were that I should put everything aside until I became a woman. "When will that be? I asked myself." During that time, my only friends were going to school, church, and home. For some people reaching the age of eighteen would be adulthood. But for me it was still abiding by the rules and regulations of my parents. The rules in my classrooms were not harsh to me because I was so afraid, I always try to do the right things at the right time. At the age of twenty yrs old I broke the rules by having a child. My parents were very upset but then it was all their fault.

After my daughter was born I though this would be freedom for me but it was not. I find myself still abiding by these rules. I am still afraid to stay out late. There are so many things that "I" am presently doing at the age of 26 yrs, which I can recalled I use to do 10 years ago. I am a very scared person who is trying to find happiness and the will to become a real adult.

Discipline must be maintained through out life. But, from my experience too many harsh rules can scar an individual through out life.

Accomplished writing? Not yet. But we find no cryptic sentences or vague, rambling generalizations. We see a smaller percentage of errors; a clear beginning, middle, and end; and sufficient details to raise the hair on the back of our necks.

221

Phyllis has become conscious of how readers read, and she has *written* to that consciousness. Awareness of how people read--the process they go through to make meaning--does not refer here to the notion of audience in its narrow sense of "who is the person out there reading this?" A broader key question must occupy the writer: *"Exactly how does my reader read, and, therefore, what must I do to help my reader function?"*

II

The answer, I have come to see, can be found in psycholinguistic theories of the reading process, from the work of Frank Smith, David Pearson, Kenneth and Yetta Goodman, Judith Langer, and others.[4] For the purposes of this discussion, I will unify the various models around four common elements; I do so recognizing fully that the models differ in their details and that lively debates rage within reading circles about the contrastive merits of each model.

A. Reading is a text-processing activity. It is a complex interaction of page, eye, and brain. Meaning is made during reading by the association of ideas represented on the page to ideas already known to the reader. This making of meaning is central to comprehension and to learning.

B. Prior knowledge in the reader's brain permits new information to be learned. New information is hooked into the old; the context in place is hospitable to expansion. But if a reader has little prior knowledge about a given subject, he or she can assimilate only a limited amount of new information at any one time. For example, were I to be asked to learn from a text on astrophysics, I would have trouble. I would be a very basic, slow reader. I know almost nothing about the field in general, about the technical jargon, or even about the conventional sentence structures used by most writers on the subject; my prior knowledge is scant. On the other hand, many basic writers I know could easily learn from an issue of *Popular Mechanics,* a magazine I find almost as difficult to comprehend as an astrophysics textbook. These readers have considerable prior knowledge of the subjects covered as well as the jargon, prose structures, and visuals.

C. A reader uses prior knowledge to make predictions about what will come next in a text. A reader predicts everything from words ("Once upon a _____ ") to concepts ("The arguments for giving up cigarettes are many. For example, _____"). Without a preconscious anticipating and estimating of what to expect next, reading would proceed at an excruciatingly slow pace. The brain fills in as it goes along. If each new word were a total surprise, the brain would be unable to make connections and would not, therefore, comprehend. I cannot read astrophysics well because I have no idea what to expect next--in words or concepts.

D. Precision in predicting is not needed. Indeed, it is often undesirable. When predicting, a reader does not have to forecast the precise words that come next. Semantic and structural equivalents work just as well. Approximations are entirely acceptable for the making of meaning. For example, should someone read "John's car was blue" for "John's auto was blue," no injury to the meaning would take place. This so-called "miscue" aids meaning; good readers miscue well. (At first, some of us who teach English are offended by the notion that relative imprecision is acceptable, but the overriding priority for essential comprehension is not aesthetics but efficient substitution. Distractions at the making-meaning level of comprehension have to be minimal.)

Almost ten years ago, my search for evidence of these unseen associative activities led me to study readers of Braille. Does the theory hold up when people must perceive through their fingers, letter by letter?

Braille, I learned, is taught in stages. First, students are given readiness materials to touch so that they can come to distinguish, for example, a circle from a square, and one grouping of circles from another. Next, the alphabet is described, with each letter and number represented by a different configuration within a cell of only six tiny dots. Braille readers must learn minute differences in the feel of each letter and number. Letters are then combined to make words. Finally, after students are minimally familiar with the letters, the concept of Braille contractions is introduced. A Braille contraction is a few letters that represents an entire word: for example, *imm* stands for *immediate, afn* stands for *afternoon,* and *onef* stands for *oneself.*

Many Braille teachers tell their students to begin reading text by 1) using the left forefinger as a placeholder for staying at the beginning of each line of text as it is being read, and 2) using the right forefinger to move across the line feeling the letters. At the end of each line, the reader is told to bring the right forefinger quickly back to meet the placeholding left forefinger and then to move both fingers down one line.

Learning to read Braille demands enormous concentration and brute determination. A high threshold for frustration is essential, and a good sense of humor helps.

Brenda (name changed) had all these qualities. I observed her at The Lighthouse in New York City, a respected training and counseling enter for the blind. Brenda was 15 years old, bright, outgoing, curious, and outspoken. For example, the first day that I was with her teacher, Brenda wasn't expecting a visitor, but she knew instantly before we could say anything that someone extra was in the room. My procedure had been to wait to be introduced by the teacher, explain why I was here, and ask if I could observe. Brenda didn't give me a chance to be so formal. She fired questions at me: Are you sighted or blind? Are you black or white (I am white, Brenda is black)? Can I look at your face (she called me "four eyes" from then on)? When I told her that I wanted to observe how people learned to read Braille, she told me I need search no further. She had the answer. Motivation. Nothing else mattered. She couldn't learn Braille before because she had not wanted to badly enough, she said. She told me to be sure to write down everything she was saying. I did.

My observations of Brenda, and others, demonstrated for me the validity of psycholinguistic theories. My observations led me, also, to think about what I call "closeness to text," the concept that I'll discuss presently concerning the integration of reading and writing instruction.

Observation 1: Brenda was reading aloud about library research. She came to the words "file cards." She read "index cards." The teacher corrected her. Brenda tossed her hand as if waving the teacher off and said brusquely, "I know, I know. Same thing." She had made a good substitution, she had predicted well, and she did not want her meaning-making activity to be interrupted.

Observation 2: The teacher was called out of the room for a few minutes. The instant the door shut, Brenda said to me "Don't tell," and she began touching the Braille with all fingers (except the thumb) of her right hand. She moved across each line. She read aloud more slowly, but she read well. She explained, "My friends at the center (a live-in facility for blind teenagers) showed me. They don't do it the way you're supposed to. They showed me you gotta move fast, or you don't make it all out." Brenda's friends had discovered that they needed to get beyond each letter in order to look *through,* not *at,* words represented on a page.

Observation 3: When I told Brenda that I was impressed with her system, she suggested that I see one of the vocational teachers. He was blind. He read with all ten fingers. His hands moved rapidly. He read aloud as well as any schooled adult might. When he turned to a new page, he lightly rubbed his hand across the page before he went to the top of the page to start reading——an anticipating activity that sighted people do with a flick of their eyes. When he read, he used his right hand to move ahead——anticipating——and his left hand to "see" the words.

III

To make meaning of texts, Braille readers do all that they can to distance themselves from the letters represented on the page. The closer they are to the text, the more they have to look at each letter, and the worse they read. They must access their prior knowledge to create meaning, so they have to avoid focusing at the letter level.

Braille writers, I should note, have an almost impossible task. Braille typewriters do not exist. (Today, computer printers that type out in Braille have begun to make a difference, although they are very expensive and not widely available.) To write, a blind person has to tap out each letter of each word using a Braille Writer, which resembles a template. To read the written text, a writer must detach the Braille Writer and touch the dots. Erasing is impossible. Revising is difficult labor. Not surprisingly, few blind people want to write. They cannot scrawl. They get bogged down. They have to stay too close to their text to allow meaning to flow from their words.

Braille readers and writers made me realize that what I call "closeness to text" matters very much. When a reader is very close to a text--reading word by word or phrase by phrase—meaning cannot be made and comprehension is impossible. The brain is concentrating on "calling" the words rather than on making associations derived from prior knowledge. *Closeness to text hurts a reader.* To make meaning from the written page, a reader must scan quickly enough to engage actively with the ideas represented on the page. There must be enough pace or speed for the brain to do its work. For comprehension of ideas, the reader must look through, not at, the text.

Many basic writers stay too close to their texts, writing word by word. They need distance. Exhortations to postpone editing until ideas are drafted onto paper don't work. (The many other basic writers who tend to dash off their writing without rereading or revising are, in my opinion, merely being adaptive; they cannot write when they get too close to their texts so they go to the opposite extreme to get something on paper.) Raising basic writers' consciousness about the reading process helps give them distance from their texts so that they can more successfully make meaning with their language.

I offer here a half dozen ways to integrate reading into a writing classroom. Once the underlying principles are in hand, teachers can devise many other ways to suit their particular teaching style.

1. Teaching Writers How Readers Read: Students take easily to the four elements of the reading process I discuss above. I give them an introduction similar to the one I give in seminars for writing teachers who want to learn about reading. I use the same handouts and overhead transparencies, including some diagrams. I tell them about Brenda. I tell them about my sister being a researcher for an ETS study that observed how children learn to read and how beginning readers miscue.

2. Teaching Writers How Writers Read: Although little has been written about the subject, reading one's own prose during composing is a very different process from reading another's prose. When they read their evolving texts, writers must simultaneously read at three different distances, as if they were wearing trifocals. In close, they must look at letters and at words. At an intermediate distance, they must look at matters of style and arrangement. At far range, they must look through the words, not at them, to make meaning. Experienced readers shift deftly among these three degrees of closeness to text. Inexperienced readers, however, need to become conscious of the differences. They need to know that they have options.

Let me be clear: This is not like insisting that students revise for meaning before they edit for correctness. That dictum is unfair, sometimes crippling for some students, because of students' varying learning styles. Some writers chew on a word to propel themselves into pages of drafting; other writers draft many pages in order to find one word. Telling students how writers read gives students the power of information. We can then trust them to use that information for making choices.

3. Demonstrating the Concept of Prior Knowledge: Many basic writers have low self-esteem. When they hear about the concept of prior knowledge, they assume that they have none. They are impressed, therefore, when they can "fill in the blanks" of a cloze application to a simple paragraph. Material on three levels of difficulty yields more dramatic results. Moving from the less to the more difficult, students can see that new knowledge becomes prior knowledge rather quickly. This works best if the reading is done on three different days, with the previous piece(s) reread on day two and day three.

225

4. Demonstrating the Concept of Prediction: Making the predicting process in reading concrete helps basic writers write better because they understand what a reader needs in order to read well. I use what I call "prediction sessions"[6] with much success; in fact, they can become so popular that they can take over a course and often have to be curtailed after a while. Prediction sessions are a class or group activity in which a group leader reveals the sentences in a writer's (always a volunteer and always anonymous) essay or paragraph, stopping at the end of each sentence so that the other students can predict the gist of the next sentence. The writer, especially at the beginning of the semester, is almost always surprised to find that the readers expect more elaboration of ideas and more cohesion.

Here is the first draft of a paragraph about crime by Roy (name changed). As you read each sentence, imagine what you might predict to be the gist of the next sentence.

New York City is one of the most densely populated cities in the world. It cannot be compared to other cities when it comes to crime. Killings and beatings of our elderly citizens by teenagers in "the big apple" are the most hideous crimes committed. Crime is on the rampage morning, noon, and night in New York City.

Here is Roy's third draft, after two prediction sessions on his work.

Crime is a reality that haunts New York City night and day. Do you want to take a subway from Manhattan to the Bronx? You'd better hold on tight to your purse or make sure that your wallet is not in your back pocket. Muggers and pickpockets will be happy to relieve you of your money--or even your life. A favorite target of thieves is our elderly citizens as they ride the subway or walk the streets. Old people are easy marks for cruel teenagers who like to beat and kill old people. One reason for so much theft in New York City is drug abuse. Junkies want their fix, but first they want our money. The "big apple" has a worm in it.

5. Training Students to Score Holistically: Basic writers are not very good at scanning text. This keeps them too close to their texts when they write and when they read. Once they learn the technique of holistic scoring (using a batch of anonymous essays that have been scored by experts), they become more distanced from their texts, often with the result that they write more fluently and easily.

6. Reading Aloud: Most basic writing students were not read to as children. Their mind's ear against which they can test the sound and rhythm of their writing is underdeveloped. Reading aloud every day helps students learn to listen for meaning. They create meaning as they listen, a process they can become conscious of. My evidence for the success of this activity is the frequency with which students ask for a selection to be reread, or want to read the selection aloud themselves when they are in groups. None of this is to suggest a quick fix. But teaching about reading in writing classrooms helps students learn about learning, about making meaning, and about constructing their worlds.

Phyllis illustrates this. I wrote her this past summer at the address I had on file to explain that I had been delayed in publishing her writing because my husband had been very ill, and that I hadn't had the time to write the article I was planning. I wanted her to know that I would be using it in this article. She wrote back:

Dear Dr. T.:
   I was pleased to receive your letter and to learn that your husband is in excellent health again. I am very happy, and as you can see from the above address, there is a little change. This is because I am now living in my own apartment with my daughter. Her name is Rosemary. Enclosed is a little picture of her.
                                                Yours truly,
                                                Phyllis

Becoming can happen.

Notes

1.   I am indebted to Robert F. Hogan, Executive Director of the National Council of Teachers of English (NCTE) for nineteen years until 1981, for alerting me to the implied distinctions among these verbs.

2.   I am indebted to Ann E. Berthoff for my first contact with the terms "making of meaning" and "meaning-making." I recommend her powerful book *The Making of Meaning: Metaphors, Models, and Maxims for Writing Teachers* (Montclair, NJ: Boynton/Cook, 1981). For example:

> In composing, we make meanings. We find the forms of thought by means of language, and we find the forms of language by talking thought.... I believe we can best teach the composing process by conceiving of it as a continuum of making meaning, by seeing writing as analogous to all those processes by which we make sense of the world. (69)

3.   For more information about college students from strongly oral traditions, see Thomas J. Farrell, "Literacy, the Basics and All That Jazz," *College English* 38 (1977): 443-59; and Lynn Quitman Troyka, "Perspectives on Legacies and Literacy in the 1980's," *College Composition and Communication* 33 (1982): 252-62.

4.   For those unfamiliar with this field, I recommend highly Frank Smith, *Understanding Reading,* 3rd ed. (New York: Holt, 1982).

5.   A good introduction to Braille can be found in Claudell S. Stocker, *Teacher's Manual: Modern Methods of Teaching Braille: Book One and Book Two* (Louisville: American Printing House for the Blind, 1970). 1970.

6.   For a detailed discussion of "prediction sessions," see my paper "The Writer as Conscious Reader." Until it appears in the forthcoming *Sourcebook for Basic Writers,* edited by Theresa Enos, to be published by Random House, it can be found in the ERIC files, Document ED 198 549, July 1981.

CHANGING BUSINESS AS USUAL:
READER RESPONSE IN THE CLASSROOM

Daniel Sheridan[5]

> . . . I should like to see our classrooms more often places in which we have the courage to admit to our students that the actual business of recreating a work is difficult and tricky and sometimes frustrating, but always exciting and challenging.
> Louise Rosenblatt, "A Performing Art"

> Reader-response theory is a gesture toward opening up dialogue with students and problematizing questions of authority, but it can only be a significant gesture when appropriated by teachers who recognize the forces against which such freedom must contend.
> Marjorie Roemer, "Which Reader's Response?"

I

Louise Rosenblatt's "A Performing Art," with its description of a reading centered classroom--one which focuses on the act of reading, in all of its complexity--was published in 1966. And yet I would venture to say that such a classroom is as rare now as it was then. This seems odd, for those twenty-five years have witnessed two developments which should have moved us further toward that goal. We have seen the rise of a "readerly" criticism, which has served to shift attention from the "what" to the "who" of reading, from the static text to the reader who creates meaning from that text. And we have seen the concurrent rise of writing theory, in which, analogously, the "who" has supplanted the "what" in a process approach. But while composition theory has helped transform the writing classroom, no such process approach has taken hold in the teaching of literature. The act of writing is central to the composition course, but the act of reading, as Rosenblatt describes it, is merely assumed in most literature courses.

The act of reading--it is necessary, I think, to phrase it this way. For reader-response theory asks us to consider reading, first and foremost, as something we do with texts. In Rosenblatt's formulation, the reader is "not a blank tape registering a ready-made message. He [is] actively involved in building up a poem for himself out of his responses to the text" *(The Reader 10)*. This "building up" process is a creative journey, not a linear process of information retrieval, and thus it can be difficult for passive readers who look for meaning in the text itself. Viewed this way, reading is an intense mental activity--but not merely that. Reader-response theory also asks us to see reading as a purposeful act (in which the reader's goal, like the aesthetic aim of building up a literary work, helps determine the outcome), a social act (which takes place in a real context, often

---

[5]From *College English* 53 (November 1991): 804-14.

in the company of others), as well as a deeply personal act (an investment of ourselves in the experience which Rosenblatt calls the "poem").

Reader-response theory, then, asks us to think seriously about readers and the act of reading, although this does not mean that we thereby dismiss the importance of the text. In Rosenblatt's view, the text constrains the act of reading, directing and shaping it. The literary experience, the "poem," is centered on neither the text nor the reader: what the reader brings to the text is important, but response is always structured by the language of the text. The literary experience, to use Rosenblatt's term, is a "transaction," in which neither the text nor the reader can be seen as the sole repository of meaning. Of the various metaphors that Rosenblatt uses to explain this transaction--dance, music, electrical circuitry--perhaps the most helpful is that of ecology. Like interdependent elements in an ecological system, the reader and the text act upon each other in the creation of the literary work.

A theory like this, it would seem, could be adapted readily to the classroom, for unlike some literary theory--deconstruction, for example--reader-response appears to be homegrown, familiar in its vocabulary, and almost automatically student-centered. Moreover, some of its main proponents-- Fish, Bleich, Holland, and Rosenblatt herself--have all written from the standpoint of classroom teachers. In addition, there is a small but available body of work which attempts to apply their ideas to the classroom: the work of Robert Probst and Russell Hunt, for example, and any number of articles in *College English, Reader,* and *English Journal* during the past ten years. This would seem to exempt reader-response theory from the charge, recently leveled by Charles Moran and Elizabeth Penfield, that "unlike composition theory, contemporary literary theory has remained somehow remote from our talk about classroom practice" (1).

Reader response is part of our *talk* perhaps, but what I want to argue here is that it has only with difficulty become part of our behavior. For there are forces that militate against a reading--centered classroom. In Marjorie Roemer's view, the problem is political, and the main issue is one of authority--who holds power in the classroom, whose response matters. I agree that issues of authority and freedom are indeed crucial in a reading-centered pedagogy, and yet I believe it would be a mistake to demand too much at this stage. As Roemer herself suggests, reader-response theory is, as yet, merely a gesture in the direction of a democratized classroom. So I would like, for the moment, to focus more strictly on current practice. From this standpoint the central question is this: can we teach in a reader-response mode without making reading itself central to the classroom? And if, as I suspect, the answer is "no," how can we go about making the act of reading central to our work? I'd like to suggest that the place to begin is with the routines, the "business as usual," of the literature classroom.

II

Business as usual consists of this: a teacher assigns a familiar text; students do the reading outside class; later, the teacher (prepared with the weight of canonical knowledge) discusses the text with students; still later, if writing is to be done, students write interpretive papers on the text. This is, of course, a generalization, but I think it is fairly accurate. For though teaching styles differ and some classes are more student-centered than others, the routine of assign-read-discuss-write is fairly constant. It is the way I was taught in college. It is what I see when I look around, both in colleges and in secondary schools. Until recently, it is the way I structured my own classes. But it is, I think, a routine that is hostile to reader-response teaching.

Supporting this routine are unspoken rules, some of which I will be discussing here. There are the rules of preparation: teachers should read the text in advance and come to class prepared; students are expected only to "do the reading." There are rules about reading: it takes place outside the classroom; class time is for interpretation. And rules about writing: when writing about literature, students must argue a point based on a coherent reading of the whole text. These, and many other rules, are implied by the routine I have described, and like all rules they are supported by a set of beliefs, not all of them consistent with the literary theory which we think guides our teaching.

The rules of preparation, for example, are based on a number of beliefs, none of which seem very hospitable to a reader-response approach: that student response has less value than teacher knowledge; that student readings are naive, teacher readings interpretive; that the teacher's proper role is that of the authority, the expert; that texts can be mastered through preparation. The rules about reading and writing suggest more beliefs: that reading and interpreting are different activities; that reading need not (or cannot) be taught; that the result of instruction should be coherent readings of the text. If these beliefs are embedded within our practice, it would seem that Roemer is correct when she says that English teachers are, more often than not, "the unconscious purveyors of a constellation of unexamined values" (918).

We learn these values chiefly through experience, especially in our lives as students in other people's literature courses. We incorporate them in our practice because, as Janet Emig has pointed out, we seldom have a coherent theory of learning to accompany our theories of literature (88-89). On the college level at least, we are not used to "classroom talk" and thus often discuss teaching in naive ways. We might assume, for example, that theory directly affects practice--whereas nothing could be further from the truth. Or we take for granted that teacher talk makes a great deal of difference, that what we say in the classroom matters more than what we (or our students) do. And so we develop a body of practice which in turn reinforces a set of beliefs--beliefs which are all the more powerful for being largely unconscious and rarely articulated.

Thus Nancy Lester and Cynthia Onore, in their study of how teachers deal with curriculum changes, argue that all change begins by "uncovering beliefs." They cite Larry Cuban, who reminds us that teaching does not take place in a vacuum: "Teacher repertoires . . . have been shaped by the crucible of experience and the culture of teaching" (40). This "culture of teaching," a slice of which we see in business as usual, exerts a powerful influence on our practice. There are traditions (the way we were taught), institutional constraints (everything from how we order books to how students enroll), personal pressures (how things would seem to our colleagues), and a host of other concerns which have little to do, on the surface, with our theory of literature.

Theory matters, of course, but we also need to take a critical look at our practice if we are to change it. For we might read, write, and dream about transactional reading and yet continue to teach as we did in the heyday of the New Criticism. That is fine if our aim is the analysis of texts a la "close reading" or the transmission of information about texts a la "literary studies." These might be worthy aims in upper-division courses where students are more fluent readers of literature and where learning *about* texts is the main business. But on the introductory level at least, we ought to be aiming, at something like what Rosenblatt describes--a reading-centered classroom. We thus need to acknowledge the forces which work against change. As Roemer suggests, the freedom implied by reader-response theory will not be achieved without struggle. One part of that struggle will involve business as usual: we need to examine the rules of the classroom in a serious way--and then consider breaking them.

III

The rules are so complex and so mutually reinforcing that one scarcely knows where to begin, so let me suggest that we start with the rules of preparation. It is axiomatic, I think, that teachers come to class prepared, that they know more about the text than do their students. And indeed, it seems reasonable to expect this of teachers; it is, as some students tell me, "what you are paid for." Break this rule and one hardly seems to be teaching at all.

But there are problems with "preparation" in the standard sense--that is, boning up on critical interpretations and background knowledge. For one thing, it fosters the notion that the teacher is the repository of a canonical wisdom superior to anything a student might know. And this becomes a way of exerting authority. We might not like to admit it, but much of our status in the classroom depends on keeping the student in an inferior position as a reader. In the end, this situation reinforces a false distinction between the way students and teachers read, the former being a naïve process of picking up information, the latter an inspired act of interpretation. As Gordon Pradl puts it, the teacher is primed to put on "the great performance," something quite different from the "primary" encounters with the text which characterize student reading (67-68).

One way to change the situation is to read, along with students, a poem or other short text which the teacher has not seen before. This is what Pradl recommends, as do Probst, Newkirk, and others--not perhaps as a regular activity but as a timely reminder of what reading is really like. The point is to bring reading actively and dramatically into the classroom, reading with "all the false starts, contradictions, and digressions" (Pradl 68). Reading with our students this way, naked and unprepared, is not of course to assume the stance of a naive reader: we, like our students, have experience and prior knowledge to work with. But it is an adventure, which is precisely why it works so well. As Newkirk points out, the reason for working this way is to "look for trouble," to find problems and struggle with them. Or as Probst puts it, this kind of activity "allows you to be wrong, to make mistakes, to be convinced by the sharper insights of someone else--in other words to engage in the natural activities associated with learning and thinking" (33).

I am not certain how "natural" any kind of teaching activity can be, this one included, but I know from experience that it can make a considerable difference in the dynamics of the classroom. Authority, in the sense of text-mastery, is now subject to challenge, and can be replaced by the communal effort to work through a text and discover its various meanings. This is not to say that the classroom becomes democratic or even necessarily more student-centered though the chances for the latter are certainly increased. For when "expertise" comes to mean the learning and thinking of reading as opposed to the great performance of a teacher, it becomes possible to talk about that difficult, tricky, frustrating, exciting and challenging process that Rosenblatt describes. This process is not just a memory; it is taking place in the presence of all. Finally, the myth of the static text is dispelled. A work, so read, is demonstrably not a stable thing; coming into being through several readings, it is an experience, language taking shape as we read.

232

And that--the notion that meaning is created through reading, not lifted magically from the text or unlocked by professorial keys--is precisely what many students need to see. These are the students who are least able to read aesthetically, the ones who passively await the instructor's word on the "theme" of a text. These are the students who literally do not know "how we got there"' when we offer them ingenious readings of a text. They believe in magic; they think we are special, not recognizing that our specialness lies in our experience as readers rather than in a "gift" denied to more pedestrian souls. They are not good readers of literature, but neither are they stupid or incapable. Never having learned what it means to read for more than "information," they need to be shown, not told, what it means to struggle with a challenging text and make meaning from it.

But this, it might be argued, is a mere trick, something to do every once in a while to make a point, but hardly a replacement for the routine of the literature course. I agree, although I believe we can read this way with our students more often than one might think. We can rely on our colleagues for recommendations of texts to assign; we can ask students to bring texts to class; and we can learn, in the end, to prepare for class in a different way--focusing more on the reading process than on the "readings" we have to offer students. Nonetheless, the mind boggles at an entire course orchestrated around unfamiliar texts. Moreover, any such technique will have only a limited effect as an isolated activity within the general structure of business as usual. What we need is a change in the routine itself.

IV

Nothing is more ingrained than the regular business of assigning whole texts to be read and then discussing them after the fact. It is the way college literature courses have always (it seems) been taught. It is the way we organize instruction, a title on the course schedule indicating the "reading" to be done for that date. It is what students and colleagues expect. And, admittedly, it is the most efficient way to "cover" the material. Changing this routine, then, violates one of the basic commandments of college teaching: Thou shalt not read in class.

Upon reflection, however, we can see that this law is based on the premise that students already know how to read, so we do not have to concern ourselves with the process. And this, in turn, implies some beliefs about reading: that it is a skill which, once learned, remains static; that reading, thus divorced from interpretation, is alike for most readers; that reading for an aesthetic aim is familiar to students. None of these, I'd argue, are true, which should at least give us pause. Nor does it seem very logical, if we are aiming at a classroom in which reading is central and response really matters, to adhere to a routine that banishes reading or treats it as mere memory.

It follows that we should spend at least some time reading in class. Plunt suggests a variety of useful activities, as do Probst, Corcoran, and others. Their techniques differ in certain ways, but have points in common: a text is begun in class; discussion takes place "in process" (that is, reading and talk about reading take place alternately); expectations and predictions play a prominent role in discussion; and, finally, the making of meaning from the text is treated as a communal activity. Whether the text is read orally or silently, whether the teacher reads or relegates this task to students, whether we follow a formal routine (like the Directed Reading/Thinking Activity) or handle the discussion informally--these are important decisions, but they need not concern us here. The main point is that reading is being made public in the classroom.

With a short story, for instance, discussion might begin with the author and title, students being asked to make predictions about the experience of reading. Some version of what Plunt calls "interrupted reading" (35-52) would follow: chunks of the text would be discussed and further predictions made. The class would end on this note, the remainder of the reading to be done for the next meeting, at which time a discussion of the entire text would take place. With a novel, obviously, proportionally less of the text would be read in class, but the same principle would hold true. With poems, on the other hand, where re-reading is crucial, it is useful to read and respond, read again and respond, and then read at least one more time. Newkirk recommends a variation, using written responses, but the effect is similar: response to the poem is "sandwiched" between readings.

Devoting class time to reading has serious consequences. Since the goal of discussion is not to offer full-blown interpretations but to describe what the reader is thinking and feeling, students are faced with a new set of demands. Generally, the "talkers" still talk, but now one hears more from students who have previously been silent. Discussion is livelier and more genuine, although it is sometimes disconcerting to discover the associations and attitudes which influence student reading. All those idiosyncracies, so richly deplored by I. A. Richards, do indeed drive the reading process. What is remarkable—and what seems to impress students the most--is that, given this diversity, we have anything in common as we read. In the end they are impressed as much by the power of the text--the "open-meshed woven curtain" which Rosenblatt has described as a shaper of meaning (*The Reader* 76)--as they are by the multiplicity of responses.

There are other consequences as well. In the economy of the classroom, where time is a valuable commodity, time spent on reading and in-process talk is obviously not being devoted to more standard after-the-fact discussion. Not all students approve. There are some who want more time spent on interpreting the text as a whole; they want to dig in more. So do I. I too regret the loss of discussion time, although I have more faith in the in-process discussions than do these students. Others are disturbed by the lack of closure in a reading-centered classroom; they want answers and they expect them to come from the teacher. Here, obviously, I disagree, though I can sympathize. "So much is left hanging," complain my engineering and business students. They are right. All I can do is smile and remind them that this is one thing they can learn from an English class.

V

Bringing reading into the classroom makes it public and communal, but there remains the more strictly personal dimension. The individual reader's transaction with the text, whether it is shared or not, is always central to the experience of literature. Our own histories as readers will surely bear this out, as will our memories of literature classes. We recall those teachers for whom literature was a living experience; we remember those discussions which stimulated controversy and sharings; but mostly we think of "the reading," the actual encounters with the texts--and what we wrote about them.

Writing is the complement to talk in the literature classroom, and it is the best way to uncover the deeply personal side of reading. As Rosenblatt suggests, writing and reading are so interconnected that "each can serve as a stimulus and support to the other" ("Writing and Reading" 25). Hence the attention paid to response statements, from Bleich's suggestions in *Readings and Feelings* to the more recent work of Corcoran and Probst. Such short writing tasks can be focused or general, can be shared or kept private, can be assigned singly or in sequence. What matters most is that they be kept informal and that they take place frequently. For their value is not so much to record thought as it is to explore responses. It is exploratory writing to enhance exploratory reading.

Reading journals fulfill a similar purpose. As Leslie Stratta and John Dixon suggest, journals "leave room for responses that are immediate, tentative, interim, fragmentary, but not yet deliberately shaped" (186). The key word, I think, is "tentative," which is precisely the element that many of my students struggle when I suggest that they focus on problems and questions, especially those that are difficult to answer. They want, instead, to say something definitive about the work, somehow ending it so they can move on to another task, so their early entries express likes and dislikes (if you "like" something, that puts an end to it) or they paraphrase (if you say what the poem says, you are done with it). I read these entries and ask for more. Sometimes I provide a format for entries or a stimulus to write; sometimes I show samples of my own journal entries or have students read each other's journals. But in the end it is the general tenor of the course that leads to change in the journals: when students see that exploration, not closure, is the aim, their journals start to become interesting.

Response statements and reading journals are important features of a new pedagogy, but we need also to reconsider the other writing assignments we give. The traditional thesis/support paper, in which a student is asked to prove a point about the text, has its own kind of validity, but it is hardly in keeping with the basic aims of reader-response theory. We need assignments that ask students to explore reading, not tasks that, to use Mariolina Salvatori's phrase, produce "excessive closure, excessive containment of possible alternative meanings, which reveals itself in a type of 'blocked' writing" (14). At least on the introductory level, we need to move away from argumentation in the direction of description and exploration. And these new assignments need to be rigorous and challenging, yet possible--not academic tasks so difficult that we would never undertake to write them ourselves.

One obvious and fairly traditional route to this kind of writing is that of "creative writing." Following the lead of Kenneth Koch, Joseph Tsujimoto argues that the teaching of poetry ought not to be divorced from the writing of it. He has created a series of poetry writing assignments that, although devised for middle school children, work quite well on the college level. Similar adaptations for fiction or drama seem possible. In a variation of this approach, Peter Adams recommends what he calls "dependent authorship." Like the time-honored "write a new ending" task, these come in a variety of shapes and sizes: imaginative reconstructions, additions to the text, continuations, epilogues, dreams, and altered endings. Adams argues persuasively that imaginative tasks in which students take on the role of the author allow them to "discover and explore elements of their response to the work that they could not grasp or articulate in any other way" (121).

Both creative writing and dependent authorship have the advantage of being field-tested, but neither asks the student to deal directly with the actual process of reading. In addition to these, then, we might consider a more self-conscious approach to writing about reading. With this in mind I have been experimenting with a multi-part assignment, what I call "the paper of many parts." Students are asked to do several things to a text: respond to it, paraphrase it, write a parody of it, do some research on it, interview another reader about it, and then to say something about the experience of reading it. "Reading," for this assignment, means going through all these steps. Students must live with a work for some time, thinking and solving problems and learning; they must handle the text in different ways, treating it with a little disrespect; and, in the end, they write more compelling and more interesting papers than they ever did with my more traditional assignments.

VI

The teaching techniques I have mentioned so far are obviously not a formula for teaching in a reader-response mode. They are a mere beginning, a tentative move in a certain direction. They make me, I fancy, a little more "a teacher of reading," a little less "a professor of literary studies." And in saying that, I must add that I am not yet prepared to abandon the main tradition entirely. A survey course for English majors presents its own set of teaching problems, as does a graduate course in Victorian literature. This is why I have limited my suggestions to introductory literature courses, where I believe the need to address the experience of reading is most urgent.

On the other hand, I see no reason not to structure upper-division or graduate courses this way. For the issue here is not just helping students to become better readers of literature. As I suggested at the start, our routines of the classroom are enactments of what we believe to be true about literature, about reading, about learning. What is bothersome about the assign-read-discuss routine is the implied lack of interest in reading, as well as the message that texts are static things to be "gotten" before they are talked about. Any course, I believe, can benefit from challenging those assumptions.

So I believe in changing the routines, in breaking the rules. They are important rules, worthy of being broken. They touch close to the heart of the matter, the problem of bringing reading into the classroom so that it can be examined and discussed, so that we can learn from the way others read. This is a fundamental change, one that would flow from--and lead to--an altered sense of how authority is exerted in the classroom. I do not mean this in any romantic sense. Mary Rose O'Reilley might well be right in saying that power cannot, and should not, be given away: "Whether we like it or not as teachers, we have inherited our fathers' light saber and we have to learn how to use it. The worst thing we can do is pretend we don't have power" (146). On the other hand, Roemer is quite correct in saying that reader-response theory should be a move toward "problematizing questions of authority," a way of "making room for contesting views and urging serious, committed, personal interchanges" (920).

It remains to be seen where the teacher is ideally situated in such a classroom. Is it as a master-reader, someone who functions primarily as a model for students? Is it as discussion leader, the first-among-equals who orchestrates the talk of a reading community? Or is it something more eclectic and perhaps more traditional--model reader, discussion leader, expert lecturer, each as the situation demands? This at least is the way I see things at present: my role might shift several times in the course of one class period, depending on what I perceive to be the needs of the students. And that suggests that, at least for the present, I am not overly concerned about the "purity" of my practice. I am aware of disparities between theory and practice (would Stanley Fish approve?) and inconsistencies in my own behavior (can one be a master-reader and still do justice to the responses of others?) And yet these are problems which attend practice of any sort. There is really no way to preserve one's innocence and remain a teacher.

What matters most, I think, is that we take practice seriously enough to change it, in spite of the inconsistencies that result. To do otherwise is to fall into a cynical paralysis. Realistically we know that the odds against the creation of a true "community of readers" are overwhelming. They are described eloquently by Walter Slatoff in his argument "against detachment": "In such an environment [as the typical college course] it comes to seem an entirely reasonable act to ask about Auden's line 'We must love one another or die' only how it relates to the rest of the poem or what its meter is or to reproduce it as an item on an identification quiz" (260). Slatoff offers no "cure" for the general conditions that lead to this kind of teaching, but he does suggest that we could improve things "by revealing our own real experience with the books we teach, by actually hearing our students' responses and seeking to deepen them rather than label or grade them, in short by trying to change the classroom from a spectacle of instruction into a room full of human readers" (260).

A room full of human readers. So simple a goal, yet so difficult to achieve. But in working toward that goal, we will have humanized the literature classroom. We will have let in all the ideas and attitudes, the frustrations and meanderings, the feelings and beliefs, all the messy stuff that makes the reading process so rich and varied. We will have let in life itself. And we will have told the truth about reading--that it is characterized first by chaos and only later by a tentative sort of order; that it proceeds through circularity as well as linearity; that guesswork is as important as logic; that certainty is an illusion; that mistakes are worth making; and that, in the end, the joy of literature comes as much from multiplicity and ambiguity as it does from unity and coherence. We will have shown students that "literature" and "reading" are not two different things and that the classroom is a place for literature to happen.

Works Cited

Adams, Peter. "Writing from Reading: 'Dependent Authorship' as a Response." Corcoran and Evans 119-52.

Bleich, David. *Readings and Feelings: An Introduction to Subjective Criticism.* Urbana, IL: NCTE, 1975.

Corcoran, Bill. "Teachers Creating Readers." Corcoran and Evans 41-74.

Corcoran, Bill, and Emrys Evans, eds. *Readers, Texts, Teachers.* Upper Montclair, NJ: Boynton/Cook, 1987.

Emig, Janet. "Our Missing Theory." Moran and Penfield 87-96.

Hunt, Russell. "Toward a Process-Intervention Model in Literature Teaching." *College English* 44 (1982): 345-57.

Lester, Nancy, and Cynthia Onore. *Learning Change: One School District Meets Language Across the Curriculum.* Portsmouth, NH: Boynton/Cook, 1990.

Moran, Charles, and Elizabeth Penfield. *Conversations: Contemporary Critical Theory and the Teaching of Literature.* Urbana, IL: NCTE, 1990.

Newkirk, Thomas. "Looking for Trouble: A Way to Unmask Our Reading." *College English* 46 (1984): 756-66.

O'Reilley, Mary Rose. "'Exterminate . . . the Brutes'--And Other Things That Go Wrong in Student-Centered Teaching." *College English* 51 (1989): 142-46.

Pradl, Gordon. "Close Encounters of the First Kind: Teaching the Poem at the Point of Utterance." *English Journal* 76 (1987): 66-69.

Probst, Robert. *Response and Analysis: Teaching Literature in the Junior and Senior High School.* Portsmouth, NH: Boynton/Cook, 1988.

Roemer, Marjorie G. "Which Reader's Response?" *College English* 49 (1987): 911-21.

Rosenblatt, Louise. "A Performing Art." *English Journal* 55 (1966): 999-1005.

_____. *The Reader, the Text, the Poem: The Transactional Theory of the*

Literary World. Carbondale: Southern Illinois UP, 1978.

_____. "Writing and Reading." *Reader 20* (1988): 7-31.

Salvatori, Mariolina. "The Pedagogical Implications of Reader-Response Theory." *Reader* 16 (1986): 1-19.

Slatoff, Walter. "Against Detachment." *College English* 32 (1970): 255-60.

Stratta, Leslie, and John Dixon. "Writing and Literature: Monitoring and Examining." Corcoran and Evans 174-96.

Tsujimoto, Joseph. *Teaching Poetry Writing to Adolescents.* Urbana, IL: NCTE, 1988.

THE ART OF COLLABORATIVE LEARNING:
MAKING THE MOST OF KNOWLEDGEABLE PEERS

Kenneth A. Bruffee[6]

Late last spring, a colleague of mine at a university out West--I'll call him Jim--wrote and asked if I would read a manuscript of his. He felt he was finally ready for someone to take a close look at it.

Jim's an old friend. I dashed off a note saying of course I'd read it, with pleasure. At the beginning of June, which luckily for both of us was right at the end of exams, I got a weighty package in the mail--279 pages plus notes. I read it, scribbled clouds of barely decipherable marginal notes, and drafted a six-page letter to Jim congratulating him on first rate work, suggesting a few changes and mentioning one or two issues he might think through a bit further.

He phoned to thank me when he got the letter and asked some questions. We then spent an hour or so discussing these questions and supporting AT&T in the manner to which it has become accustomed.

Before the snow blows, I expect I shall see some of Jim's manuscript again. I doubt that he needs another reading, but I'm happy to do it if he wants me to. I learned a lot reading his book. We both learned something talking out the few stickier points in it. Anyway, I owe him one. He did the same for me five years ago, when I was thrashing about in the terminal throes of the book I was finishing. His name appeared prominently on my acknowledgments page; I suppose mine will appear prominently on his.

The experience I have just described is familiar to most readers of *Change.* To enjoy such an experience, you don't have to write a book. All you have to do is work with an intelligent, compatible committee on an interesting grant proposal or a new development plan for your college. You know how it can go. Joe gets an idea and sketches it out in a couple of pages. Mary says, hey, wait a minute--that makes me think of.... Then Fred says, but look, if we change this or add that. . . . In the end everyone, with a little help from his and her friends, exceeds what anyone could possibly have learned or accomplished alone.

If I'm right that this kind of experience is familiar, then no one reading this article is a stranger to collaborative learning, however strange the term may be. Jim and I are peers. When Jim asked me to read his work and I agreed, we became an autonomous collaborative learning group of two with the task of revising and developing the written product of one of its members.

The term collaborative learning has become increasingly familiar today because it is applied not only to voluntary associations such as my work with Jim, but also to teaching that tries to

---

[6]From <u>Change</u> (March/April 1987): 42-47.

imitate that experience in college and university classrooms. Teachers of writing at institutions throughout the country are discovering that teaching students in a variety of ways to work productively on their writing demonstrably improves students' work.

And it is not just writing teachers who are interested. Clark Bouton and Russell Y. Clark's useful book, *Learning in Groups,* reports on the way collaborative learning is being applied in subjects from business management to medicine to math. And there is at least one physics lab manual in the country (at Montana State University) that presents an extended rationale of collaborative learning on its front cover.

Perhaps more to the point for some of us, at least one trenchant article exists that explains collaborative learning for the benefit of faculty and administrators who find themselves evaluating teachers. Harvey S. Wiener's "Collaborative Learning in the Classroom: A Guide to Evaluation" suggests ways to tell when teachers are using collaborative learning most effectively. It is also, therefore, a useful guide to effective use of collaborative learning for teachers.

Admittedly, there is not much research to date on the effects of collaborative learning in college and university education. But recent work on its effect in primary and secondary schools is relevant. Surveys of research by David Johnson *(Psychological Bulletin 89)* and by Shlomo Sharon *(Review of Educational Research 50)* tend to support the experience of college and university instructors who have used collaborative learning. Students learn better through non-competitive collaborative group work than in classrooms that are highly individualized and competitive. Robert E. Slavin's *Cooperative Learning* reports similar results.

Interest in collaborative learning in colleges and schools is motivated in part by these results. It is motivated also by the observation that the rest of the world now works collaboratively almost as a universal principle. Japanese "Theory-Z" quality circles on the factory floor aside, there is hardly a bank, legal firm, or industrial management team that strives--much less dares--to proceed in the old-fashioned individualistic manner. Physicians are increasingly collaborative, too, although they prefer to call it "consultation." At Harvard Medical School, *25* percent of each entering class currently studies in collaborative groups, bypassing systematic lecture courses almost entirely.

Interest in collaborative learning is motivated also by recent challenges to our understanding of what knowledge is. This challenge is being felt throughout the academic disciplines. That is, collaborative learning is related to the social constructionist views promulgated by, among others, the philosopher Richard Rorty *(Philosophy and the Mirror of Nature)* and the anthropologist Clifford Geertz. These writers say (as Geertz puts it in his recent book, *Local Knowledge)* that "the way we think now" differs in essential ways from the way we thought in the past. Social constructionists tend to assume that knowledge is a social construct and that, as the historian of science Thomas Kuhn has put it, all knowledge, including scientific knowledge, "is intrinsically the common property of a group or else nothing at all." (See Bruffee, "Social Construction, Language, and the Authority of Knowledge: A Bibliographical Essay," *College English* 48 [Dec. 1986]: 77-90.)

Collaborative learning is related to these conceptual changes by virtue of the fact that it assumes learning occurs among persons rather than between a person and things. It even turns out that some teachers who are using collaborative learning have found that social constructionist assumptions enhance their understanding of what they are trying to do and give them a better chance of doing it well.

So, although the term "collaborative learning" may be unfamiliar for some, collaborative learning itself is not new. Our understanding of its importance to higher education began in the late 1950s with Theodore Newcomb's work on peer group influence among college students *(College Peer Groups, The American College,* ed. Nevitt Sanford) and with M. L. J. Abercrombie's research on educating medical students at University Hospital, University of London. Newcomb demonstrated that peer group influence is a powerful but wasted resource in higher education. Abercrombie's book, *The Anatomy of Judgement,* showed medical students learning the key element in successful medical practice, diagnosis--that is, medical judgment--more quickly and accurately when they worked collaboratively in small groups than when these worked individually.

Abercrombie began her important study by observing the scene that most of us think is typical of medical education: the group of medical students with a teaching physician gathered around a ward bed to diagnose a patient. Then she made a slight but crucial change in the way that such a scene is usually played out. Instead of asking each individual medical student in the group to diagnose the patient on his or her own, Abercrombie asked the whole group to examine the patient together, discuss the case as a group, and arrive at a consensus--a single diagnosis agreed to by all.

When she did this, what she found was that students who learned diagnosis collaboratively in this way acquired better medical judgment faster than individual students working alone.

With the exception of small, recently instituted experimental programs at the medical schools of the University of New Mexico and Harvard University, Abercrombie's conclusion has had little impact as yet on medical school faculties anywhere, in Britain or America. But when I read the book in 1972, a dozen years or so after it was published, her conclusion had an immediate and, I believe, positive impact on my thinking about university instruction and eventually, on the role I see myself in as a classroom instructor.

The aspect of Abercrombie's book that I found most illuminating was her evidence that learning diagnostic judgment is not an individual process but a social one. Learning judgment she saw, patently occurs on an axis drawn not between individuals and things, but among people. But in making this observation, she had to acknowledge that there is something wrong with our normal cognitive assumptions about the nature of knowledge. Cognitive assumptions, she says, disregard "the biological fact that [the human being] . . . is a social animal." "How [do] human relationships," that is, relations among persons, she asked, "influence the receipt of information about apparently non-personal events?"

In trying to answer this question, Abercrombie makes the brilliant observation that, in general, people learn judgment best in groups; she infers from this observation that we learn judgment well in groups because we tend to talk each other out of our unshared biases and presuppositions. And in passing, she drops an invaluable hint: The social process of learning judgment that she has observed seems to have something to do with language and with "interpretation."

These three principles underlie the practice of collaborative learning. One thing that college and university instructors most hope to do through collaborative learning is increase their students' ability to exercise judgment within the teacher's field of expertise, whatever that field is.

But there is today another thing that instructors hope to do through collaborative learning. They hope to raise their students' level of social maturity as exercised in their intellectual lives. In doing so, instructors are trying to prepare their students for the "real world." They are preparing them to enter law, medicine, architecture, banking, engineering, research science--any field, in fact, that depends on effective interdependence and consultation for excellence.

This discovery that excellent undergraduate education also depends on effective interdependence and consultation awaited the work of William Perry. Perry's book, *Forms of Intellectual and Ethical Development in the College Years,* has made an indelible impression on the thinking of many college and university instructors, but not in every instance for the right reason. Like Abercrombie, Perry makes cognitive assumptions about the nature of knowledge, and most readers to date have found his developmental "scheme" of greatest interest.

Yet Perry himself is not entirely comfortable with the cognitive assumptions underlying his scheme. He has read Thomas Kuhn's *The Structure of Scientific Revolutions,* and acknowledges that our current view that "knowledge is contextual and relative" is only the most recent phase in a tendency toward the assimilation of cultural diversity that needs for its fulfillment "a new social mind."

As a result, again like Abercrombie, Perry implies that the central educational issue today hinges on social relations, not on cognitive ones: relations among persons, not relations between persons and things. Learning as we must understand it today, he concludes, does not involve people's assimilation of knowledge; it involves people's assimilation into communities of knowledgeable peers. Liberal education today must be regarded as a process of leaving one community of knowledgeable peers and joining another.

Perry's discomfort with this conclusion when it comes to educational practice, however, suggests that he himself may never have quite recognized the full implications of his study. He denies that the creating of communities of knowledgeable peers among students is a legitimate part

243

of rationally and consciously organized university education. He prefers to rely on "spontaneity" to organize knowledge communities among students. He politely dismisses as unprofessional attempts to foster communities among students by using "particular procedures or rituals." Students must independently manage their "identification with the college community" as they go about "divorcing themselves" from the communities they have left behind.

Fortunately, Perry quotes liberally from his raw material--statements made by a sizeable number of informants among the Harvard College undergraduate body. And these undergraduates are not at all as ambivalent as Perry seems to be about regarding learning as a social process. Many of them see their undergraduate education quite explicitly as a difficult, perhaps even treacherous passage from one homogeneous community--the one they came from--to another homogeneous community--the college community of their student peers.

This "marrying into" the new community of students at college is clearly, as the students describe it, an informal, autonomous variety of collaborative learning that challenges students to define their individuality not as starkly and lonesomely independent, but as interdependent members of their new undergraduate community.

The more formal varieties of collaborative learning organized by instructors in classrooms imitate this informal type. And they imitate the "real world" interdependence and consultation that goes on in much business and professional work, including the work my friend Jim and I did together on his book and mine. In classroom collaborative learning, typically, students organized by the teacher into small groups discuss a topic proposed by the teacher with the purpose of arriving at consensus, much as Abercrombie's medical students practiced diagnosis on patients chosen by the teaching physician. Or students may edit each other's writing, or tutor each other, or develop and carry through assigned (or group-designed and teacher-approved) projects together.

But this classroom work, however collaborative, differs in striking ways from autonomous, "real world" interdependence. Classroom collaborative learning is inevitably no more than *semi-autonomous*, because students don't usually organize their own groups or choose their own tasks, as Jim and I did. In most cases, teachers design and structure students' work for maximum learning as part of a course of study. And teachers evaluate the work when it is completed, comparing it with professional standards and the work other students have done, both currently and in the past.

Now, to be accurate to a fault, of course, Jim and I were not an absolutely autonomous group either, any more than any interdependent consultative professional work is. Like most independently organized groups--such as political clubs, golf foursomes, and sand-lot baseball teams--he and I organized our working group on our own initiative for our own purposes, but we played the game, so to speak, by a set of rules we held in common with many other such groups.

The mores, conventions, values, and goals of our professional organization (in our case, the Modern Language Association), of that motley class of human beings called "university faculty," of promotion and tenure committees whose values are probably similar at Jim's college and mine, and so on--these large institutional communities determine to some extent what Jim and I did and said, how we did it and said it, and in point of fact, that we were doing it and saying it at all. Institutional motives and constraints always apply when people prepare themselves to take a hand in what is going on in the prevailing economic, legal, and educational world.

Formed within the immediate confines of a college's institutional structure, however, working groups in a collaborative learning classroom are clearly semi-autonomous. Like the New York Yankees, a Boy Scout troop, or the United States Supreme Court, their collaboration is organized by a larger institutional community and with its sanction. Group members abide by the conventions, mores, values, and goals of that institution. The autonomy of classroom groups derives from the fact that once the tasks are set and the groups organized, instructors step back, leaving peers to work in groups or pairs to organize, govern, and pace their work by themselves and to negotiate its outcome.

That this partial autonomy is the key to the impact of collaborative learning is evident when we compare semi-autonomous work with work that is entirely non-autonomous. The work of non-autonomous groups cannot reasonably be called collaborative learning at all. Like life in a Trappist monastery or an army platoon, in which activity is rigorously controlled, classroom group work is non-autonomous whenever instructors do not step back from the groups of working students, but rather "sit in" on them or "hover," predetermining the outcome of the work and maintaining the students' direct dependency on the teacher's presence, resources, and expertise.

Degree of autonomy is the key to collaborative learning because the issue that collaborative learning addresses is the way authority is distributed and experienced in college and university classrooms. It would be disingenuous to evade the fact that collaborative learning challenges our traditional view of the instructor's authority in a classroom and the way that authority is exercised.

This issue is much too complex to go into here. But perhaps we can get a provocative glimpse of the possible rewards that might accrue from pursuing it further if we take a brief look at the nature and source of the authority of knowledge in any autonomous working group. Return for a moment to my friend Jim and me at work together on his manuscript. What was the source of the authority exercised in that work? Where was it placed and how did it get there? Not to put too fine a point on it, where did I get the authority to comment on his writing?

The answer, of course, is that Jim and I together generated the authority in our group of two. And to occur at all in this way, that generation of authority required certain conditions. For starters, we like each other. We have read each other's stuff. We respect each other's intelligence. We have similar interests. We have worked together professionally in other circumstances. In short, we were *willing* to collaborate.

It was under these conditions that Jim *granted* me authority over his work by asking me to read it. The authority of my knowledge with regard to his manuscript originated primarily with him.

I mean "primarily" here in the strongest possible sense. My authority began with his request, and the principal claim to the validity of my authority resulted from that request.

Furthermore, and equally important, when I responded positively, I agreed to *take on and assert* authority relative to him and his work. In that sense the authority of my knowledge with regard to his manuscript originated primarily not only with his granting me the authority, but also with my accepting it, both, of course, in a context of friendliness and good grace.

Willingness to grant authority, willingness to take on and exercise authority, and a context of friendliness and good grace are the three ingredients essential to successful autonomous collaboration. If any of these three is missing or flags, collaboration fails. These three ingredients are essential also to successful semi-autonomous collaboration, such as classroom collaborative learning.

But when instructors use semi-autonomous groups in classes, the stark reality is that willingness to grant authority, willingness to take it on and exercise it, and a context of friendliness and good grace are severely compromised. Classroom authority does not necessarily begin--as Jim's and mine began--with the participants' (that is, the students') willing consent to grant authority and exercise it. In a classroom, authority still begins in most cases with the representative or agent of the institution, the instructor. Furthermore, except in highly unusual classrooms, most students start the semester as relative strangers. They do not begin, as Jim and I did, as friends. It is not surprising that, as a result, in many classrooms students may at first be wary and not overly eager to collaborate.

That is, collaborative learning has to begin in most cases with an attempt to *re-acculturate* students. Given most students' almost exclusively traditional experience of classroom authority, they have to learn, sometimes against considerable resistance, to grant authority to a peer ("What right has he got to . . . ?"), instead of the teacher. And students have to learn to take on the authority granted by a peer ("What right have I got to . . . ?"), and to exercise that authority responsibly and helpfully in the interest of a peer.

Skillfully organized, collaborative learning can itself re-acculturate students in this way. Once the task is set and the groups organized, collaborative learning places students working in groups on their own to interpret the task and invent or adapt a language and means to get the work done. When the instructor is absent, the chain of hierarchical institutional authority is for the moment broken. Students are free to revert to the collaborative peership that they are quite used to exercising in other kinds of extracurricular activities from which faculty are usually absent.

Of course, students do not always exercise effective collaborative peership in classrooms, especially at first because they have all so thoroughly internalized our long-prevailing academic prohibitions against it. And it need hardly be added that non-autonomous groups, in which the instructor insists on remaining in direct authority even after the task is set and the groups organized, cannot re-acculturate students in these ways, because the chain of hierarchical institutional authority is never broken.

Because we usually identify the authority of knowledge in a classroom with the instructor's authority, the brief hiatus in the hierarchical chain of authority in the classroom that is at the heart of collaborative learning in the long run also challenges, willy-nilly, our traditional view of the nature and source of the knowledge itself. Collaborative learning tends, that is, to take its toll on the cognitive understanding of knowledge that most of us assume unquestioningly. Teachers and students alike may find themselves asking the sorts of questions Abercrombie asked. How can knowledge gained through a social process have a source that is not itself also social?

This is another aspect of collaborative learning too complex to go into here. But raising it momentarily gives us a hint about why collaborative learning may empower students to work more successfully beyond the confines of college or university classrooms. Collaborative learning calls on levels of ingenuity and inventiveness that many students never knew they had. And it teaches effective interdependence in an increasingly collaborative world that today requires greater flexibility and adaptability to change than ever before.

WHAT I WISH I HAD KNOWN ABOUT PEER-RESPONSE GROUPS BUT DIDN'T

Ronald Barron[7]

When I was in high school, students did not show their compositions to classmates until after the teacher had rendered a verdict in the form of a grade. If the grade was good enough, we let our friends see it; if the grade was not good enough, we lost the paper as quickly as possible.

When I started to teach composition, I wasn't surprised when my students reacted in the same way. What point could there be in having another student read your paper? Teachers, not students, knew what constituted good writing, and I as their teacher wrote elaborate comments on their papers to teach them how to become better writers. Most of my comments were wasted words because my students paid as little attention to them as I had paid to the comments written by my teachers. My intentions were good, but my methods were not.

Now I use peer-response groups in my composition classes--and most of my students benefit because they get feedback and assistance from their peers prior to writing the final draft of their compositions. The quality of their papers has convinced me that students can and should use peer-response groups to improve their writing.

But response groups have not always worked well for me. When I first used them, they were failures because I merely assigned students to groups and expected them to know what to do. I did not teach them how to use response groups effectively. The critical factor in determining the success or failure of the method is what happens before students get into their groups to read each other's papers. The groups by themselves are not a panacea.

Prior to working in response groups, students must understand the purpose. They need to learn that evaluating the worth of the papers written by other members of the group is not the primary goal of good responders. Nor is an "error hunt" a valuable approach to the task. Instead, members of effective response groups treat the papers they are examining as "works in progress" and recognize that their goal is to serve as sympathetic readers suggesting methods for writers to use in improving their papers. Ideally a dialogue should be created between the writer and other members of the group which clarifies the intent of the writer's essay and sharpens the way it is achieved. This mind-set is not easy to establish, but it is critical in achieving success with response groups.

How do I promote this mind-set? Modeling of the process is essential. My experience with response groups has convinced me that usually when students are not on task in their groups, it is because they do not know what to do or they do not understand why the task is important, or a

---

[7]From *English Journal* 80 (September 1991): 24-32.

combination of these two reasons. Therefore, students need to study what peer-response groups do and then practice using peer-response techniques.

Modeling Peer-Response Groups

Published Models

Student Writers at Work, Second Series (1986, New York: St. Martin's), edited by Donald McQuade and Nancy Sommers, provides a useful first step in introducing peer response. (I use the second series, but the other volumes in the series work equally well.) McQuade and Sommers provide a brief introduction to the process, recommending the use of what they call *observations, evaluations,* and *end comments* in responding to papers. *Observations* are non-judgmental statements about what writers have done in composing drafts of the paper. These statements may address any component of the essay from the content or organizational level to the sentence or word level. The observations may cause writers to revise their papers, or they may reassure writers that what they attempted to do is recognizable to an independent reader. *Evaluations* move beyond merely describing what the writer has done to assessing the strengths and weaknesses of the draft under consideration by the group. However, the responsibility and authority to do something about the evaluations rest with the writer of the essay. A viable option for any writer is to ignore the comments made by members of the response group. Finally, *end comments* provide writers with guidance which should help them set goals for the next draft of the essay and formulate an achievable plan of revising to meet those goals. McQuade and Sommers provide students with a clear explanation of the tasks they will be asked to perform for each other, but even more valuable are the student examples included in the text. The examples are particularly useful because students can see how four experienced peer responders commented on the text and how writers made use of or, in some cases, disregarded the comments of their peers.

Student Models from Former Students

Although McQuade and Sommers' text is useful in teaching effective peer-response techniques, other methods and other terminology can be used to accomplish the same goal. One alternative method I have used is to duplicate particularly good examples of peer-response work done by my own students during the previous year. These examples not only provide good models for current students to study, but they also help create credibility for the task: if students from previous classes have been able to handle the task efficiently, so can the students in my present classes. A variation is to have a group of students from the previous year's class conduct a mock peer-response conference for students presently taking the class. This approach has two primary assets: students can see how effective peer responders work, and they can ask those effective peer responders questions about what they have observed. Usually the question-and-answer session leads to unsolicited testimonials from the experienced peer responders, thus making the technique more attractive to the inexperienced students. A final alternative method involves videotaping a good response group. Although this method does not allow students to question the participants, it does have the advantage of being easier to schedule than a live mock conference. Any of these methods should provide students with a clear conception of what they will be expected to do in their own response groups.

In-Class Practice with Teacher's Draft

Once peer response has been introduced, the next step is in-class practice. For the first practice sessions, I provide students with an early draft of a paper I have written. During the past few years I have tried two different methods for conducting these practice sessions: (1) having the students go through the paper individually and then using the following class period to list their comments on the board, following the listing with a discussion and evaluation of the worth the comments might have to someone revising the paper, or (2) having students work in groups preparing a "master" copy for their group, duplicating the master copies from individual groups, and devoting a class session to a discussion of what the groups suggested. The first method is quicker and entails slightly less work for the teacher, but I prefer the second method because it is closer to the type of activity I expect students to perform when they respond to drafts in their own groups.

For the modeling to be effective, teachers must be willing to let students respond to early drafts of their own writing, an experience which can be intimidating the first time, particularly if they want students to believe they are "experts" on writing. Revising the paper extensively prior to giving it to students defeats the purpose of the activity and usually is recognized by students. A polished paper severely limits the opportunities students have for suggesting revision options, sending the message to students that they cannot provide useful advice about how to improve a paper. Although it may be intimidating, allowing students to respond to an early teacher-written draft does pay dividends for students and for teachers. Students are more willing to share their writing with other students if their teacher has done the same thing first. Also, students see that even experienced writers need to revise their papers, sometimes extensively, to clarify their writing and to achieve quality final copies. Finally, students learn that inexperienced writers are capable of helping even experienced writers improve their compositions. The benefits to teachers? Students are more willing to approach peer response with an open mind, reserving judgment until after they have worked with their group for the first composition assignment of the class. More important, students write more effective and more interesting papers. What more could any teacher who has to read those compositions ask for?

But I don't stop with the "mock" peer editing session. For the session to have maximum benefit, I revise my draft using the students' comments. The revised copy is then given to students, and we discuss where I followed their advice and where I ignored it. More important, we discuss why I followed the course of action I did. Ideally, if time allows, students should be given a second chance to respond to the "revised" copy.

Wouldn't professional models work just as well or better than teacher drafted examples, particularly if the teacher were able to find examples of work-in-progress? My answer to the question is "no." Use of professional models allows some students to use the "cop-out" that "so-and-so should be able to do that because they are professional writers, but I'm not a

250

professional so don't expect me to do the same thing." However, I have one even stronger objection to the use of professional models. One of the almost cliched phrases about writing instruction is the injunction to students to "show not merely tell" while they are writing. The same "rule" should also apply to instruction about the writing process. I believe I project greater sincerity and have a greater impact on students if I "show" how a technique works for me rather than merely "telling" students what they should do.

In-class practice sessions should be repeated later in the course. These "refresher" sessions can focus on what is and isn't working in the students' own groups. These latter sessions will be done from a position of knowledge which makes them extremely valuable to students.

Forming Peer-Response Groups

How many people should peer-response groups have, and how should their composition be determined? Trial and error has taught me that four people is probably the best size for a group. Assuming a fifty-five- to sixty-minute class period, an efficient peer group can provide useful feedback on four papers. Also, a four-member group seems to facilitate discussion of the paper. If a group gets too large, some students may be left out of the discussion, or a teacher may have to institute some "rule" to ensure equal participation opportunities. Neither alternative is desirable. On the other hand, if a group is too small, students do not get sufficiently diversified responses to their papers, thus limiting the value of peer response.

The membership of peer-response groups can be determined in a wide variety of ways, ranging from random assignment to balancing groups so all of the best or all of the poorest writers do not end up together. Since rapport contributes to the effectiveness of a group, I allow students the option of setting up their own peer groups; however, I tell them I will rearrange the groups if they do not function effectively. After the peer-group practice sessions, my students select their own groups if they have a preference. Students who do not express a preference are randomly assigned to groups. One suggestion I offer students prior to selecting their groups is that they probably should not be in a group with their best friends since they would likely seek their responses anyway. They will derive the most benefit by getting additional responses from students they would not normally ask to read their papers.

Periodic teacher monitoring of groups is extremely important and enables teachers to recognize problems and to try to solve them before they become critical. If problems arise that cannot be resolved, I change the composition of the groups. But using response groups is not a "miracle method" which works equally well with all students. Teachers need to understand that there may be some students who do not function well with any group. In such cases teachers have to work with those students to try to improve their group participation, but in the end they may have to be content with placing these students in groups where they do the least harm.

How often should peer groups meet, and what should they actually do?

I schedule peer groups to meet twice for each composition assignment. The first time the groups meet they focus on the global components of the composition such as the organizational pattern, additional material that may be needed, places where the paper could use emphasis or clarification, and unrelated or unnecessary material that may sidetrack the reader. These global components should be the subject of the first session because problems at the sentence and word level may change or disappear as the writers make large structural or conceptual changes during the revising process. To keep the focus on these larger components of a composition rather than on more limited items, I suggest that students read their papers to each other rather than exchange written drafts. However, I strongly recommend that students take notes during the discussion of their papers so they will not forget the advice they receive from their peer group. When students revise their drafts, they decide which advice has merit and which advice doesn't match their goals for the composition.

For the second peer session I require students to exchange drafts because the focus of this session should be on the word, sentence, or paragraph level, for example, sentence variety, word choice, punctuation, and the like. I also encourage students to provide copies of their papers to other group members prior to the day of the response group meeting. This practice allows other members of the group to provide a studied response rather than being restricted to a first impression.

Although I would like to devote more time to response groups, the time available in my composition course prevents it. However, my students are encouraged to convene their groups outside of class when and if they feel the need. As the course progresses and students learn the benefits of peer response, groups meet more frequently on their own, or at least individuals exchange drafts of their compositions outside of class. I even see students going outside of their own group for additional feedback--probably the major testimonial to the value they place on peer feedback. Success with their first papers makes students believers in the technique.

Where does the teacher fit into the writing process once students learn the importance of peer response? First, teachers sit in on group sessions to determine how efficiently the groups are operating. During those observations teachers can expect to be asked for advice about the draft under consideration by the group. In these situations I attempt to act as any other member of the group, giving my frank response to the draft but consciously resisting the temptation to take over the group. A second way teachers can participate is by making individual conference time available for students who request it. In other words, the use of response groups does not preclude teacher input, but it does change the nature of the input. Rather than the teacher determining when and what input is necessary, students determine when they need such input and what specific help they require. Sometimes students request a great deal of help with a particular assignment; at other times they feel quite content to proceed on their own with little or no teacher assistance. I consciously strive to become only one source of advice about how to write a composition, rather than trying to be a "writing seer" who knows all and tells all about how to complete the assignment. This approach to composition closely resembles the way students will have to handle writing outside of school.

Prior to having students write a first draft, I have them study effective models, usually strong papers written by students during the previous year, but sometimes I also use professionally written examples. We then spend class time discussing the unique qualities of the types of writing students will be expected to do, as well as trying to reach a consensus about what makes the models effective. When students discuss what makes a piece of writing effective, they have a better understanding of how to write a composition of their own which incorporates those priorities. The discussion of quality papers can also lead to teacher and/or student-generated guide sheets which can be used both by the response groups in suggesting revisions of works-in-progress and by the teacher in evaluating final compositions.

What are the qualities of successful response groups?

My observation of and participation in peer-response groups leads me to believe that success requires the following conditions:

1. *Tolerating and respecting other members in the group.* Good response-group members recognize that although all compositions need to be comprehensible to other people, not all papers have to be written in the same way and for the same purpose. "Variety is the spice of life" may be a cliche, but it is a cliche containing more than a kernel of truth when applied to writing. Students should also recognize that not all members of their group will be of equal value to them at the same point in the writing process, but by the time they have "finished" their papers, all group members will have been of some value to them. The diversity of skills available within the group is one of the major assets of peer response. Some people ask effective questions about the content and purpose of the composition which may help writers clarify their meaning. Other people are more effective at suggesting alternative wording or phrasing both to clarify meaning and to avoid repetitious patterns. Finally, some people are most comfortable dealing with spelling, punctuation, and other components of final editing. In short, relying on one person for response limits the value of the technique.

2. *Working outside of class.* If students have revised their drafts to the best of their own ability prior to meeting with the group, the group will be able to devote its time to what the writers could not accomplish on their own. In addition, writers will have an incentive for seeking the response of others, either to find out how well their own revisions have worked or to seek better alternatives than they have been able to generate on their own. By contrast, students defeat the purpose of response-group meetings if they come to their sessions unprepared or poorly prepared. The group cannot respond well to a rough draft of a composition if it is so rough that peers cannot follow it. This observation may seem obvious, but as most experienced teachers know, common sense is not always common in the classroom, so it is probably a good idea to make the point about preparation with students while discussing effective peer response.

3. *Focusing the group response.* Writers should think about what kind of assistance they are seeking from the group. As they draft their papers, I recommend that students write reminders for

themselves about the nature of the advice they need, so they will not forget to ask about those items during their group sessions. Indicating the assistance they need increases the likelihood that the responses writers receive will be functional and on target. Otherwise, students may get "shotgun" responses, random responses which might help them revise, but which more often than not seem to miss the very areas where the writers need help. This approach also helps to make clear that the final responsibility for the assignment lies with the writer, not with the group. Group members advise, but writers have to decide which advice to follow, particularly since they may get conflicting advice. A side benefit of this procedure is that while they are constructing questions to focus the attention of their group, writers sometimes see options for revising they did not recognize while they were concentrating on the print copy of their paper.

4. *Presenting alternatives, not ultimatums*. The phrasing of suggestions for revision is as important as the nature of the comments. The key point for students to remember is that they are making *suggestions*. Presenting alternatives for revision makes clear to writers that group members want to help them improve their papers while at the same time allowing the writers to maintain ownership of their compositions, an important consideration if students are going to improve as writers. Presenting ultimatums about ways to revise accomplishes the reverse. Self-assured writers resent the way they are treated by the group and tend to ignore advice, good or bad, that they receive. For less confident writers, the consequences can be even worse. Even if they produce a strong final paper, they have no real sense of ownership of what they have produced. A more likely occurrence, however, is that their final draft will lack a consistent voice or point of view because they tried to incorporate all the advice they received without exercising any judgment about its value or the way it conformed to their intentions in composing the paper. In the end, these less-confident writers will have received reinforcement for their belief that they do not write well nor will they ever be able to write well.

5. *Indicating both strengths and areas where revision is needed*. Students do not always know, or at least they are not always sure, what is most effective in their own papers. Sometimes writers can be too close to their own compositions. Fresh ideas and phrasing do not always seem original because the writer has worked with those items over a period of time. Reading a draft supportively by focusing on its strengths also provides the writer with an incentive for revising. The time spent clarifying and polishing seems worthwhile if the writer believes the paper contains material someone else wants or needs to know. A good guideline for peer responders is to attempt to apply the biblical golden rule, "Do unto others as you would have them do unto you," when discussing the draft of someone's composition.

I encourage groups to set as a goal producing the four best papers in the class, not just one good paper. As one student said in her evaluation of my composition course this year, "When someone in my group got an A on a paper, I also felt like I had received an A." Although that ideal goal of producing the four best papers is not always attainable, how will students and, for that matter, their teachers know if it can be reached unless students try to accomplish it? Trying sometimes leads to pleasant surprises. A more realistic group goal should be to produce four papers which are all better than what individual writers could have produced on their own. That goal is within the capabilities of all students.

One of the purposes of a composition course should be to make students more confident and more independent writers. Peer-response groups help accomplish this purpose. In addition, good responders tend to become better writers. For most students, as their ability as responders improves, their ability to revise their own compositions also improves because they have a better sense of how to approach the task.

However, teachers should not expect all members of response groups to gain the same benefits from the experience. Teachers need to tolerate some partial failures even though they may have worked extensively with individuals trying to improve their performance. The important point to keep in mind is not to junk the technique because it does not work well with all students. Also, teachers may not experience as much success with peer response groups as they wish the first time they try them. My own experience is a good case in point. Experience and modification of the technique to fit the individual personalities of teacher and students are necessary for success with peer-response groups, just as with almost every other effective teaching technique. However, teachers who devote time and effort to instruction in the use of response groups will be rewarded when students write better papers, feel more confident about their writing skills, and view writing as a positive experience rather than one to be avoided.

RESEARCH AS A SOCIAL ACT

Patricia Bizzell and Bruce Herzberg[8]

"Research" can be defined in several ways. First, it may mean discovery, as in the discovery of new information about the world by a researcher. We often call this work "original" research and think of the researcher as a solitary genius, alone in a study or, more likely, a laboratory. Second, "research" may mean the recovery from secondary sources of the information discovered by others. This is often the way we think of student research: students go to the library to extract information from books for a research paper. These two definitions call for some examination.

The first kind of research——discovery——seems more valuable than the second kind—recovery. Discovery adds to the world's knowledge, while recovery adds only to an individual's knowledge (some might add, "if we're lucky"). No matter how we protest that both kinds of research are valuable, there is a distinctly secondary quality to recovery. After all, recovery is dependent entirely upon discovery, original research, for its materials. Discovery actually creates new knowledge, while recovery merely reports on the results of the work of those solitary geniuses.

Common sense tells us that students, with rare exceptions, do not do original research until graduate school, if then. Students and teachers quite naturally share the feeling that research in school is, thus, mere recovery. Consequently, students and teachers often conclude that students are not likely to produce anything very good when they do this kind of research. Indeed, one cannot be doing anything very good while piling up the required number of facts discovered by others. Research-as-recovery seems to justify writing a paper by copying others' accounts of what they have discovered.

If we try, however, to remedy the defects of the research-as-recovery paper by calling for actual discovery, we run into more problems. Those who hope to do original research must know, before anything else, where gaps exist in current knowledge. And, of course, knowing where the holes are requires knowing where they are not. For most (perhaps all) students, this takes us back to research-as-recovery, that plodding effort to find out some of what others have already figured out.

Even research that evaluates sources of information, relates the accounts of information to one another, frames an argument that ties them together, and either reveals something important about the sources themselves or develops into a new contribution on the same topic requires, like discovery, a grasp of a field of knowledge that students cannot be expected to have.

The problem with both kinds of research, then, hinges on knowledge itself. The popular image of the solitary researcher in the lab or the library does not hint at the problem of knowledge-—that these people are workers in knowledge who need knowledge as a prerequisite to their work.

[8]From Patricia Bizzell and Bruce Herzberg, The Clearing House 60 (March 1987): 303-306.

According to the popular image, they simply find facts. If that were all, presumably anyone could find them. But we know that is hardly the case. What successful researchers possess that our students typically do not is knowledge, the shared body of knowledge that helps scholars define research projects and employ methods to pursue them. Invariably, researchers use the work of others in their field to develop such projects and consult others in the field to determine what projects will be of value. In short, all real research takes place and can only take place within a community of scholars. Research is a social act. Research is always collaborative, even if only one name appears on the final report.

This, then, is the third definition of research: a social, collaborative act that draws on and contributes to the work of a community that cares about a given body of knowledge. This definition is also a critique of the popular images that we have been examining. For, by the social definition of research, the solitary researcher is not at all solitary: the sense of what can and should be done is derived from the knowledge community. The researcher must be in constant, close communication with other researchers and will likely share preliminary results with colleagues and use their suggestions in further work. Her or his contributions will be extensions of work already done and will create new gaps that other researchers will try to close. Finally, his/her work of discovery is impossible without continuous recovery of the work of others in the community.

The social definition also allows us to revise the notion of research-as-recovery, for the recoverer in a community of knowledge is not merely rehashing old knowledge or informing himself/herself about a randomly chosen topic—he/she is interpreting and reinterpreting the community's knowledge in light of new needs and perspectives, and in so doing creating and disseminating new knowledge. The activity of interpretation reveals what the community values and where the gaps in knowledge reside. "Study knows that which yet it doth not know," as Shakespeare recognized long ago.

In many fields, the activities of synthesis and interpretation are primary forms of research. Think, for example, of the fields of history, philosophy, art and literary criticism, even sociology, economics, and psychology. But the important point is that no field of knowledge can do without such work. Clearly, the lab-science image of research is inaccurate, unrepresentative, and unhelpful. Research as a social act makes far more sense

This new definition of research changes what it means for students to do research in school. In what ways do students participate in knowledge communities? One well-known and successful research assignment—the family history—suggests that in this very real community, student researchers find material to be interpreted, contradictions to be resolved, assertions to be supported, and gaps to be filled. They share the information and interpretations with the rest of the community, the family, who do not possess such a synthesis and are grateful to get it. But how do students fit into academic knowledge communities that are so much larger and colder than the family?

First, we must recognize that secondary and middle level students are novices, slowly learning the matter and method of school subjects. But they need not master the knowledge of the experts in order to participate in the sub-community of novices. They will need to know what other students know and do not know about a subject that they are all relatively uninformed about. In other words, they need to have a sense of what constitutes the shared body of knowledge of their community and a sense of the possible ways to increase that knowledge by useful increments. Imagine the classroom as a neighborhood in the larger academic community. Students contributing to the knowledge of the class are engaged in research in much the same way that expert researchers contribute to the larger community. They find out what is known—the first step in research—and identify what is unknown by sharing their knowledge amongst themselves. Then, by filling in the gaps and sharing what they find, they educate the whole community.

There are several practical implications for re-imagining research in this way:

1. The whole class must work in the same area of inquiry—not the same topic, but different aspects of the same central issue. A well-defined historical period might do: by investigating work, play, social structure, literature, politics, clothing styles, food, and so on, students would become local experts contributing to a larger picture of the period. We will look at other examples later.

2. Students will need some common knowledge, a shared text or set of materials and, most of all, the opportunity to share with each other what they may already know about the subject. By collaborating on a questionnaire or interviewing each other, students learn valuable ways of doing primary research.

3. They will need to ask questions, critically examine the shared knowledge, and perhaps do some preliminary investigation to determine what the most tantalizing unknowns may be. Here again, some free exchange among class members will be helpful.

4. The exchange of ideas must continue through the process of discovery. Like expert researchers, students need to present working papers or colloquia to the research community, distribute drafts and respond to feedback, and contribute to the work of others when they are able. Finally, their work must be disseminated, published in some way, and made available to the group. The early framework of the research community ought not to be reduced to a way to introduce the regular old term paper.

A perfectly good way to choose the general area of research for a class is simply to choose it yourself. Teachers represent the larger community and can be expected to know something about the topic at hand and provide guidance, so if the topic interests the teacher, all the better. Of course, the teacher can lean toward topics that may interest the class. Students may be asked to choose from among several possibilities suggested by the teacher, but it is likely to be needlessly daunting to the students to leave the whole selection process to them. Among the possibilities for class topics: utopia, Shakespeare's England, Franklin's America, the jazz age, the death of the dinosaurs, the year you were born, images of childhood, the idea of school, work, and play; wealth and poverty, country and city, quests and heroes, creativity—it's easy to go on and on.

Central texts can be books, photocopied selections, a film, or videotapes. More's Utopia might work for some classes, but a utopian science fiction book might be better for others, and the description of the Garden of Eden, a well-known utopia is only three pages long. Shakespeare plays are easy to come by, as is Franklin's *Autobiography* or selections from it. Not every topic will require such materials, of course. For some topics, the students' interviews or other initial responses might be compiled into the central text.

The shared knowledge of the group might be elicited through alternate writing and discussion sessions, the students answering questions like "what do you know about x?" or "what would you like to know about x?" Interviews and questionnaires also work, as noted. All of this preliminary reading, writing, and discussion will help to create a sense of community and give students a jump-start on writing for the group, rather than for the teacher. Needless to say, the teacher ought not to grade and need not even read such preliminary work, beyond requiring that it be done.

Identifying a gap in the group's knowledge and choosing a topic for individual research may still be difficult, and it helps to be armed with suggestions if the students run out of ideas or need to be focused. Have a list of questions about utopias, a list of attempted utopian communities, the names of prominent figures in the period under discussion, some key ideas or events or issues to pursue, and so on. Students may not see, in the central text, problems like class differences in opportunities for schooling, or assumptions about the place of women, or attitudes linked to local or historical circumstances. If discussion and preliminary research do not turn them up, the teacher can reasonably help out. We need not pretend that we are inventing a new field of inquiry, but we must beware of the temptation to fall back on assigned topics.

Having students share drafts and give interim reports takes time, but it is usually time well spent. Students can learn to provide useful feedback to other students on drafts of papers--teachers should not read every draft. Students acting as draft-readers can respond to set questions (what did you find most interesting? what do you want to learn more about?) or work as temporary collaborators in attacking problem areas or listen to drafts read aloud and give oral responses. Other kinds of sharing may be worthwhile. Annotated bibliographies might be compiled and posted so that resources can be shared. Groups might lead panel discussions to take the edge off formal oral presentations. Reading aloud and oral reporting are good ways, too, of setting milestones for writing, and public presentation is important for maintaining the sense of community. Oral reports, by the way, tend to be better as drafts than as final presentations——the feedback is useful then, and anxiety about the performance is muted. Publishing the final results is the last step——copies of the papers might be compiled with a table of contents in a ring binder and put on reserve in the school library, for example.

These activities do not eliminate problems of footnote form and plagiarism, but in the setting of a research community, the issues of footnoting and plagiarism can be seen in a fresh light. Students should be able to articulate for themselves the reasons why members of a community would want to enforce among themselves (and their novices) a common and consistent method of citation. When knowledge exists to be exchanged, footnotes facilitate exchange. So too with plagiarism: members of the community would love to see themselves quoted and footnoted, but not robbed.

An excellent way to teach citation and reinforce community cohesion is to ask students to cite each other. How do you cite another student's paper, especially in draft form? How do you cite an oral report? How do you thank someone for putting you onto an idea? These citation forms may be used rarely, but they are good ways to stir up interest in the need for and uses of footnotes.

If the students are discovering the process of drafting, peer-review, and interim reports for the first time, the problems of discussing work-in-progress may come up in that context. Many students have learned that it is wrong to look at someone else's paper and will just be learning about the way professionals share and help each other with their work. A good place to see how collaboration works is to look at the pages of acknowledgments in books. Students will find, in all of their textbooks, long lists of people who are acknowledged for help in the process of writing. Writing their own acknowledgments will allow students to talk about how their ideas were shaped by others, especially by those who cannot reasonably be footnoted.

If the social act of research is successful, students have the opportunity to learn that knowledge is not just found, but created out of existing knowledge. And if people create knowledge, it is reasonable to expect knowledge to change. What people regard as true may be something other than absolute fact. Indeed, it may be only a temporary formulation in the search for better understanding. We can hope that our students will develop ways to evaluate knowledge as a social phenomenon and progress toward a critical consciousness of all claims to knowledge.

REVISION STRATEGIES OF STUDENT WRITERS
AND EXPERIENCED ADULT WRITERS

Nancy Sommers[9]

Although various aspects of the writing process have been studied extensively of late, research on revision has been notably absent. The reason for this, I suspect, is that current models of the writing process have directed attention away from revision. With few exceptions, these models are linear; they separate the writing process into discrete stages. Two representative models are Gordon Rohman's suggestion that the composing process moves from prewriting to writing to rewriting and James Britton's model of the writing process as a series of stages described in metaphors of linear growth, conception-incubation-production.[1] What is striking about these theories of writing is that they model themselves on speech: Rohman defines the writer in a way that cannot distinguish him from a speaker ("A writer is a man who . . . puts his experience into words in his own mind"--p. 15); and Britton bases his theory of writing on what he calls (following Jakobson) the "expressiveness" of speech.[2] Moreover, Britton's study itself follows the "linear model" of the relation of thought and language in speech proposed by Vygotsky, a relationship embodied in the linear movement "from the motive which engenders a thought to the shaping of the thought, *first* in inner speech, *then* in meanings of words, and *finally* in words" (quoted in Britton, p. 40). What this movement fails to take into account in its linear structure--"first . . . then . . . finally"--is the recursive shaping of thought by language; what it fails to take into account is *revision*. In these linear conceptions of the writing process revision is understood as a separate stage at the end of the process--a stage that comes after the completion of a first or second draft and one that is temporally distinct from the prewriting and writing stages of the process.[3]

The linear model bases itself on speech in two specific ways. First of all, it is based on traditional rhetorical models, models that were created to serve the spoken art of oratory. In whatever ways the parts of classical rhetoric are described, they offer "stages" of composition that are repeated in contemporary models of the writing process. Edward Corbett, for instance, describes the "five parts of a discourse"--*inventio, dispositio, elocutio, memoria, pronuntiatio*--and, disregarding the last two parts since "after rhetoric came to be concerned mainly with written discourse, there was no further need to deal with them,"[4] he produces a model very close to Britton's conception *[inventio]*, incubation *[dispositio]*, production *[elocutio]*. Other rhetorics also follow this procedure. and they do so not simply because of historical accident. Rather, the process represented in the linear model is based on the irreversibility of speech. Speech, Roland Barthes says, "is irreversible":

"A word cannot be retracted, except precisely by saying that one retracts it. To cross out here is to add: if I want to erase what I have just said, I cannot do it without showing the

---

[9]From *College Composition and Communication* 31 (December 1980): 378-88.

eraser itself (I must say: *'or rather . . .' 'I expressed myself badly . . .'*); paradoxically, it is ephemeral speech which is indelible, not monumental writing. All that one can do in the case of a spoken utterance is to tack on another utterance."[5]

What is impossible in speech is *revision:* like the example Barthes gives, revision in speech is an afterthought. In the same way, each stage of the linear model must be exclusive (distinct from the other stages) or else it becomes trivial and counterproductive to refer to these junctures as "stages."

By staging revision after enunciation, the linear models reduce revision in writing, as in speech, to no more than an afterthought. In this way such models make the study of revision impossible. Revision, in Rohman's model, is simply the repetition of writing: or to pursue Britton's organic metaphor, revision is simply the further growth of what is already there, the "pre-conceived" product. The absence of research on revision, then, is a function of a theory of writing which makes revision both superfluous and redundant, a theory which does not distinguish between writing and speech.

What the linear models do produce is a parody of writing. Isolating revision and then disregarding it plays havoc with the experiences composition teachers have of the actual writing and rewriting of experienced writers. Why should the linear model be preferred? Why should revision be forgotten, superfluous? Why do teachers offer the linear model and students accept it? One reason, Barthes suggests, is that "there is a fundamental tie between teaching and speech," while "writing begins at the point where speech becomes impossible.[6] The spoken word cannot be revised. The possibility of revision distinguishes the written text from speech. In fact, according to Barthes, this is the essential difference between writing and speaking. When we must revise, when the very idea is subject to recursive shaping by language, then speech becomes inadequate. This is a matter to which I will return, but first we should examine, theoretically, a detailed exploration of what student writers as distinguished from experienced adult writers *do* when they write and rewrite their work. Dissatisfied with both the linear model of writing and the lack of attention to the process of revision, I conducted a series of studies over the past three years which examined the revision processes of student writers and experienced writers to see what role revision played in their writing processes. In the course of my work the revision process was redefined as *a sequence of changes in a composition--changes which are initiated by cues and occur continually throughout the writing of a work.*

Methodology

I used a case study approach. The student writers were twenty freshmen at Boston University and the University of Oklahoma with SAT verbal scores ranging from 450-600 in their first semester of composition. The twenty experienced adult writers from Boston and Oklahoma City included journalists, editors, and academics. To refer to the two groups, I use the terms *student writers* and *experienced writers* because the principal difference between these two groups is the amount of experience they have had in writing.

Each writer wrote three essays, expressive, explanatory, and persuasive, and rewrote each essay twice, producing nine written products in draft and final form. Each writer was interviewed three times after the final revision of each essay. And each writer suggested revisions for a composition written by an anonymous author. Thus extensive written and spoken documents were obtained from each writer.

The essays were analyzed by counting and categorizing the changes made. Four revision operations were identified: deletion, substitution, addition, and reordering. And four levels of changes were identified--word, phrase, sentence, theme (the extended statement of one idea). A coding system was developed for identifying the frequency of revision by level and operation. In addition, transcripts of the interviews in which the writers interpreted their revisions were used to develop what was called a scale of concerns for each writer. This scale enabled me to codify what were the writer's primary concerns, secondary concerns, tertiary concerns, and whether the writers used the same scale of concerns when revising the second or third drafts as they used in revising the first draft.

Revision Strategies of Student Writers

Most of the students I studied did not use the terms *revision* or *rewriting*. In fact, they did not seem comfortable using the word *revision* and explained that revision was not a word they used, but the word their teachers used. Instead, most of the students had developed various functional terms to describe the type of changes they made. The following are samples of these definitions:

Scratch Out and Do Over Again: "I say scratch out and do over, and that means what it says. Scratching out and cutting out. I read what I have written and I cross out a word and put another word in; a more decent word or a better word. Then if there is somewhere to use a sentence that I have crossed out, I will put it there."

Reviewing: "Reviewing means just using better words and eliminating words that are not needed. I go over and change words around."

Reviewing: "I just review every word and make sure that everything is worded right. I see if I am rambling; I see if I can put a better word in or leave one out. Usually when I read what I have written, I say to myself, 'that word is so bland or so trite,' and then I go and get my thesaurus."

Redoing: "Redoing means cleaning up the paper and crossing out. It is looking at something and saying, no that has to go, or no, that is not right."

Marking Out: "I don't use the word rewriting because I only write one draft and the changes that I make are made on top of the draft. The changes that I make are usually just marking out words and putting different ones in."

Slashing and Throwing Out: I throw things out and say they are not good. I like to write like Fitzgerald did by inspiration, and if I feel inspired then I don't need to slash and throw much out."

The predominant concern in these definitions is vocabulary. The students understand the revision process as a rewording activity. They do so because they perceive words as the unit of written discourse. That is, they concentrate on particular words apart from their role in the text. Thus one student quoted above thinks in terms of dictionaries, and, following the eighteenth century theory of words parodied in *Gulliver's Travels,* he imagines a load of things carried about to be exchanged. Lexical changes are the major revision activities of the students because economy is their goal. They are governed, like the linear model itself, by the Law of Occam's razor that prohibits logically needless repetition: redundancy and superfluity. Nothing governs speech more than such superfluities; speech constantly repeats itself precisely because spoken words, as Barthes writes, are expendable in the cause of communication. The aim of revision according to the students' own description is therefore to clean up speech; the redundancy of speech is unnecessary in writing, their logic suggests, because writing, unlike speech, can be reread. Thus one student said, "Redoing means cleaning up the paper and crossing out." The remarkable contradiction of cleaning by marking might, indeed, stand for student revision as I have encountered it.

The students place a symbolic importance on their selection and rejection of words as the determiners of success or failure for their compositions. When revising, they primarily ask themselves: can I find a better word or phrase? A more impressive, not so cliched, or less hum-drum word? Am I repeating the same word or phrase too often? They approach the revision process with what could be labeled as a "thesaurus philosophy of writing"; the students consider the thesaurus a harvest of lexical substitutions and believe that most problems in their essays can be solved by rewording. What is revealed in the students' use of the thesaurus is a governing attitude toward their writing: that the meaning to be communicated is already there, already finished, already produced, ready to be communicated, and all that is necessary is a better word "rightly worded." One student defined revision as "redoing"; "redoing" meant "just using better words and eliminating words that are not needed." For the students, writing is translating: the thought to the page, the language of speech to the more formal language of prose, the word to its synonym. Whatever is translated, an original text already exists for students, one which need not be discovered or acted upon, but simply communicated.[7]

The students list repetition as one of the elements they most worry about. This cue signals to them that they need to eliminate the repetition either by substituting or deleting words or phrases. Repetition occurs, in large part, because student writing imitates--transcribes--speech: attention to repetitious words is a manner of cleaning speech. Without a sense of the developmental possibilities of revision (and writing in general) students seek, on the authority of many textbooks, simply to clean up their language and prepare to type. What is curious, however, is that students are aware of lexical repetition, but not conceptual--repetition. They only notice the repetition if they can "hear" it; they do not diagnose lexical repetition as symptomatic of problems on a deeper level. By rewording their sentences to avoid the lexical repetition, the students solve the immediate problem, but blind themselves to problems on a textual level; although they are using different words, they are sometimes merely restating the same idea with different words. Such blindness, as I discovered with student writers, is the inability to "see" revision as a process; the inability to "re-view" their work again, as it were, with different eyes, and to start over.

The revision strategies described above are consistent with the students' understanding of the revision process as requiring lexical changes but not semantic changes. For the students, the extent to which they revise is a function of their level of inspiration. In fact, they use the word *inspiration* to describe the ease or difficulty with which their essay is written, and the extent to which the essay needs to be revised. If students feel inspired, if the writing comes easily, and if they don't get stuck on individual words or phrases, then they say that they cannot see any reason to revise. Because students do not see revision as an activity in which they modify and develop perspectives and ideas, they feel that if they know what they want to say, then there is little reason for making revisions.

The only modification of ideas in the students' essays occurred when they tried out two or three introductory paragraphs. This results, in part, because the students have been taught in another version of the linear model of composing to use a thesis statement as a controlling device in their introductory paragraphs. Since they write their introductions and their thesis statements even before they have really discovered what they want to say, their early close attention to the thesis statement, and more generally the linear model, function to restrict and circumscribe not only the development of their ideas, but also their ability to change the direction of these ideas.

Too often as composition teachers we conclude that students do not willingly revise. The evidence from my research suggests that it is not that students are unwilling to revise, but rather that they do what they have been taught to do in a consistently narrow and predictable way. On every occasion when I asked students why they hadn't made any more changes, they essentially replied, "I knew something larger was wrong, but I didn't think it would help to move words around." The students have strategies for handling words and phrases and their strategies helped them on a word or sentence level. What they lack, however, is a set of strategies to help them identify the "something larger" that they sensed was wrong and work from there. The students do not have strategies for handling the whole essay. They lack procedures or heuristics to help them reorder lines of reasoning or ask questions about their purposes and readers. The students view their compositions in a linear way as a series of parts. Even such potentially useful concepts as "unity" or "form" are reduced to the rule that a composition, if it is to have form, must have an introduction, a body, and a conclusion, or the sum total of the necessary parts.

The students decide to stop revising when they decide that they have not violated any of the rules for revising. These rules, such as "Never begin a sentence with a conjunction" or "Never end a sentence with a preposition," are lexically cued and rigidly applied. In general, students will subordinate the demands of the specific problems of their text to the demands of the rules. Changes are made in compliance with abstract rules about the product, rules that quite often do not apply to the specific problems in the text. These revision strategies are teacher-based, directed towards a teacher-reader who expects compliance with rules--with pre-existing "conceptions"--and who will only examine parts of the composition (writing comments about those parts in the margins of their essays) and will cite any violations of rules in those parts. At best the students see their writing altogether passively through the eyes of former teachers or their surrogates, the textbooks, and are bound to the rules which they have been taught.

Revision Strategies of Experienced Writers

One aim of my research has been to contrast how student writers define revision with how a group of experienced writers define their revision processes. Here is a sampling of the definitions from the experienced writers:

Rewriting: "It is a matter of looking at the kernel of what I have written, the content, and then thinking about it, responding to it, making decisions, and actually restructuring it."

Rewriting: "I rewrite as I write. It is hard to tell what is a first draft because it is not determined by time. In one draft, I might cross out three pages, write two, cross out a fourth, rewrite it, and call it a draft. I am constantly writing and rewriting. I can only conceptualize so much in my first draft-- only so much information can be held in my head at one time; my rewriting efforts are a reflection of how much information I can encompass at one time. There are levels and agenda which I have to attend to in each draft."

Rewriting: "Rewriting means on one level, finding the argument, and on another level, language changes to make the argument more effective. Most of the time I feel as if I can go on rewriting forever. There is always one part of a piece that I could keep working on. It is always difficult to know at what point to abandon a piece of writing. I like this idea that a piece of writing is never finished, just abandoned."

Rewriting: "My first draft is usually very scattered. In rewriting, I find the line of argument. After the argument is resolved, I am much more interested in word choice and phrasing."

Revision: "My cardinal rule in revising is never to fall in love with what I have written in a first or second draft. An idea, sentence, or even a phrase that looks catchy, I don't trust. Part of this idea is to wait a while. I am much more in love with something after I have written it than I am a day or two later. It is much easier to change anything with time."

Revising: "It means taking apart what I have written and putting it back together again. I ask major theoretical questions of my ideas, respond to those questions, and think of proportion and structure, and try to find a controlling metaphor. I find out which ideas can be developed and which should be dropped. I am constantly chiseling and changing as I revise."

The experienced writers describe their primary objective when revising as finding the form or shape of their argument. Although the metaphors vary, the experienced writers often use structural expressions such as "finding a framework," "a pattern," or "a design" for their argument. When questioned about this emphasis, the experienced writers responded that since their first drafts are usually scattered attempts to define their territory, their objective in the second draft is to begin observing general patterns of development and deciding what should be included and what excluded. One writer explained, "I have learned from experience that I need to keep writing a first draft until I figure out what I want to say. Then in a second draft, I begin to see the structure of an argument and how all the various sub-arguments which are buried beneath the surface of all those sentences are related." What is described here is a process in which the writer is both agent and vehicle. "Writing," says Barthes, unlike speech, "develops like a seed, not a line,[8] and like a seed it confuses beginning and end, conception and production." Thus, the experienced writers say their drafts are "not determined by time," that rewriting is a "constant process," that they feel as if (they) "can go on forever." Revising confuses the beginning and end, the agent and vehicle; it confuses, *in order to find,* the line of argument.

After a concern for form, the experienced writers have a second objective: a concern for their readership. In this way, "production" precedes "conception." The experienced writers imagine a reader (reading their product) whose existence and whose expectations influence their revision process. They have abstracted the standards of a reader and this reader seems to be partially a reflection of themselves and functions as a critical and productive collaborator--a collaborator who has yet to love their work. The anticipation of a reader's judgment causes a feeling of dissonance when the writer recognizes incongruities between intention and execution, and requires these writers to make revisions on all levels. Such a reader gives them just what the students lacked: new eyes to "re-view" their work. The experienced writers believe that they have learned the causes and conditions, the product, which will influence their reader, and their revision strategies are geared towards creating these causes and conditions. They demonstrate a complex understanding of which examples, sentences, or phrases should be included or excluded. For example, one experienced writer decided to delete public examples and add private examples when writing about the energy crisis because "private examples would be less controversial and thus more persuasive." Another writer revised his transitional sentences because "some kinds of transitions are more easily recognized as transitions than others." These examples represent the type of strategic attempts these experienced writers use to manipulate the conventions of discourse in order to communicate to their reader.

But these revision strategies are a process of more than communication; they are part of the process of *discovering meaning altogether*. Here we can see the importance of dissonance; at the heart of revision is the process by which writers recognize and resolve the dissonance they sense in their writing. Ferdinand de Saussure has argued that meaning is differential or "diacritical," based on differences between terms rather than "essential" or inherent qualities of terms. "Phonemes," he said, "are characterized not, as one might think, by their own positive quality but simply by the fact that they are distinct."[9] In fact, Saussure bases his entire *Course in General Linguistics* on these differences, and such differences are dissonant; like musical dissonances which gain their significance from their relationship to the "key" of the composition which itself is determined by the whole language, specific language (parole) gains its meaning from the system of language (langue) of which it is a manifestation and part. The musical composition--a "composition" of parts--creates its "key" as in an over-all structure which determines the value (meaning) of its parts. The analogy with music is readily seen in the compositions of experienced writers: both sorts of composition are based precisely on those structures experienced writers seek in their writing. It is this complicated relationship between the parts and the whole in the work of experienced writers which destroys the linear model; writing cannot develop "like a line" because each addition or deletion is a reordering of the whole. Explicating Saussure, Jonathan Culler asserts that "meaning depends on difference of meaning."[10] But student writers constantly struggle to bring their essays into congruence with a predefined meaning. The experienced writers do the opposite: they seek to discover (to create) meaning in the engagement with their writing, in revision. They seek to emphasize and exploit the lack of clarity, the differences of meaning, the dissonance, that writing as opposed to speech allows in the possibility of revision. Writing has spatial and temporal features not apparent in speech--words are recorded in space and fixed in time--which is why writing is susceptible to reordering and later addition. Such features make possible the dissonance that both provokes revision and promises, from itself, new meaning.

For the experienced writers the heaviest concentration of changes is on the sentence level, and the changes are predominantly by addition and deletion. But, unlike the students, experienced writers make changes on all levels and use all revision operations. Moreover, the operations the students fail to use--reordering and addition--seem to require a theory of the revision process as a totality--a theory which, in fact, encompasses the *whole* of the composition. Unlike the students, the experienced writers possess a nonlinear theory in which a sense of the whole writing both precedes and grows out of an examination of the parts. As we saw, one writer said he needed "a first draft to figure out what to say," and "a second draft to see the structure of an argument buried beneath the surface." Such a "theory" is both theoretical and strategical; once again, strategy and theory are conflated in ways that are literally impossible for the linear model. Writing appears to be more like a seed than a line.

Two elements of the experienced writers' theory of the revision process are the adoption of a holistic perspective and the perception that revision is a recursive process. The writers ask: what does my essay as a *whole* need for form, balance, rhythm, or communication? Details are added, dropped, substituted, or reordered according to their sense of what the essay needs for emphasis and proportion. This sense, however, is constantly in flux as ideas are developed and modified; it is constantly "re-viewed" in relation to the parts. As their ideas change, revision becomes an attempt to make their writing consonant with that changing vision.

The experienced writers see their revision process as a recursive process--a process with significant recurring activities--with different levels of attention and different agenda for each cycle. During the first revision cycle their attention is primarily directed towards narrowing the topic and delimiting their ideas. At this point, they are not as concerned as they are later about vocabulary and style. The experienced writers explained that they get closer to their meaning by not limiting themselves too early to lexical concerns. As one writer commented to explain her revision process, a comment inspired by the summer 1977 New York power failure: "I feel like Con Edison cutting off certain states to keep the generators going. In first and second drafts, I try to cut off as much as I can of my editing generator, and in a third draft, I try to cut off some of my idea generators so I can make sure that I will actually finish the essay." Although the experienced writers describe their revision process as a series of different levels or cycles, it is inaccurate to assume that they have only one objective for each cycle and that each cycle can be defined by a different objective. The same objectives and sub-processes are present in each cycle, but in different proportions. Even though these experienced writers place the predominant weight upon finding the form of their argument during the first cycle, other concerns exist as well. Conversely, during the later cycles, when the experienced writers' primary attention is focused upon stylistic concerns, they are still attuned, although in a reduced way, to the form of the argument. Since writers are limited in what they can attend to during each cycle (understandings are temporal) revision strategies help balance competing demands on attention. Thus, writers can concentrate on more than one objective at a time by developing strategies to sort out and organize their different concerns in successive cycles of revision.

It is a sense of writing as discovery--a repeated process of beginning over again, starting out new--that the students failed to have. I have used the notion of dissonance because such dissonance, the incongruities between intention and execution, governs both writing and meaning. Students do not see the incongruities. They need to rely on their own internalized sense of good writing and to see their writing with their "own" eyes. Seeing in revision--seeing beyond hearing--is at the root of the word *revision* and the process itself; current dicta on revising blind our students to what is actually involved in revision. In fact, they blind them to what constitutes good writing altogether. Good writing disturbs: it creates dissonance. Students need to seek the dissonance of discovery, utilizing in their writing, as the experienced writers do, the very difference between writing and speech--the possibility of revision.

NOTES

1. D. Gordon Rohman and Albert O. Wlecke, "Pre-writing: The Construction and Application of Models for Concept Formation in Writing," Cooperative Research Project No. 2174, U.S. Office of Education, Department of Health, Education, And Welfare; James Britton, Anthony Burgess, Nancy Martin, Alex McLeod, Harold Rosen, *The Development of Writing Abilities* (11-18) (London: Macmillan Education, 1975).

2. Britton is following Roman Jakobson, "Linguistics and Poetics," in T. A. Sebeok, *Style in Language* (Cambridge, Mass: MIT Press, 1960).

3. For an extended discussion of this issue see Nancy Sommers, "The Need for Theory in Composition Research," *College Composition and Communication* 30 (February, 1979); 46-49.

4. *Classical Rhetoric for the Modern Student* (New York: Oxford University Press, 1965), p. 27.

5. Roland Barthes, "Writers, Intellectuals, Teachers," in *Image-Music-Text*, trans. Stephen Heath (New York: Hill and Warner, 1977), pp. 190-91.

6. "Writers, Intellectuals, Teachers," p. 190.

7. Nancy Sommers and Ronald Schleifer, "Means and Ends: Some Assumptions of Student Writers," *Composition and Teaching*, II (in press).

8. *Writing Degree Zero* in *Writing Degree Zero and Elements of Semiology*, trans. Annette Lavers and Colin Smith (New York: Hill and Wang, 1968), p. 20.

9. *Course in General Linguistics*, trans. Wade Baskin (New York, 1966), p. 119.

10. Jonathan Culler, *Saussure* (Penguin Modern Masters Series: London: Penguin Books, 1976), p. 70.

MAKING ASSIGNMENTS, JUDGING WRITING, AND ANNOTATING PAPERS: SOME SUGGESTIONS

Richard L. Larson[10]

Whether or not they follow a syllabus prepared by the head of the writing program or by a departmental committee, or develop their own assignments, or do some of both, new teachers are usually responsible for three of the central acts performed by any teacher of writing: giving students their assignments (or invitations) for writing, making judgments about students' writing (whether in the form of grades, advice about revision, or summary analyses), and offering comments about students' papers. I offer here some suggestions to new teachers about how they might perform each of these acts.

Writing Assignments

Assignments not only tell the students what they are expected to write about, they define (taken as a group) the emphases and structure of the course, and signal some of the values held by the teacher. Furthermore, if the assignments are written out, they act as examples of the teacher's own writing. So the instructions should be as thoughtfully prepared and as precisely expressed as possible. A poor assignment, or a potentially good assignment poorly described, is always an invitation to weak papers from students. What follows is a list of questions that a teacher might consider for each writing assignment before distributing it. Considering these questions before giving out an assignment will not guarantee the effectiveness of the assignment, but doing so may enable the teacher to improve the assignment and to avoid common causes of weak papers.

Writing Assignments: Questions to Consider

1. Is the task the students must accomplish clearly defined? That is, can they see exactly what task they are called upon to perform in writing (e.g., to identify the traits of a literary character, to report the results of a survey or experiment, to propose a plan of action to meet a need, to elucidate some complex terminology, to explain some personal feelings about a situation)? Will they have a clear idea of what the paper they are to produce should do?

2. Have you a clear idea about what a desirable response to the assignment might look like? Should you share any features of this desirable response with the students? Are the bases for evaluation of their papers clear to students.

---

[10]From *Training the New Teacher of College Composition* ed. Charles W. Bridges. Champaign, Illinois: NCTE, 1986.

3. If appropriate, are the students given a clear idea of what steps or cognitive/conceptual activities they will need to undertake in writing the paper? If, for instance, the citation of certain kinds of data in support of a conclusion is required, can the students determine that such citations are required? (It is possible, of course, that some requirements will have been established in earlier assignments. But if such requirements have not been established, they should be made clear as the assignment under consideration is made.)

4. Can the assignment be completed with some success by students at different levels of ability? If not, is the limitation on how many students can do the assignment important?

5. Does the assignment demand of the students some exercise of judgment, some engagement with--resolution of--a problem? (Assignments that can be answered yes or no with little explanation, or that demand no more than a list of items, may present no challenge to the students and give them no practice in thinking out a response.)

6. Is it clear why students are asked to write this paper, that is, is it clear how the writing is related to the overall plan for the course?

7. Is the assignment likely to be of interest to the students? Is doing it likely to lead to some learning (some understandings, some conclusions) about the subject--to some recognitions that the students did not have before doing the assignment? Do the students, that is, stand to gain from the assignment something more than just another completed paper?

8. Does the assignment help the students envisage a credible writing situation--an honest purpose and an interested, responsive audience?

Judgments

Teachers ought not to view a piece of writing as a collection of separate parts (even if the essay impresses them as exactly that); they should view a piece of writing as a whole, as an act of communication undertaken by one human being for one or more others. That is to say, a piece of writing, or a spoken utterance, is an action taken in order to reach an audience; it should be judged as a total action. Difficulties with syntax, spelling, transitions, the shapes of paragraphs, and so on should be judged in perspective; the teacher might ask how these weaknesses or these difficulties affect the overall success of the author in completing the act of communication that he or she has attempted. As a reader, do I respond to this piece as the author evidently wished me to respond? Why or why not? The following questions may help teaching assistants to approach papers in this spirit, and to judge them accordingly.

Some Questions for Use in Judging a Piece of Writing

1. If the assignment that evoked the writing gives specific directions, does the writing carry out those directions?

2. What are the special characteristics (e.g., citation of certain kinds of information, inclusion of particular kinds of details, demonstration that the writer is aware of any special interests operating among members of the audience, and so on) that a paper must exhibit in order to complete the assigned task successfully? Does the essay have these features?

3. At or close to the beginning, is the author's purpose in the paper clear? Is it clear why the author comes before the reader at this time, on this subject? Is there a focus for the essay? Is it clear what problems, if any, the author is addressing? Is it clear what rhetorical or cognitive acts the author intends to complete during the paper?

4. During the paper, does the author make clear how all parts of the essay relate to the carrying out of his or her purpose, i.e., to the accomplishment of the "action" promised? If the author's purpose changes, is there an explanation of the change?

5. Is an overall plan for the whole essay evident? Is a plan evident within individual sections? Is the plan suitable to the author's purpose?

6. Is the essay as a whole coherent, that is, does the sequence of steps taken by the author in the essay remain clear, and can the reader follow the author's plan?

7. Is the essay correct in its facts?

8. Are the data cited adequate to the author's purpose? Are important data omitted or neglected?

9. Where data are interpreted, are the interpretations fair and reasonable?

10. Has the author taken care to explain important assumptions made during the paper?

11. Has the author recognized important implications of the data cited or inferences drawn?

12. Does the author avoid including data not related to his or her purpose?

13. Is the author's reasoning sound? If particular data are applied to generalizations in order to reach a conclusion, is the process followed sound?

14. At the end, has the author completed the action he or she promised? Has the author accomplished the essay's purpose? Has he or she solved (or offered a reasonable proposed solution to) the problem raised at the start?

15. Does the author's conclusion build upon, and take account of, data and reasoning in the body of the paper?

16. Is the style reasonably clear, free of distracting errors in punctuation and of syntactic features that complicate reading?

17. Does the author earn the reader's respect for his or her views?

Comments

New teachers are almost always responsible for commenting on or annotating students' papers. Sometimes they comment orally, in conferences or even in small groups or workshops. More often, they comment in writing. What follows is a group of suggestions about making written comments (though I think the same suggestions would apply to comments made in a conference, small group, or workshop). Following these suggestions, of course, will not ensure that the teacher's comments are incisive or that they highlight the same features of a paper that another teacher might highlight. But the suggestions will help teachers prepare comments that enable students to learn, and that-- perhaps as important--give students the sense that their papers have been read by thoughtful human beings who genuinely want to help them communicate their ideas more completely and effectively.

These suggestions assume that comments on students' papers should have three purposes: (1) to identify the paper's strong points as well as points in need of improvement, (2) to suggest how the student might prepare a more effective paper next time, and (3) to give the student some explanation of why the instructor reached a particular evaluation of the paper.

The suggestions also assume that an effective comment on an essay can be a powerful teaching instrument--often more influential on the student's writing than class discussions of sample papers. The comment, after all, expresses what the teacher values in writing and locates places where the student has reached those values and where the student needs to do additional work in order to reach those values. In the writing of comments, the suggestions assert, it is better to explain a criticism or proposed revision with excessive thoroughness than to offer it so sketchily that the student cannot learn from it.

Writing Comments on Students' Essays

Marginal Comments

In making marginal comments, remember that you are neither a proofreader (responsible for normalizing spelling, punctuation, and typographical style) nor an editor (responsible for improving diction, idiom, and possibly syntax) nor a judge (responsible for rendering a verdict of "good" or "bad"), but a teacher from whom students hope to get help in improving their reasoning, organization, style, and so on. If your students are to learn from what you write in the margins of their papers, your observations must be clear and self-explanatory.

1. Use marginal comments primarily to call attention to some particular strength or weakness in the paper--usually a strength or weakness of detail, or at any rate one that can be located precisely--at the point where it occurs. Usually comments that refer to the reasoning or design or style of the whole essay are better reserved for the general (final) comment.

2. Feel free to ask questions about points that the student makes, to ask for clarification, to point out (where such a comment seems appropriate) other possible views of the subject. Let the student know that you are interested in what he or she has to say to you.

3. Avoid using "?" and terse queries like "What?" or "How come?" or "So what?" If you feel that the student's reasoning is unsatisfactory (e.g., because pertinent data are omitted or because an unsound conclusion has been drawn or because the significance of an idea is not made clear), explain your judgment precisely enough to let the student know where you think his or her thinking is faulty. Do not leave the student guessing that your notation simply reveals a difference of opinion between the two of you, or believing that your opinions on the point in question are unjustifiably rigid. Better fewer marginal comments well explained than a large number of cryptic, uninformative jottings.

4. In general, avoid arguing with the student. Focus on passages in which the student might demonstrably have improved what he or she has done. If the matter on which you are tempted to comment is simply a source of disagreement between the two of you on a point where reasonable people might differ, omit the comment. Avoid asking a student to "explain" a point on which his or her reasoning is fairly obvious or self-evident. Ask for explanation only when the reasoning is in fact hidden and needs to be disclosed. Try not to quibble over matters of diction and sentence structure that reflect only differences between your taste and that of the student. Comment on style only when you can propose a visible improvement over the student's way of expressing an idea.

5. Do not hesitate to note places where the student's thinking is especially effective, his or her style especially pleasing, his or her organization notably well planned, and so on.

General (Final) Comments

The purpose of the general comments is to record your overall impression of the paper and, more important, to point out goals for the writer to seek in revising that paper or in writing his or her next paper. Most comments should not be merely judgments about the paper at hand, although, of course, some comments that analyze a paper in detail can imply constructive suggestions for revision or for the elimination of recurrent weaknesses in the student's writing. The list that follows sums up the characteristics a good general comment may have; it is not a list of items to be included in every general comment you write.

1. Unless the mechanics and syntax are hopelessly inept (sometimes, to be sure, they are), make the general comment more than a list or summary of such errors. Play down mechanical difficulties where possible.

2. Show respect for the student's paper; recognize that it is the student's work--the student's property. Try not to treat it as if the student were doing something for you. Try not to treat the paper as if the principal difficulty were that the student did not do what you wanted him or her to do or what you thought he or she ought to do. Work, if possible, from the student's perspective as well as from your own. Leave the student believing, after reading your comment, that the essay still belongs to him or her and that you are out to help the student to do better what he or she wanted to do-- or to help the student improve his or her choice of subject or perspective or emphasis so that he or she can earn the reader's respect more successfully.

3. Point out strengths or good features of the essay wherever you can, rather than focusing exclusively on weaknesses. (This suggestion does not imply, however, that you should pore over a bad paper in search of a trifling virtue on which to comment.) If the paper marks an improvement over the student's earlier work, say so and tell why you think so.

4. In part, at least, let your general comments inform the student how well he or she met the problems posed by the assignment. Deal with this point even if you plan to devote most of the comment to matters not related to the student's handling of the specific assignment.

5. Concentrate on the most important difficulties of substance, structure, and style that affect the paper as a whole. If the reason for criticism of some features of the paper is not obvious, suggest why these features are indeed weaknesses and, where possible, propose changes that would have improved the paper. Be sure that the student can see why you think he or she should have done things differently; make clear how the proposed changes would improve the paper. Such comments are especially important if you ask your students to revise their papers. Specify in the comment what the student's principal aims should be in revising.

6. Try to see that the comment is constructive--that it has "transfer value." That is, try to help students to improve their work on future papers. To achieve this purpose, search out fundamental features that may be in need of improvement: factual inaccuracies, unclear assertions, lack of coherence between sentences and paragraphs, reliance on unrecognized and undefended assumptions, excessively abstract diction, unsound generalizations or conclusions based on inadequate evidence, and so on. Describe and illustrate these features so that students will understand them and can learn to recognize them as they revise rough drafts of future papers. Call particular attention, if possible, to difficulties that recur in successive essays by the same student.

7. Let your general comment support, and be supported by, the marginal comments; the two sets of observations should work together. Often you will be able to illustrate comments on the paper by referring to difficulties pointed out in detail in marginalia. But the general comment should not be merely a disjointed summary or repetition of the marginal comments. It must bring your separate

responses to the paper into focus; it must give the student a coherent assessment of the paper as a whole.

8. Unless you have developed a special relationship with the student in which irony will not be misinterpreted, take care that your comments are not ironic, sarcastic, condescending, or inclined to belittle the student as a person. Irony can only anger students; it does not instruct them. Slangy, flippant admonitions (e.g., "Don't slit your wrists over this grade") should be avoided; a teacher should give more thoughtful and beneficial advice.

9. Focus your comment on the paper, not on the personality or motivation of its author. Even making assumptions about what led the writer to adopt a particular attitude or discuss a specific subject is usually unwise. Of course, if parts of a paper are ambiguous or if the emphasis is fuzzy, you can and should ask the writer which of two or three possible meanings he or she intended to convey, or whether you are correct in believing that the writer meant to emphasize a particular point.

Finally, one implication in point 4 above bears repeating: comments on students' papers should bear some relationship to what the student was asked to accomplish in the essay. As has been suggested earlier, it is wise to anticipate, when planning an assignment, the features that will result in success or failure in students' work and perhaps to anticipate the kinds of comments one might need to make on that work. Such advance planning may help strengthen the assignment; it may also simplify and accelerate the process of responding to students' work.

I hope that following these three sets of suggestions will help instructors work more successfully at the point where, finally, the real teaching of writing occurs: at the point where the instructor evokes and responds to students' writing. Students learn to write by writing; the teacher best fulfills his or her professional responsibility by helping to ensure that students are encouraged and guided toward their best writing.

LEARNING TO PRAISE

Donald A. Daiker[11]

In *A Moveable Feast,* Ernest Hemingway recounts his first meeting with F. Scott Fitzgerald. One night while Hemingway is sitting with friends at the Dingo Bar in Paris, Fitzgerald unexpectedly walks in, introduces himself, and proceeds to talk nonstop about Hemingway's writing, especially "how great it was." Hemingway reports that he was embarrassed by Fitzgerald's lavish compliments--not because he felt flattered by them, but because he and his fellow expatriates "still went under the system, then, that praise to the face was open disgrace" (Hemingway 1964, 150).

The distrust of praise among American writers abroad seems to have rubbed off on composition teachers at home. In a 1985 study at Texas A&M University, Sam Dragga analyzed forty freshman essays that had been graded and marked by four randomly chosen and traditionally trained teaching assistants. They wrote a total of 864 comments on the essays, but only 51 of them were comments of praise. This means that 94% of the comments focused on what students had done poorly or incorrectly, only 6% on what had been done well (Dragga 1986). The same pattern apparently prevails in high school as well. A study of responses by thirty-six secondary English teachers revealed that although 40% of their end-of-paper comments were positive, the percentage of positive marginal comments was a meager .007% (Harris 1977). The conclusion that college composition teachers find error more attractive than excellence is consistent with a pilot study of my own conducted in 1982 at Miami University (Daiker 1983). I asked twenty-four colleagues to grade and comment on "Easy Street," a student essay chosen because it combines strength with weakness in both content and style (see pp. 108). I asked my colleagues to mark the essay as if it had been submitted in their freshman composition course. They made a total of 378 separate markings or comments on the student essay: 338, or 89.4%, of them cited error or found fault; only 40, or 10.6%, of them were comments of praise. What may make the predominance of correction over commendation even more significant is that during the previous month, a departmental memorandum reported scholarly consensus on two matters of grading: (1) an instructor should not mark every writing error, because students cannot psychologically cope with a deluge of deficiencies; and (2) an instructor should use praise and positive reinforcement as a major teaching strategy.

Scholarship notwithstanding, composition teachers have traditionally withheld praise from papers they have considered less than perfect. A case in point is the well-known "Evaluating a Theme," published in the *Newsletter of the Michigan Council of Teachers of English* (Stevens 1958). The issue consists of twenty-five responses--twenty-one by college teachers, four by secondary teachers--to a single composition, and the issue's popularity carried it through sixteen

---

[11] From *Writing and Response: Theory, Practice, and Research,* ed. Chris Anson. Urbana, Illinois: NCTE, 1989.

printings. According to my figures, the proportion of criticism to praise is roughly the same as in the Texas A&M and Miami studies; the Michigan teachers identified nine errors or problems for every instance of praiseworthy writing. Just as important, fifteen of the twenty-five teachers found nothing in the paper deserving of praise. In three of those instances, college professors sufficiently skilled to ferret out thirty flaws apiece in a brief essay could not--or would not--identify a single source of strength. Their wholly negative comments reminded me of a grade appeal procedure in which I was asked to evaluate eight compositions written for a colleague's freshman English class. I read the compositions in order, paper one through paper eight, and I read them with increasing despair--not because of what the student had written, but because in responding to a semester's worth of writing, my colleague had offered not a single word of praise. Not an idea, not an example, not a sentence or clause or phrase or punctuation mark--nothing, apparently, merited a compliment. I began to wonder why the student was appealing only a grade, and I had visions of Bartleby the scrivener at work in a dead-letter office.

Francis Christensen observed a quarter century ago that there are two sharply contrasting points of view toward the teaching of English (Christensen 1962). The first he calls the "school" tradition, the second the "scholarly" tradition. The school tradition, nourished by a view of language that regards all change as decay and degeneration, encourages instructors to respond to student writing primarily by identifying and penalizing error. Because of the school tradition, it has long been common to speak of "correcting" themes. There is no clearer embodiment of the negative and narrowly conformist values of the school tradition than the popular correction chart. The 1985 "Harbrace College Handbook Correction Chart," to take a recent example of the species, provides seventy-one correction symbols for instructors to use and students to interpret. Why are correction symbols needed? Why write "d" rather than "diction," or "frag" rather than "This is not a complete sentence because it lacks a verb"? Presumably because instructors find so many errors to mark that not enough time remains for them to use whole words or complete sentences themselves. Significantly, what the correction charts never include is a symbol for approval or praise.

To become teachers of English in a "positive, joyous, creative, and responsible sense," Christensen urges us to replace the inert, rule-encumbered school tradition with more enlightened scholarly views. For several decades now, composition scholars have reported the value of praise in improving student writing. Paul B. Diederich (1963, 1974), senior research associate for the Educational Testing Service, concluded from his research in evaluation that "noticing and praising whatever a student does well improves writing more than any kind or amount of correction of what he does badly, and that it is especially important for the less able writers, who need all the encouragement they can get" (1974720). Since writing is an act of confidence, as Mina Shaughnessy reminds us (1977, 85), it is not surprising that the scholarly tradition emphasizes responding with encouragement. Ken Macrorie (1968) recommends that we "encourage and encourage, but never falsely" (688). E. D. Hirsch (1977), who believes that written comments may turn out to be "the most effective teaching device of all" (159), agrees that "the best results are likely to be produced by encouragement" (161). For William F. Irmscher, "the psychology of positive reinforcement . . . should be the major resource for every writing teacher" (1979, 150). All of these individuals would support Diederich's statement that "The art of the teacher--at its best--is the reinforcement of good things" (1963, 58).

Praise may be especially important for students who have known little encouragement and, in part for that reason, suffer from writing apprehension. Writing apprehension is a measure of anxiety established through the research of John Daly and Michael Miller (1975b). According to these researchers, the highly apprehensive writer is one for whom anxiety about writing outweighs the projection of gain from writing. Because they fear writing and its consequences, "high apprehensives" seek to avoid writing situations: they are reluctant to take courses in writing, and they choose academic majors and occupations with minimal writing requirements. When they do write, they use language that is significantly less intense than people with low writing apprehension; that is, they are more reluctant to take a stand or to commit themselves to a position. They try to play it safe not only by embracing neutrality, but by saying less: in response to the same assignment, high apprehensives write fewer words and make fewer statements than low apprehensives (Daly 1977; Daly and Miller 1975a; Daly and Shamo 1978; Holland 1980). The problem for highly apprehensive writers is circular. Because they anticipate negative consequences, they avoid writing. Yet the avoidance of writing--the lack of practice--leads to further negative consequences: writing of poor quality that receives low grades and unfavorable comments. One's attitude toward the act of writing, Daly concludes, clearly affects not only how one writes and how often one writes, but even how others evaluate that writing (Daly 1977). What may be equally important--since writing is a powerful and perhaps even unique mode of learning (Emig 1977)--is that by systematically avoiding writing situations, high apprehensives close off opportunities for learning and discovery.

But the cause of writing apprehension may suggest its cure--or at least its treatment. A major cause of writing apprehension is past failure or a perception of past failure; high apprehensives perceive their writing experiences as significantly less successful than low apprehensives. Daly says that the "highly apprehensive writer expects, due to a history of aversive responses, negative evaluations for writing attempts. This expectation likely becomes self-fulfilling" (1977, 571). These "aversive responses" include negative comments on assignments and low grades on papers and in writing courses. The connection between writing apprehension and teacher response is supported by the research of Thomas C. Gee (1972). Working with 139 eleventh graders, Gee found that students whose compositions received either criticism alone or no commentary at all developed significantly more negative attitudes toward writing than students whose compositions received only praise. Moreover, after just four weeks, students who received only negative comments or none at all were writing papers significantly shorter than those of students who were praised.

Since positive reinforcement, or its lack, is so crucial to a student's level of writing apprehension (Daly and Miller 1975c), one way of reducing apprehension is by allowing students to experience success with writing. They will experience success, of course, whenever their writing is praised. For students who do not share their writing with others--and high apprehensives fear negative responses from their peers as well as their instructors--the writing teacher is likely their only potential source of praise.

But praise, however beneficial as a remedy for apprehension and as a motivator of student writing, is more easily enjoined than put into practice. Dragga notes in his study, for instance, that the four teaching assistants trained in praiseworthy grading all experienced "difficulty in labeling and explaining the desirable characteristics of their students' writing." He concludes that teacher training must emphasize explicit criteria for praiseworthy grading. The title of this article implies that praise does not flow readily from the marking pens of writing teachers; it must be learned. Still, an instructor's conscious decision to praise the work of students is a promising starting point. Sometimes all that's needed is a gimmick. My own method is to allow myself nothing but positive comments during an initial reading of a student paper; I lift my pen to write words of praise only. Another practice is to ask, just before moving to another essay, "Have I told Melissa two or three things about her paper that I like?" R. W. Reising's technique is even more effective: he has developed a grading form that requires him to write one to three positive comments before he even considers noting a weakness (1973, 43).

But sometimes what we need is not a gimmick but understanding. We need to understand that what deserves praise is, for a teacher of writing, a relative and not an absolute question. As Ben Jonson says, "I will like and praise some things in a young writer which yet, if he continue in, I cannot but justly hate him for the same" (1947, 617). Following relative standards, we are in no sense dishonest or condescending in praising one writer for what we might ignore or criticize in another--even within the same class. Diederich urges us to praise everything a student has done that is "even a little bit above his usual standard"(1974, 20).

After all, we follow relative standards in most of the teaching we do outside the classroom. In helping children learn how to talk or how to color or how to swim, we don't hold them up to the absolute standards of Demosthenes, van Gogh, or Mark Spitz; we don't even expect them to match their older friends or siblings. In fact, we praise them for the most modest achievements. I still remember trying to help my six-year-old daughter Pam learn how to hit a softball in our backyard on Winthrow Avenue. Although I pitched the ball as gently as I knew how, trying to make it eminently hittable, Pam just could not get her bat on the ball. We tried all sorts of minor adjustments in her batting stance--hands held together, feet placed further apart, head turned at a more acute angle--but Pam kept missing. Despite my encouragement, she was losing heart in the enterprise. Finally, on perhaps the thirtieth pitch, Pam did hit the ball--nothing like solid contact, but still a distinctly audible foul tip. Of course, I jumped up and down; of course, I shouted "Way to go, Pammy!"; and of course, she smiled. I praised her lots more when she managed first a foul pop, then a dribbler to the mound, and then a genuine ground ball. As a high school student, Pam started at first base for the varsity softball team.

Even with relative standards, a commitment to positive reinforcement, and perhaps a gimmick or two, most of us could benefit from some practice in praise. For that purpose, let's work

281

with an essay written several years ago by a Miami University freshman in response to an open assignment.

Easy Street

The crowd screams and chants, as a bewildered contestant nervously jumps up and down in search of help. Excitedly, Monty Hall comments on the washer and dryer behind box number two in trade for the big curtain where Carol Marroll is standing. The contestant, with glamour and greed in her eyes; wildly picks the curtain. But when raised there stands a 300 pound cow munching on a bail of hay. Embarrassed and sad, the woman slowly sits down.

The old American ideal of hard work and get ahead had traditionally been one followed by many men. But with the arrival of the twentieth century, their seems to be anew way to get ahead. The new American ideal of something for nothing. It seems to have taken the place of honest work. In our popular television game shows, the idea of being able to win prizes and cash by just answering a few simple questions seems to thrill the average American. It is so popular and fascinating that the morning hours are consumed with five or six hours of the programs. The viewer is thrown into a wonderland where everything is free for the taking. The reason for such interest in these programs is that they show life as most of us really wish it to be--soft, easy, free. Our society now enjoys the simplicities of life, and our television game shows exemplify that.

One of the newest of all American dreams is to win a state lottery. What easier way is there to become a millionaire with such a small investment? The state makes it as easy as just reading a couple of numbers off a card, or scratching away a secret spot. Who hasn't at least once in their life, dreamed of hitting the big one, and living off the fat the rest of their life; without ever having to work again? Our country clubs, local junior football teams, even our churches have lotteries now thriving on that dream.

In our whole vocabulary their is no word that can command as much attention as the word "free." It sums up our modern culture and feelings. Advertisers use the word as frequently as possible knowing its strong effect on the public. The idea of giving something away without the consumer having to pay for it has made many a company successful.

The old American ideal seems to have moved over for the new. No longer does a man have to work late or get up early. By just guessing the right tune in five notes; he could be ordering caviar in the morning rather than toast.

When "Easy Street" was evaluated by college instructors, grades ranged from *B* to *F*, with *C and C-* by far the most common. But my colleagues found much to praise even in an essay they rated average or slightly below average in quality. Their comments of praise are categorized below, according to the four levels Nina Ziv (1984) used in her study of teacher response: conceptual, structural, sentential, and lexical.

A.   Conceptual Level

1.   "Your thesis--that the new American ideal is 'something for nothing'--is strong and clear."
2.   "Your thesis is interesting and clear, and your use of particular, graphic details to support the thesis greatly aids your reader's understanding. The conversational tone of your paper also helps the reader understand you."
3.   "The content of this paper is interesting & to the point, the essay is fairly well unified, and you show the ability to use effective details."
4.   "There is much that is strong here; your sense of detail is good and your ideas are insightful."
5.   "You have provided some excellent examples which capture the essence of the 'new' American ideal."
6.   "Your ideas are brilliant, and the way you have argued your point is convincing. Keep up with original and thought-provoking ways of looking at life around you."
7.   "I like the scope of your commentary, which moves from the initial, interest-provoking example, to the statement of American ideals in paragraph #2, to the further example--of the state lottery--in paragraph #3."
8.   "You come across as being perceptive and as concerned about an important trend in our culture."
9.   "Your ideas here are strong and clear" (refers to second paragraph).
10.   "Your paper has fine unity and some precise illustrations."

B.   Structural Level

1.   "The paper is well-organized and well-focused, with some nice paragraph transitions."
2.   "Good details" (refers to next-to-last sentence of first paragraph and to middle sentence of third paragraph).
3.   "An effective opening paragraph—good detail!"
4.   "Well put, effective use of specific detail" (refers to last sentence of third paragraph).
5.   "A superb choice of topic—and a good natural organization from specific to general—from private to public—and from analysis to significance."
6.   "Effective introduction—your detailed description gets the reader interested and draws him into your analysis."
7.   "Good strategy for your opening: you caught my attention."
8.   "Good details here" (refers to opening sentences of third paragraph).
9.   "I like this" (refers to the whole of first paragraph).

10.   "I got a good first impression of this paper. You've started off well with an anecdote that gives the reader a good visual picture and gets her into your thesis."

C. Sentential Level

1.   "Good sentences" (refers to middle sentences of second paragraph).
2.   "Good parallelism" (refers to third sentence of third paragraph and to first two sentences of last paragraph).
3.   "Very nice pair of sentences—clear and concise" (refers to first two sentences of fourth paragraph).
4.   "Effective closing image. Good!"
5.   "Nice structure" (refers to last sentence of fourth paragraph).

D. Lexical Level

1.   "Good—effective word choice here" (refers to "chants, as bewildered contestant").
2.   "You have a vigorous and full vocabulary."
3.   "Nice title."
4.   "Nice series—good climax" (refers to "soft, easy, free" of second paragraph).
5.   "Nice phrase" (refers to "with glamour and greed in her eyes").

Although these positive comments show that "Easy Street" has much to praise, instructors marking the paper more readily recognized error than they identified strengths, especially on the sentential and lexical levels. For example, many instructors pointed out the dangling modifier in the next-to-last sentence of the first paragraph ("But when raised"), but no one applauded the effective use of appositive adjectives ("Embarrassed and sad") as modifiers in the following sentence. It seems clear that we have been better trained to spot comma splices and fragments and other syntactic slips than to notice when students take risks: Only one of two dozen evaluators commended the student for "soft, easy, free," a notable instance of series variation with the coordinating conjunction eliminated. Instructors routinely called attention to the misused semicolon in "By just guessing the right tune in five notes; he could be ordering caviar in the morning rather than toast." Far fewer heard the interesting sentence rhythms created by the sophisticated use of repetition.

So perhaps we need to go back to school ourselves to learn how to recognize what merits praise in student writing. A good starting point for syntax are the chapters on free modifiers in *Notes Toward a New Rhetoric* (Christensen and Christensen 1978) and in *The Writer's Options* (Daiker, Kerek, and Morenberg 1986), and the articles on coordination by Winston Weathers (1966) and Robert L. Walker (1970). But probably even more useful are sessions at conferences, at department meetings, and at workshops for teaching assistants in which we help each other learn what to praise and how to praise. But, if we listen to students, the "how" may not be all that important. At the same time that students tell us that criticism must be specific to work--a comment like "diction" or "logic" or "awkward" is almost always misunderstood unless explained in detail-- they receive even vague compliments like "nice" and "good" and "well written" with gratitude and thanksgiving (Hayes and Daiker 1984). Don Murray once casually remarked at a Wyoming Conference on Freshman and Sophomore English that one of his favorite responses to student writing begins with the five words "I like the way you." He told us we could complete the sentence in any way we chose: "I like the way you use dialogue here" or "I like the way you started your paper with a story" or "I like the way you repeated the key word *animal* in this paragraph."

In his preface to John Gardner's *On Becoming a Novelist,* Raymond Carver (1983) recalls his experience as a college freshman in Gardner's creative writing class at Chico State College. Carver remembers, above all, that Gardner lavished more attention and care on his work than any student had a right to expect. Although Gardner would cross out what he found unacceptable in Carver's stories and add words and even sentences of his own, he was always looking to find something to praise. When there was a sentence, a line of dialogue, or a narrative passage that he liked, something that he thought "worked" and moved the story along in some pleasant or unexpected way, he'd write "Nice" in the margin or else "Good!" And seeing these comments, my heart would lift. (xvi-xvii). It's a good bet that genuine praise can lift the hearts, as well as the pens, of the writers who sit in our own classrooms, too.

References

Carver, R. 1983. Preface to *On Becoming a Novelist,* by J. Gardner, xvi-xvii. New York:Harper.

Christensen, E. 1962. Between Two Worlds. Paper delivered to the California Association of Teachers of English, February, San Diego. Reprinted in *Notes toward a New Rhetoric,* edited by F. Christensen and B. Christensen, [1967] 1978.

Christensen, F., and B. Christensen, editors. [1967] 1978. *Notes Toward a New Rhetoric: Nine Essays for Teachers.* 2nd ed. New York: Harper.

Daiker, D. A. 1983. The Teacher's Options in Responding to Student Writing. Paper presented at the annual Conference on College Composition and Communication, March, Washington, D.C.

Daiker, D. A., A. Kerek, and M. Morenberg. 1986. *The Writer's Options: Combining to Composing.* 3rd ed. New York: Harper.

Daly, J. A. 1977. The Effects of Writing Apprehension on Message Encoding. *Journalism Quarterly* 54:566-72.

Daly, J. A., and M. D. Miller. 1975a. Apprehension of Writing as a Predictor of Message Intensity. *The Journal of Psychology* 89:175-77.

Daly, J. A., and M. D. Miller. 1975b. The Empirical Development of an Instrument to Measure Writing Apprehension. *Research in the Teaching of English* 9:242-49.

Daly, J. A., and M. D. Miller. 1975c. Further Studies on Writing Apprehension: SAT Scores, Success Expectations, Willingness to Take Advanced Courses and Sex Differences. *Research in the Teaching of English* 9:250-56.

Daly, J. A., and W. Shamo. 1978. Academic Decisions as a Function of Writing Apprehension. *Research in the Teaching of English* 12:119-26.

Diederich, P. B. 1963. In Praise of Praise. *NEA Journal* 52:58-59.

Diederich, P. B. 1974. *Measuring Growth in English.* Urbana, Ill.: National Council of Teachers of English.

Dragga, S. 1986. Praiseworthy Grading: A Teacher's Alternative to Editing Error. Paper presented at the Conference on College Composition and Communication, March, New Orleans, La.

Emig, J. 1977. Writing as a Mode of Learning. *College Composition and Communication* 28:122-28.

Gee, T. C. 1972. Students' Responses to Teacher Comments. *Research in the Teaching of English* 6:212-21.

Harris, W. H. 1977. Teacher Response to Student Writing: A Study of the Response Pattern of High School Teachers to Determine the Basis for Teacher Judgment of Student Writing. *Research in the Teaching of English* 11:175-85.

Hayes, M. F., and D. A. Daiker. 1984. Using Protocol Analysis in Evaluating Responses to Student Writing. *Freshman English News* 13:1-4, 10.

Hemingway, E. 1964. A *Moveable Feast.* New York: Scribners.

Hirsch, E. D., Jr. 1977. *The Philosophy of Composition.* Chicago: University of Chicago Press.

Holland, M. 1980. The State of the Art: The Psychology of Writing. Paper presented at the Inland Area Writing Project's Summer Writing Conference, July, University of California at Riverside.

Irmscher, W. F. 1979. *Teaching Expository Writing.* New York: Holt, Rinehart, and Winston.

Jonson, B. 1947. Timber, or Discoveries. *In Ben Jonson, vol. 8,* edited by C.H. Herford Percy and E. Simpson. Oxford, England: Clarendon.

Macrorie, K. 1968. To Be Read. *English Journal* 57:688-92.

Reising, R. W. 1973. Controlling the Bleeding. *College Composition and Communication* 24:43-44.

Shaughnessy, M. 1977. *Errors and Expectations: A Guide for the Teacher of Basic Writing.* New York: Oxford University Press.

Stevens, A. K., editor. 1958. Evaluating a Theme. *Newsletter of the Michigan Council of Teachers of English* 5 (6). Ann Arbor: Michigan Council of Teachers of English.

Walker, R. L. 1970. The Common Writer: A Case for Parallel Structure. *College Composition and Communication* 21:373-79.

Weathers, W. 1966. The Rhetoric of the Series. *College Composition and Communication* 17:217-22.

Ziv, N. D. 1984. The Effect of Teacher Comments on the Writing of Four College Freshmen. In
New Directions in Composition Research, edited by R. Beach and L. S. Bridwell, 362-80. New York: Guilford.

BRINGING PRACTICE IN LINE WITH THEORY:
USING PORTFOLIO GRADING IN THE COMPOSITION CLASSROOM

Jeffrey Sommers[12]

Portfolio assessment in the composition classroom offers not a methodology but a framework for response. Rather than provide definitive answers to questions about grading criteria and standards, the relationship between teacher and student, and increased paper loads, the portfolio approach presents an opportunity for instructors to bring their practice in responding to student writing in line with their theories of composing and pedagogy. My essay proposes to take an exploratory look at how portfolio evaluation compels instructors to address a number of important, and long-lived, issues underlying response to student writing. When an instructor chooses to use a portfolio system, certain other decisions must inevitably follow, and it is the implications of these decisions that I propose to examine most closely.

As the writing process has become the focus of composition classes over the past three decades, it seems an almost natural evolution for portfolio evaluation to have entered the classroom. Emphasizing the importance of revision to the composing process--regardless of which theoretical view of composing one takes--ought to lead to a classroom practice that permits, even encourages, students to revise. While such revision can, of course, occur in a classroom in which the writing portfolio is not in use, the portfolio itself tends to encourage students to revise because it suggests that writing occurs over time, not in a single sitting, just as the portfolio itself grows over time and cannot be created in a single sitting. Elbow and Belanoff argue that a portfolio system evaluates student writing "in ways that better reflect the complexities of the writing process: with time for freewriting, planning, discussion with instructors and peers, revising, and copy editing. It lets students put these activities together in a way most productive for them" (this volume 14).

Additionally, the portfolio approach can help students discover that writing is indeed a form of learning. Janet Emig has argued that writing "provides [a] record of evolution of thought since writing is epigenetic as process-and-product" (128). Portfolios provide a record of that record. Emig also describes writing as "active, engaged, personal--notably, self-rhythmed" (128). The notion that writing occurs over time in response to the rhythms created by the individual writer--a notion that makes eminent sense when one considers that no two writers seem to work at precisely the same pace and that no two pieces of writing seem to take form at the same pace even for the same writer--is another excellent argument for using portfolios. The portfolio approach allows writers to assemble an *oeuvre* at their own pace, within the structure of the writing course and its assignments, of course. Nevertheless, the portfolio by its very nature suggests self-rhythm because some pieces will require more drafts than others, even if explicit deadlines are prompting their composition.

---

[12]From *Portfolios: Process and Product* ed. Pat Belanoff and Marcia Dickson. Portsmouth, New York: Boynton/Cook, 1991.

For good cause then have portfolio systems of evaluation become commonplace in composition classrooms. But with these portfolios also come serious issues about grading standards and criteria, about how teachers and students relate to one another, about how teachers handle increased paper loads. Before examining how these issues might be resolved, perhaps it is time to acknowledge that this essay has yet to define *portfolio*. I have deliberately avoided doing so for two reasons: first, *portfolio* is a familiar-enough term and not really all that mysterious, and thus what I have written so far should be comprehensible to my readers; second, no consensus exists about just what a portfolio is or should be, however familiar the concept may seem. In fact, two distinctly different models of portfolios exist, each compelling its adherents to address the central issues of response in very different theoretical ways.

The first model is described well by James E. Ford and Gregory Larkin, who use as an analogy an artist's portfolio. Each student's work is "collected, like the best representative work of an artist, into a 'portfolio'" (951). We are to see students in the role of free-lance commercial artists approaching an art director at an advertising agency with a large portfolio case containing their "best representative work." Such a model is easily transferred into the writing classroom. Students in the writing course produce a certain number of written documents during the term, agreeing in advance that only a specified number of those documents will be graded by the instructor. Commercial artists would never compile a portfolio that consisted of every piece of work they had done and neither do the students; the idea is to select a representative sampling that shows the creators at their best.

This portfolio model most likely grows out of instructors' concern with grading criteria and standards. Ford and Larkin, as the title of their article suggests, came to the portfolio as a means of guaranteeing grading standards. Instructors are justified in upholding rigorous standards of excellence because their students have been able to revise their work and select their best writing for evaluation. As Ford and Larkin comment, "A student can 'blow' an occasional assignment without disastrous effect" (952), suggesting that the instructor is being eminently fair. Elbow and Belanoff, in the context of a programmatic portfolio-assessment project, make a similar argument, one equally applicable to the individual composition classroom. "By giving students a chance to be examined on their best writing--by giving them an opportunity for more help--we are also able to demand their best writing" (this volume 13). This portfolio system "encourages high standards from the start, thereby encouraging maximum development" (Burnham 137).

To Ford and Larkin, Burnham, and Elbow and Belanoff, a portfolio is a sampling of finished products selected by the student for evaluation. Although the instructor using this model may very well be concerned with the students' development as writers, as Burnham's remark indicates, essentially this portfolio model is grade driven and could be accurately labeled a *portfolio grading system*. It is grade driven because the rationale for using the portfolio framework grows out of an understanding that the student's written work will ultimately be evaluated.

However, portfolio grading, paradoxically, not only grows out of a concern for eroding standards, but also out of a concern for the overemphasis upon grades in writing courses. Christopher Burnham calls the students' "obsession" with grades a "major stumbling block" (125) to effective learning in the composition classroom and turns to portfolio grading as a means of mitigating the students' obsession with grades. Burnham concludes that the portfolio system "establishes a writing environment rather than a grading environment in the classroom" (137).

Thus, by addressing the issue of responding to the student's writing, Burnham wants to change the relationship between the student and the instructor. He wants to create a more facilitative role for the instructor, in accordance with suggestions about response from Donald Murray, Nancy Sommers, and Lil Brannon and C. H. Knoblauch. He not only wants to allow students to retain the rights to their own writing, he wants them to assume responsibility for their writing, asserting that portfolio grading "creates independent writers and learners" (136).

The question then of when and what to grade becomes quite significant. Although grading criteria must be established by instructors who employ portfolio grading, new criteria for grading the final drafts do not generally need to be developed. Presumably, instructors will bring to bear an already developed set of criteria for grading, applying these criteria rigorously to designated papers, thus protecting the integrity of their standards.[2] Nonetheless, a crucial question arises: when will student work receive a grade: at midterm, only at the end of the term, with each submission? Some instructors grade every draft and revision as students submit them, some grade only the revisions, some grade only papers designated as final drafts. In some portfolio-grading systems, the students select a specified number of final drafts at midterm and a second set at end of the term, while in other systems, all grading occurs at the end of the term.

Instructors using portfolio grading must decide when to offer grades. Grading every draft keeps the students informed, but, because even a temporary grade has an air of finality to many students simply because it is a grade, this policy may undercut the idea that each draft may potentially develop into a finished product. Grading revisions only may encourage the grade-obsessed student to revise if only to obtain a grade, thus introducing revision to some students who may otherwise lack the motivation to revise, but also reinforcing the primacy of grades.

By deferring grades until the end of the term, instructors can extend the duration of the "writing environment" that Burnham hopes to substitute for the "grading environment" in the course. However, if students are indeed obsessed with grades, as he argues, then it seems likely that for a substantial number of students, or perhaps for all of the students to varying extents, there will always be a grading environment lurking beneath the writing environment of the course. If instructors respond effectively and frequently and confer with students individually, they can keep students informed of their approximate standing in the course, possibly deflecting their grade anxiety, but it is disingenuous to claim that portfolio grading removes grade obsession. If the portfolio ultimately produces an accumulation of individual grades, grade obsession cannot really be eliminated although it certainly can be reduced.

Yet a larger issue arises, an issue related to one's pedagogical assumptions about the significance of grades. Burnham discusses the portfolio system as a means of leading to student development, a development inevitably measured by the final grades earned by the student's portfolio. Inherent in this model is the idea that students can improve the writing, and thus the grade, by revising and selecting their best work. Inevitably, then, instructors using portfolio grading must address the issue of grade inflation. Although one of the motivating forces behind portfolio grading, as we have seen, is protecting grading standards, the system itself is designed to promote better writing by the students, and it stands to reason that many students are going to be submitting portfolios that consist of writing better than they might be able to produce in a classroom employing a traditional grading system. Will instructors raise the standards so high that even the improved writing in the portfolios falls into the usual grading curve? Or, and this seems much more likely, will the grades themselves on the whole be somewhat higher because of the portfolio approach despite higher standards? Should higher grades be of significant concern to instructors? Do higher grades mean "grade inflation"? What is the role of grades in writing courses? Portfolio grading compels instructors to consider these important questions.

Finally, portfolio grading presents problems to instructors in handling the paper load. Since most programs suggest or stipulate a certain number of assignments per term, instructors using the portfolio system must determine how they will count assignments. Will newly revised papers count as new assignments? By doing so, the instructor can keep the paper load from mushrooming. Let's focus on a course that requires seven papers in a semester (the situation at my institution), with the understanding that the portfolio will consist of four final drafts selected by the student. If instructors count revisions of papers 1 and 2 as papers 3 and 4, their paper load will be less because students will still only produce seven drafts for them to read. On the other hand, the students' options at the end of the term will be reduced by this method of counting; they will have to select four final drafts from only five different pieces in progress. To ensure students the full choice of seven, however, instructors commit themselves to more responding. In our hypothetical case, they will read at least nine drafts, seven first drafts, and revisions of the first two papers. Thus a routine decision actually has important pedagogical implications.

Several methods of controlling the paper load do exist. One is to divide the term in half, asking students to produce two mini-portfolios. At midterm, for instance, in the situation already described, students are required to submit two final drafts for grading out of the first four assigned papers. At the end of the term, students must select two of the final three assigned papers for grading. Thus the paper load is under greater control because the students cannot continue work on the first four papers after midterm. On the other hand, Burnham's desire to create a writing environment rather than a grading environment will be affected because grades will become of primary concern not once but twice during the term.

Another method for controlling the paper load is to limit the number of drafts students may write of individual papers. Without such a limit, some students will rewrite and resubmit papers almost weekly, adding greatly to the paper load; of course, one can argue that such students are developing as writers in an important way. Deadlines for revisions of papers can also be used to control the paper load since "real" writers always work under deadlines. They may revise and revise and revise, but ultimately they must conclude. Instructors may allow students to revise a given assignment as often as they wish but within a designated period of time. Another method of controlling the paper load is to limit the number of revisions students may submit at one time or to designate specific times when revisions may be submitted. Late in the term, industrious students may have revisions of three or four different assignments ready to be submitted; some limit on the number they may hand in at one time can help instructors manage the course more effectively. Stipulating that revisions can be handed in only on certain days can allow instructors to plan their time for responding more efficiently.

Eventually, the end of the term arrives, and for many instructors using portfolio grading, the paper load explodes. Portfolios of four papers or more per student come in at the end of the term and must be graded quickly in order to submit final grades on time. Holistic grading can make the paper load manageable as instructors offer no comments but just a letter grade on each final draft.

Grading portfolios at the end of the term undeniably requires more time than grading a single final exam or final paper would. However mundane these questions of handling the paper load may seem, the answers one supplies affect the entire portfolio grading system because many of these decisions may influence the relationship between students and their instructors, and some may influence, or be influenced by, instructors' grading criteria and standards.

To sum up then, a portfolio grading system defines a portfolio as a sampling of students' finished writing selected by the students for evaluation. Portfolio grading offers instructors a means of keeping their grading standards high while employing their usual grading criteria, it presents one potential method for reducing students' obsession with grades and transforming the classroom environment into one more engaged with writing than grading, and it increases instructors' paper loads. Instructors' decisions about when to grade and how to manage the paper load raise complications because they affect the relationship between instructors and their students. Thus, teachers planning on implementing portfolio grading need to consider carefully how they will do so in a way that will keep their practice in line with their own theoretical assumptions about writing and about composition pedagogy.

The second, newer, portfolio system model I will call the "holistic portfolio." The holistic portfolio is a response to continued theorizing about the nature of the composing process. Louise Wetherbee Phelps argues that theories underlying teaching practices evolve toward greater depth, and she sketches a hierarchy of response models to student writing beginning with one she labels "evaluative attitude, closed text" (49). In this model, the instructor treats the student text as "self-contained, complete in itself . . . a discrete discourse episode to be experienced more or less decontextually" (50). This concept of response to a text views reading as evaluation; instructors responding in this model may speak of "grading a stack of papers." The next response model described by Phelps is one she calls "formative attitude, evolving text" (51). Instructors read students' drafts as part of a process of evolution, thus entering into and influencing the students' composing process. In this model of response, instructors locate "learning largely in the actual composing process" (53).

Phelps describes a third model of response as "developmental attitude, portfolio of work": "Whereas the first group of teachers reads a 'stack' of papers and the second reads collected bits, scraps, and drafts of the composing process, the third reads a 'portfolio' of work by one student" (53). Phelps elaborates on two ways to work with portfolios, describing first the portfolio grading model we have already examined, which she dubs "the weak form." In this approach, she writes, "teachers continue to read and grade individual papers attempting to help students perfect each one" (53). As Phelps has described the models of response, we can see that she has first described portfolio assessment used in a programmatic approach to large-scale decision making about student proficiency and placement. Her second model fairly accurately describes the portfolio-grading approach of Ford and Larkin and Burnham, elaborated upon somewhat in her depiction of "the weak form" of her third response model.

In the second method of using portfolios, Phelps also describes a different portfolio system. Some instructors employ portfolios because they wish to respond from a "*developmental perspective*." From this perspective, the student writing "blurs as an individual entity" and is treated as a sample "excerpted from a stream of writing stimulated by the writing class, part of the 'life text' each literate person continually produces" (53). Phelps concludes:

The reader's function is [to read] through the text to the writer's developing cognitive, linguistic, and social capacities as they bear on writing activities. The set of a single writer's texts to which the reader has access, either literally or through memory, is the corpus from which the reader tries to construct a speculative profile of the writer's developmental history and current maturity. (53)

This definition of portfolio no longer serves as an analogy to the commercial artist's carefully assembled portfolio of a representative sampling of her best work. Instead it more closely resembles an archivist's collection of a writer's entire *oeuvre*. Instructors do not deal with selected writings but evaluate the entire output of the student writer. The implications of such a definition are quite different from those of the portfolio grading model defined by Ford and Larkin, Burnham, and Elbow and Belanoff.

While portfolio grading systems are driven by pedagogical concerns with fair grading as well as with composing process theory, the holistic portfolio system is primarily driven by a pedagogical concern with composing process theory. Although Knoblauch and Brannon's polemic *Rhetorical Traditions and the Teaching of Writing* does not discuss portfolio evaluation, its view of the composing process might very readily lead to it. Knoblauch and Brannon describe the "myth of improvement" that has stifled writing instruction by focusing on the kind of evaluation Phelps details in her first model of response (evaluative attitude, closed text). Knoblauch and Brannon suggest that "the most debilitating illusion associated with writing instruction is the belief that teachers can, or at least ought to be able to, control writers' maturation, causing it to occur as the explicit consequence of something they do or ought to do" (165). This illusion is reductionist, leading to a view of the writing course "in minimal functionalist terms" (165). This "myth of improvement" has produced a definition of teaching and curricular success that stresses "trivial but readily demonstrable short-term 'skill' acquisitions" and has led some teachers "to imagine it is fair to 'grade on improvement,' mistaking a willingness to follow orders for real development" (165).

While Knoblauch and Brannon's book remains controversial, their critique of "the myth of improvement" cogently articulates many instructors' reservations about grading practices based on the artificial academic calendar, a system that demands students learn at a given pace, defined by a ten-week quarter, a fourteen-week trimester, or a sixteen-week semester. Knoblauch and Brannon conclude by arguing that "symptoms of growth--the willingness to take risks, to profit from advice, to revise, to make recommendations to others--may appear quickly, even if improved *performance* takes longer" (169).

For instructors whose conception of the composing process is compatible with the developmental schemes underlying Knoblauch and Brannon's book and Phelps's third model of response, the holistic portfolio should have great appeal. It presents these instructors with difficult decisions, however, in the same areas that the portfolio grading system presented its practitioners: grading criteria and standards, the teacher-student relationship, and handling the paper load.

While upholding grading standards was the catalyst for portfolio grading, holistic portfolio systems appear to be less concerned with the notion of grading standards, at least in traditional terms. Because the holistic portfolio system does not focus instructors' attention on specific final drafts, it does present instructors with some major decisions about criteria for the final evaluation.

293

Several possibilities exist. Instructors may create a grading system that weights final drafts but also grades draft materials, notes, peer commentary, and so on. Counting the number of drafts or the variety of included materials is a way to "grade" preliminary materials. However, any counting method might distort the course's emphasis on development by encouraging students to create "phony" drafts, drafts written after the fact simply to pad the portfolio (just as many of us used to compose outlines *after* completing high school term papers as a way of meeting a course requirement).

Another way to grade the final portfolio is more holistic, and thus probably "purer" in the sense that it avoids treating individual drafts as "collected bits, scraps, and drafts" and treats portfolios as part of "the life text" (Phelps 53). The instructor looks for "symptoms of growth," to borrow Knoblauch and Brannon's phrase--"the willingness to take risks, to profit from advice, to revise, to make recommendations to others." Those students who demonstrate the greatest growth receive the highest grades, assuming that the instructor has developed a scale that measures growth--no small assumption.

While the holistic portfolio can fit very nicely into a developmental view of the composing process, it presents great difficulties in fitting at all into a traditional academic grading system and poses serious questions for instructors about how they see their writing courses fitting into the academy. This method of evaluation works most readily in a pass/no pass grading situation, indeed is an argument for such a grading system. But pass/no pass writing courses are the exception rather than the rule. Unfortunately, neither Knoblauch and Brannon nor Phelps really addresses the issue of how to grade in a writing course that emphasizes a developmental perspective on writing. It is conceivable that an instructor holistically evaluating a set of portfolios could assign an entire class of industrious students grades of A, having developed grading criteria that emphasize "symptoms of growth"; such an instructor can have rigorous standards in that only those students who have made the effort and demonstrated the growth receive the As. However, one suspects this instructor would face a one-to-one meeting with a concerned writing program administrator or department chair sometime after submitting the final grades.

Some compromise or accommodation must undoubtedly be made by instructors, perhaps along the lines discussed earlier of weighting final drafts. The important point to make here is that instructors should be aware of how the grading criteria they develop correlate with the theory underlying their use of portfolio evaluation.

Given the problematic nature of grading holistic portfolios, why would instructors adopt this model of the portfolio system? The holistic portfolio system offers distinct advantages in defining a healthy teacher-student relationship. Burnham's hopes of creating a writing environment rather than a grading environment are more readily realized in the holistic portfolio system. Because the final portfolio will not be graded in any traditional sense, because individual grades on drafts do not occur, in theory the classroom using the holistic portfolio can indeed become a writing environment, since there is no reason for it to become a grading environment, and the instructor can truly doff the evaluator's role and don instead the facilitator's role.

Burnham praises portfolio grading for encouraging students to assume responsibility for their learning; portfolio grading "creates independent writers and learners," he concludes (137). His point is that when students know that they can control their grades through extra effort in revising and through the selection process available to them prior to final evaluation, they become more responsible and more independent; in today's terminology, they become "empowered." However, the motivation comes from a concern with grades.

In the holistic portfolio system, the students are also afforded the opportunity to become more responsible, not for their grades so much as for their development. They can indeed become independent learners, independent of traditional grading obsessions as well. The teacher and student can become "co-writers," in Phelps's phrase. The emphasis in the course falls not on improving texts as a means of improving a grade but instead falls on developing as a writer, understanding that this development is more important than grades on individual texts.

Both models of portfolios, then, hope to free students of the tyranny of the grade. The portfolio grading system does so temporarily, but also readily accommodates the traditional institutional need for grades. The holistic portfolio system can indeed free students to become learners and writers for the duration of a writing course but only if instructors have resolved the essential conflict between their course and the institution's demand for traditionally meaningful grades.

In the final area of paper load, it seems most likely that the holistic portfolio system will produce a heavier paper load than the portfolio grading system will. Any schemes to limit students' output would likely conflict with the theoretical assumptions that lead to using the holistic portfolio system. Thus students' portfolios are likely to grow in length as well as in the hoped-for depth of development. At the end of the term, instructors must read not merely a specific number of selected final drafts, but entire portfolios, certainly a slower process. Periodic reading of the growing portfolios--which instructors taking such a developmental perspective will probably wish to do-- may reduce the paper load at the end of the course since instructors can scan the familiar materials in the portfolio, but it will not significantly reduce the paper load so much as spread it out over the course of the term. Instructors contemplating a portfolio system of either sort, or a hybrid version of the two models described, are faced with the need to answer some important questions for themselves before incorporating the system into their writing classes. Louise Wetherbee Phelps concludes her discussion by commenting that her depiction of response models represents an increasing growth on the part of instructors. She argues that "experience itself presses teachers toward increasingly generous and flexible conceptions of the text and the reading task" (59). If she is correct, as I think she is, then the movement in composition classrooms toward portfolio systems of one sort or another will accelerate as the emphasis on the composing process as central to writing courses continues. As the profession continues to refine its thinking about composition pedagogy, portfolio systems seem destined to proliferate in use and to grow in significance. The portfolio system of evaluation has tremendous advantages, which are described throughout the rest of this book, but it also requires great thought on the part of instructors because a portfolio system implemented in a scattershot manner may well undercut the goals of a writing course. The portfolio offers instructors wonderful opportunities to bring their teaching practice in line with their theoretical assumptions about writing and about teaching, but that convergence can only occur if instructors ask themselves the right--and the tough--questions and work out the answers that best provide what both instructors and students need in the writing course.

Note

1. I am assuming that instructors themselves will grade the papers. Ford and Larkin describe a programmatic use of portfolio grading wherein the portfolios are graded by a team of graders not including the students' instructor. My interest in this essay, however, is in the issues faced by individual instructors who do not have the power to implement such grading practice but must conduct their own evaluations.

APPLYING DONALD MURRAY'S "RESPONSIVE TEACHING"

Chris Madigan, University of New Mexico[13]

I normally teach 3 composition classes per semester—about 75 students—and require 7 papers from each. For the last four years, I have allowed an unlimited number of revisions. The average is 3 + drafts per paper, and a few students have revised a paper a dozen times. I assign letter grades only at mid- and end-of-term, and the only mark I put on individual papers is an R (revision required) or a checkmark (revision optional). I give all other responses orally, in 10 minute office conferences that each student attends voluntarily, averaging 4 per semester. The first 14 months I began conferencing, I held 700 conferences.

If my conference procedure were the traditional one--which my students describe as "you tell me what's wrong with my paper and how to fix it"--I couldn't have survived those 700 conferences. Instead, I've used what Donald Murray calls "Responsive Teaching" and actually enjoyed them. I'd like to briefly describe "Responsive Teaching" and identify advantages and disadvantages of the method by sharing some anonymous student course evaluations and my own reflections. First, the method.

Murray explains Responsive Teaching in chapters 4, 7, 9, 17, 20, and 22-25 of *Learning by Teaching* (Boynton/Cook, 1982) and more systematically in chapters 7 and 8 of *A Writer Teaches Writing* (2nd ed., Houghton Mifflin, 1985). The writer follows language toward an evolving meaning, and the teacher follows the writer following the language. More specifically: (1) the student writes, (2) the student responds to the text (the product) or to the experience of producing it (the process), (3) the teacher listens to the student's response (rational) and to how it is presented (emotional), (4) the teacher reads (or listens to) the text from the student's perspective, (5) the teacher responds to the student's response, and (6) the student responds to the teacher's response.

Let's assume that a student has written a readable draft and appears for an appointment. As she walks in, I'll ask "What would you like to talk about today?" or "How can I help?"

She'll identify the paper she wants to discuss; and then I'll ask, "What do you like about this paper or the way you put it together? What are you pleased with?" That usually throws the writer, but I won't accept anything but a strength at this point, so she'll find something good about the paper, if only that she liked her subject.

After I've rephrased the evaluation into terms we use in class and we're both satisfied I know what we're talking about, I'll ask, "What are you not so pleased with?" Usually that answer

---

[13]From *College Composition and Communication* 39 (February 1988): 74-77.

comes very easily. Often a whole catalog of faults spills out of the writer's mouth. If so, I ask, "Of all these faults you've named [and I'll list them] which is the biggest problem?"

When I'm sure I know what the writer disliked, I'll ask, "If you were going to work on this paper some more, what one thing would you do to improve it most?" When I can rephrase that revision strategy, I say, "Okay, let's take a look at it," and I swivel my chair so the writer can look over my shoulder as I read, and I run my pencil down the margin to show where I am in the paper.

If I run into problems, I may say, "I don't understand this section. What do you mean here?" Or "I'm two pages into this and feel lost. What's your point?"

When I find good writing, I say, "I like that." When I'm amused, I laugh. Generally, though, I don't say much till I'm done, but I do a lot of nodding and chuckling, grunting and gasping.

Once I've finished reading, I swivel back around toward the writer. I recall what she was pleased and displeased with, and if I agree with the self-evaluation I'll say something like, "You're right about the organization. I never wondered where I was or where I was going next. And the conclusion is a problem. I was surprised when I turned the page and didn't find another paragraph. What are you going to do about that?"

If I thought part of the student's evaluation was off-base, I might say, "I can tell you found a topic you liked. I got excited about it too. But I don't think your grammar is the biggest problem. What I need right now is a clearer notion of what you're trying to tell me. What's your point?"

Once a draft is focused and fairly well developed, I talk about surface features. Murray says to students, "This is really good writing. Mind if I mess with it?" And then he models whatever revision will improve the piece the most. When the writer gets the idea or bristles at his "taking over," he hands it back.

When the writer finishes or gets tired of the essay, I try to make her conscious of what she's learned before she moves on: "What did you learn from writing this?" "Is this paper different from others you've written? How? See any connections among those differences?" And finally, "What are you going to work on next?"

While I'd never use all these questions in one conference, I might use all on one paper, over two or three conferences. I respond only to what the student has evaluated (one good, one bad feature) and to what I think the paper needs next because I'd prefer writers revise from a few comments than ignore many. And fewer comments keep conferences to 10 minutes. (Murray claims to use 2-minute conferences effectively, but I'm not that proficient.) Besides, I schedule class time for peer response before and after every due date so writers can get suggestions and the respondents can see the results. Therefore, because I'm not the only respondent, I don't feel obligated to give a complete error analysis. And since most students successfully revise papers I mark "revision required" but never confer about, they don't always need me anyway.

That's my version of Responsive Teaching. The teacher expects writers to evaluate and refine their own writing, asks leading questions, and tries not to side-track the self-evaluation once it begins.

How well does it work? Let me talk about student reactions first. Students report they *know more about me* and, through me, *course requirements.*

The personal contact increases motivation. One student wrote, "The personal interchange . . . makes class and school seem more human. We aren't just a number in somebody's book somewhere." Another said, "Knowing he was taking time to work personally in conferences made me want to do a better job."

Talking promotes discovery--once the initial shock wears off. As one student noted, "On my second conference, [the teacher] said `What's wrong with your paper?' I was shocked. Students shouldn't have to be put to such a judgment on themselves--I mean that would really make a student think. It did me. I figured out what was wrong with my paper and fixed it."

Hearing themselves generate new, good ideas *builds self confidence and a sense of responsibility.* Murray calls writing a "rational act in an emotional setting." Overcoming comma splices doesn't help if we simultaneously kill willingness to write. In Responsive Teaching the teacher addresses the emotional and the cognitive so students can say (as one did), "I felt I could write my way and . . . not just make it your way. I really felt like a writer, not just a machine cranking out copies of what the teacher wanted to read."

But Responsive Teaching has its problems, e.g., *carpool arrangements* that preclude frequent conferences at commuter schools, *schedule conflicts* between teacher and students, and *inadequate conference time.* More serious problems also appear.

Responsive Teaching is not for every student. Some students *can't escape being defensive* in one semester. Shy students sometimes squirm uncomfortably in conference but sometimes appreciate the chance to ask questions they wouldn't hazard in an open classroom. Grade apprehensives crave teacher-evaluation, not self-evaluation, as the most direct route possible to higher grades, and infrequent grades is the most common complaint on student evaluations.

Responsive Conferences are not for every teacher, either. They would not suit teachers who *doubt students' ability to evaluate themselves* or who *feel uncomfortable in one-to-one situations or with listening more than talking.* And these are legitimate reasons for not embracing a conference strategy.

Even teachers who attempt Responsive Teaching fall prey to fears. The worst is "not doing my job."-- It's hard letting a student maintain title to a very flawed (or even mediocre) paper submitted late in the semester. I fear we won't "fix" everything by end of term. What will the student's next writing teacher think of me? So I'm *tempted to identify all the errors,* not just what the writer can handle now. I'm tempted to extend conference beyond 10 minutes, though that's as much self-evaluation and empathic listening as we can both muster at once. I'm *tempted to "take over" the revision* when I see that 11th-hour, please-just-tell-me-what-to-do look. Nor do I always overcome those temptations. Then later, reading the revision, I am amazed at the exactness with which the writer made my corrections. And in the back of my head, I hear a whispering suspicion: "Did I do this to myself, or was I tricked?"

Despite those problems, I intend to continue conferencing because of its benefits.

Students and I enjoy a far *greater range of response*. Responsive Teaching depends on face-to-face contact, verbal and nonverbal cues. I can hear the boredom behind a halfhearted "I liked my topic" and address that. I can ask a pointed "Why should I be interested in reading this?" yet support the writer with my undivided attention. I can tell when my encouragement begins to cloy or when I've been too rough and need to ease off. What I may be too polite to say, I can groan.

I avoid lonely late-night paper reading marathons. I enjoy talking to students more than writing marginal notes. Except for 7 nights my first semester conferencing, I left my papers at school.

I enjoy *more immediate access to my students' composing processes.* Recently I asked "Why'd you use a comma here?" and discovered a rule distortion that corrected most of that writer's surface errors. I could but wouldn't have done the error analysis alone. Asking is easier and quicker.

I return papers faster. On each paper I write only an R (revision required) or a check-mark (revision optional). That doesn't take long, and if the student wants, I can mark text in conference. A week used to be the minimum time I kept papers; now it's maximum.

I may be saving time. I'm certainly giving *more and better feedback per unit of time.* I used to spend 10-20 minutes writing comments on a paper. Audiotaped critiques took less time, but I couldn't gauge writers' reactions, and they couldn't respond to my misreadings. Now students happily confront me with my misinterpretations, and I happily point out why the text induced such insanity.

The first term I used Responsive Teaching was the first semester in 13 years I turned grades in early. Last semester, needing more time for administrative duties and bowing to students' requests for written feedback, I began writing summary responses on all student papers *and* conferencing with students who wanted conferences. Compared to semesters of all-conference feedback, last semester's students averaged fewer drafts per paper, fewer excellent papers at end of term, and more canceled or no-show conferences. And I was late submitting final grades.

I'm returning to Responsive Teaching, but not just for those reasons. Responsive Teaching puts the primary responsibility for improving writing where it belongs--on the writers--and I like teaching that way.

THE FIRST FIVE MINUTES:
SETTING THE AGENDA IN A WRITING CONFERENCE

Thomas Newkirk

Freshman are usually allowed to hide--at least at large universities. Most of their courses meet in large lecture halls where they are taught by professors who don't, who really can't--learn the names of their students. In class, students listen and take notes, but do not speak. Examinations, by necessity, take the form of multiple-choice or short-answer questions, and the results are posted by Social Security number with an accompanying distribution curve to indicate where the student ranks.

The invariable exception to this pattern is freshman composition where, for better or worse, the student cannot hide. The student is called by name and, on an almost weekly basis, receives a response to his or her writing. Hiding is particularly difficult in the composition course where teacher and student meet for regular conferences in which the student must speak, explain, evaluate; where he or she must make what are often the first awkward steps in the direction of analytic conversation, the staple of the academic world. I will contend in this chapter that these meetings, and in particular the first few minutes of these meetings, constitute some of the most poignant dramas in the university.

I don't mean to overemphasize the confrontational nature of the writing conference by echoing Joe Louis's warning to Billy Conn--"You can run, but you can't hide." Most conferences seem casual, supportive; there is regular laughter and, at the end of the course, appreciation for the personal attention received. But the seemingly effortless, conversational quality of conferences belies their complexity, for both teacher and student are filling paradoxical roles. The teacher must balance two opposing mandates: on the one hand to respond to the student, to evaluate, to suggest possible revisions and writing strategies; and on the other to encourage the student to take the initiative, to self-evaluate, to make decisions, to take control of the paper. There is no neat way to reconcile these mandates, no formula to prevent missteps--just the endless prospect of gambling, of risking silence at some points and assertiveness at others.

The student meets this dilemma from the other end and fills a role at least as paradoxical. When asked the question, "What did you think of your paper?" or one of its many variants, the student knows that the question if really, "How did you (acting as a member of a community that you are not yet a member of) react to this paper?" Furthermore, the person asking the question *is* a member of that community and very likely has a better answer--at least in the opinion of the student. Yet, despite the awkwardness of the situation, the student recognizes (usually) that the question is a valid one and works to formulate an answer. So if the teacher is a gambler, the student is often the actor, pretending her or his way into a role.

To complicate matters further, both student and teacher need to come to a meeting of minds fairly early in a writing conference; they need to set an agenda, agree to one or two major concerns that will be the focus of the conference. The agenda often deals with a possible revision of the paper, but there are other possibilities: it could deal with the writing process of the student or with a paper that is yet to be written. Unless a commonly-agreed-upon agenda is established, a conference can run on aimlessly and leave both participants with the justifiable feeling that they have wasted time. The efficient setting of an agenda is particularly important in the conferences that will be analyzed in this chapter. Each lasts about fifteen minutes, and in some, part of this time is used for reading the paper. There is little time to meander.

The conferences were held as part of the freshman English course at the University of New Hampshire and occurred in the third week of the course (in most cases they were the second student-teacher conference). In virtually all sections of freshman English, students are not graded until mid-semester and then only on work that both student and instructor feel is the best produced to that point. For that reason, instructors in these early conferences are not under pressure to give or justify grades. Each conference was taped by the instructor, a first-semester teaching assistant, who transcribed the conference and then annotated it, identifying crucial junctures and critical mistakes. The procedure used by Carnicelli (1980) served as a model.

I will present the opening segments, lasting about five minutes, of three conferenced that show different ways in which agendas are negotiated or fail to be negotiated. The papers for these conferences are similar; they are first drafts dealing with personal experiences, and, like many early papers in freshman English, they lack focus. An instructor reading these papers away from the student could conceivably write a similar comment for each. But the student is present, and this presence changes the nature of the teaching act.

"It Might be Kind of Dumb..."

The paper for the following conference was entitled "My Favorite Course," five double-spaced pages which began with the student's love for horses as a child (she had a toy palomino). From this beginning she moves on to describe how she was admitted to a horsemanship course, the things she has learned so far in the course, and positive and negative points about her horse. After reading the paper (and before reading the transcript), I expected the conference to deal with the issue of focus. But it didn't, and the reason why should be evident for the opening segment (in this and the following transcriptions, T=teacher and S= student):

T: All right, now let's talk about your paper. I'm going to spend a few minutes on it now and then we'll talk about it.

S: OK [Teacher reads paper].

T: OK. Uh, why don't you tell me a little about your paper. What was it like writing it?

S: Oh, I liked it. I really like the class, you know, and I liked writing about it.

T: So you enjoyed it?

S: Yeah. It's a fun class.

T: Was it a fun paper?

302

S: Yeah. Well, you know, I wanted to write about it. Maybe it's really boring because I really just wrote it for me, but I guess I just wanted to. It, you know, doesn't say much. Just about my class.

T: Well, I enjoyed reading it. It was fun reading it. I could tell that you liked the class and I liked the way your enthusiasm really shows.

S: Yeah.

T: Was there a part that you really enjoyed writing?

S: Well, I enjoyed writing the whole paper pretty much.

T: Uh huh. Is there a part you liked best, you know, a favorite part?

S: Oh, yeah. I really liked the part about Trigger [the toy horse]. Remembering him. I still have him somewhere at home. It might be kind of dumb though, a plastic horse.

T: Oh no. I really liked that. I had a dog, a stuffed shaggy dog that I remembered while reading it. He's somewhere now. I guess everyone grows up with these animals and then keeps them forever. [Laughter.]   But I liked that part, I could really relate to it. Was there a part that you thought needed work still? You know, something you were sort of unhappy with?

S: Well, I wondered if it would be boring. You know, too long. It really doesn't say much.

T: Did you, uh, did you want it to say something? What did you want to tell me?"

S: Oh, well. I just wanted to tell you about my riding class.

T: Uh huh.

S: That's all.

T: Uh huh. Um. You know you told me about yourself, too.

S: What?

T: Well, that part about Trigger?

S: Oh yeah. [Laughs]

T: And you know, about being tested. Your dedication. Not only getting up at the crack of dawn and all, but the work. Like it sounds like you're really working your body, so it's a lot of hard work as well as fun.

This conference stumbles at the beginning over the reference to "it." In the first five exchanges, the teacher uses "it" three times, in each case referring to the paper or the writing of the paper. The student uses "it" three times, each time referring to the horsemanship class and ultimately leading her to misunderstand the teacher's question:

T: So you enjoyed it?

S: Yeah. It's a fun class.

T: Was it a fun paper?

One senses the student's lack of familiarity with the intent of the conference and her lack of awareness that the teacher's primary concern at this point in the conference is with the process of writing. The student doesn't, in fact, quite know what it means to "talk about your paper." This discomfort with the analytic intent of the conference becomes even more evident when the teacher pushes (ever so gently) for a critical evaluation of the paper.

In response to the teacher's request for an analytic judgment, the student consistently gives a global evaluation--of the paper, of the class, and, most devastatingly, of herself. When asked to tell about the writing of the paper (an implicit request for analysis), the writer replies with, "Oh, I liked it." When asked, this time more explicitly, if there was a "*part* that you really enjoyed writing," the student replies that she liked "writing the whole paper pretty much." And again later in the segment, when asked about the main point of the paper, she replies globally that she "just wanted to tell you about my riding class." The only tentative move toward an analytic view is the student's admission that she liked the part about the toy horse. For this student, the text seems to exist as a whole that cannot be differentiated into features or parts. And because she brings this frame to her paper, the teacher comes up empty in most of the exchanges.

But not totally empty. For in these replies, the student is making clear her lack of confidence in her own writing ability and her doubts about the validity of her experience as a topic for writing. In these first few minutes the student characterizes her writing as: "boring" (twice), "it doesn't say much," "it might be kind of dumb," and "too long." It is this message that the teacher picks up on and makes the focus of the conference agenda. In her analysis of the conference, the teacher wrote:

> She told me in a previous conference...[that] she is the first one of her extended family to go to college. Her self-confidence is very shaky, and she considers her acceptance into UNH to be a fluke. She doesn't think she is "college material." She has a pattern of trashing herself, telling me how "dumb" she is compared to all the "real" students around her....I have an agenda of support for her and, if possible, some sort of positive response against her habit of self-denigration.

So the teacher gambles. She focuses on supporting the student, allaying the student's fears that she is an inadequate writer and that her experiences are "boring." The gamble is that by ignoring, for a time, various technical problems in the writing and by emphasizing the positive, the writer will, in the near future, gain enough confidence to deal with these technical matters. Another gamble is

304

that this support will not be taken by the student as a definitive evaluation--"I enjoyed reading it" may be translated by the student into "This is an A paper." The teacher gambles....and waits.

"....Like a Mack Truck"

The second conference deals with an untitled paper about the function of pets. It begins in a fairly technical way with the sentence "I wonder what part domestic animals play in the ecosystem." For most of the paper, however, the writer shifts to more casual language to describe her own relationship with her dog as they went out in the woods after a snow:

> She would suddenly stop, lie on the ground and chew at the ice. Sometimes it was severe enough to cause her paws to bleed leaving red splotches on the snow. I knew it was more painful for her if I attempted to yank out the ice.

At the end of the paper, the writer returns to the more distant vocabulary of the beginning, when she concludes that "Pets are machines for us to lavish affection on or proclaim superiority over."

The paper alone suggests two major issues. The radical shift of tone after the beginning is jolting, and the conclusion comparing pets to machines seems at odds with the affectionate description of the writer's relationship with her own pet. Ironically, both teacher and student in the following excerpt agree on the central problem in the paper, yet the conference misfires badly.

T: Now, what did you think your purpose was in writing the paper?

S: Well, I was just kind of dealing with the fact that people have animals. And are nice to them. And we're really not nice to other organisms besides ourselves. You know, I wonder why people are so uncommonly nice to domesticated animals.

T: Yeah? So--ummm--did you come to any conclusion about that?

S: No. [Laughs.]

T: But at the end you say: "I have had a pet as a companion. Pets are machines for us to lavish affection on or to proclaim our superiority over." That sounds like you've come to a conclusion.

S: Well, it's more of an observation.

T: Oh. You see, I think it's a false conclusion. I mean I think you still don't know.

S: I don't.

T: And I think it's better that you don't know. I mean you're saying there ought to be some reason for this, but I love my dog.

S: Yeah.

T: And so for me the last paragraph was--I think I said that before--that you have a tendency to be asking questions and think you have to find some answer.

S: Umhumm.

T: And I don't think--I mean whatever answer you find, it's probably going to be a question and it's probably going to be inherent in the whole piece.

S: So I don't really have to....

T: You're saying, "God, this is strange, we're funny creatures." And that's the answer. You don't have to what?

S: I don't have to make it so--like I ought to stick on this conclusion--which is unnecessary.

T: And also, when you do that you tend to lapse into this scientific language that really--you sound like you've turned into a computer or something. ...Were there any parts of this that you liked better than other parts, that you enjoyed writing?

S: Yeah, I liked describing--like the skiing and walking through the woods and stuff. I enjoy writing like that. 'Cause I enjoy doing it so...

T: And were there any parts that gave you trouble?

S: I don't think so. It's kind of like--I felt that it wasn't--like I--this first part, you know, I was just wondering in general and then I kinda switched into my own experience and that wasn't too smooth, I don't think. Yeah, you know, I just--the part where I was describing what we did.

T: Yeah, well you need the--let's see: "I wonder what part domestic animals play in the ecosystem.....Domesticated animals are personalized diversions for humans." See, you've answered it too soon.

S: But .....that's like an observation.

What stands out in this conference is the domination of the teacher. She speaks more than twice as much as the student (351 to 162 words), but a word count alone does not make clear the nature of that domination. The teacher seems to have in mind what Knoblauch and Brannon (1984) call an "ideal text." She has an image of the true version which this paper should ultimately conform to. In this truer state, the paper would illustrate, through the description of the author and her pet, the reasons why we treat pets in special ways. The language of the paper would be "human" and avoid broad assertions that might *answer* the question raised in the paper; rather, the author should indicate no more certainty than to suggest that, "God this is strange, we're funny creatures." Indeed, just after the excerpt I've quoted here, the teacher offers the student language for this ideal text, urging the student to qualify her assertions with "it seems to me..."--whereupon the student reminds the teacher that their textbook tells them to avoid "it seems."

Many changes that the student might make in moving toward this ideal text *would* improve the writing. The conclusion does seem too assured, and it doesn't deal with the complexity of the question raised. The problem is the lack of negotiation in the conference. The teacher identifies a problem and suggests remedies before the student is even convinced that a problem exists. Even at the very end of this first segment, the student repeats her justification of the conclusions as "observations." Paradoxically, when given an opportunity to state her own judgment of the paper, the student identifies the mismatch between the opening and the descriptive parts which, she claimed, she enjoyed writing more than the "scientific" opening. This judgment is not really so far from the agenda the teacher opens with. The conference might have looked a great deal different if the teacher had begun by focusing on the effectiveness of the descriptive passages and then encouraged the student to fit the opening and conclusions to this effective writing.

But because the teacher's agenda is set rather inflexibly early on, she misses this and other opportunities to build on the observations of the student. The student is shut out in two ways: first, she is put on the defensive when the instructor calls her conclusion "false." Then, even when the conclusion/observation issue is momentarily dropped, the teacher doesn't hear the student's contributions. When the student attempts a summary of the teacher's suggestions about the conclusion, the teacher changes the subject:

S: I don't have to make it so--like I ought to stick on this conclusion--which is unnecessary.

T: And also, when you do that you tend to lapse into this scientific language.

It is not at all clear that the student understands what is to be done with the ending, but the teacher moves on. Similarly, she fails to follow up on the student's comments about enjoying the writing of the descriptive parts. In her analysis of the transcript, the instructor admits that when the student identifies the problem with the shift from scientific to more casual descriptive language, she "stubbornly cling[s] to my diagnosis about questions and answers."

This conference illustrates what Freedman and Sperling (1985) call "cross-purpose talk":

> With no match in focal concern, T and S will likely be talking at cross purposes and may not even be attending to what the other is saying....This cross-purpose talk manifests itself in a T-S conference when S and T each bring up a topic of concern over and over again, no matter what the other wants to focus on, indicating that T and S have different agendas for what needs to be covered in the conference. (117)

The teacher reviewing the conference put the problem a bit more bluntly: "Mea culpa. I ran over this kid like a Mack truck."

"It Just Didn't Make Sense"

The final conference excerpt deals with a paper called "Mailaholic," which attempts to explain the writer's addiction to getting letters. It starts out in a lighthearted, almost "cute" way, detailing her love of various kinds of stamps and stationery and the way she and other dorm members place unopened letters on their lunch trays to flaunt the fact that someone has written to them. Then, as in the previous paper, there is a shift in tone, and, in brief paragraphs, the writer explains what letters from mother, boyfriend, and best friend mean. At first reading, this short paper--about 700 words total--seems the least promising of the three (the word superficial comes to mind). But like an expert canoeist, the teacher follows the current of the student's language to a real insight.

T: How do you feel about this paper?

S: I don't like it. I like the topic. I like the title, but I had a hard time...I had a lot of ideas I wanted to put in...and they didn't seem to flow. Like I read the paper that you gave us Thursday...I just liked it. Like everything flowed and went together smoothly. And this, I'm like...it just doesn't say anything. I wanted to say something but I didn't say it the right way.

T: OK. Tell me what you were trying to say...in a few sentences...if you had to tell me what your paper was about.

S: How much getting a letter means to me. But I just...I don't know...I like a lot of times, you know, it just didn't make sense. It was like I didn't know how to say it.

T: Do you think you addressed that anywhere on the page?

S: Yeah. I think where I'm saying about how I go about reading a letter. You know, after I ... if there's one there...after I've gotten a letter and just sit there and let everyone see it. And then when I get in the privacy of my own room... then I read it, 'cause then I feel I'm with the person rather than having all this noise around me and I can't concentrate.

T: Yes?

S: And then if I don't get a letter... I like sort of envy them and am real jealous. And it's like they do what I do...it's wrong because they're hurting me. I do the same thing. I put it on my lunch tray and let everyone see the letter.

T: Yes?

S: I like that part of it. Maybe I just don't like the beginning or how I get into it. I don't like the transitions. Sometimes I don't see how I get where I'm going.

T: OK. Then you think that perhaps you were trying to find your topic, found it, and then ran out of it?

S: Yeah.

T: Where do you think you really started to get into it?

S: On the second page.

T: All right...

S: But I don't really dig into the mess. What I understood about it is....I think that's where I actually start talking about what I mean to say about it, you know.

T: Yes?

S: So I suppose if I just cut off the first page and start it out with the rest?

T: Yes?

S: What I should try to do....

T: What other kind of things are you trying to say?

S: Uh....

T: When you think about what getting a letter really means.

S: Well, on the last page...about when I get a letter from my boyfriend, or my best friend, or my mom....what feelings I get when I get it...a letter from them.

By this point the agenda is set. The rest of the conference explores what these feelings are, and as the writer talks, she moves beyond the juvenile tone of the original draft to an insight into her own need for letters:

S: And like I was really close to my mom this summer. So it's like I'm up here and I don't want them to forget me. And so I just want to keep grasping...you know...to make sure that life is still going on. And when I go home....everything isn't going to be the same, but it isn't going to be dramatically different.

While this observation still relies, to a degree, on the commonplace "make sure that *life is still going on,"* the writer seems to have found a reason for her need for letters.

She has been able to make these moves toward understanding because the teacher gave her room. The ratio of teacher talk to student talk differs radically from the second conference quoted earlier. Here the teacher speaks only 97 words to the student's 397, and in many of the exchanges she simply prods the student with a "yes." Such a ratio, of course, may not be an "ideal" to work towards; so much student talk could be digressive. But in this case, the student seems to be working from a global and unformed dissatisfaction with her paper to a more analytic evaluation that will guide her revision. The writer's initial evaluative responses were scattered: it doesn't "flow," it has a lot of ideas, it "doesn't say anything," and "I don't think I did it the right way." The teacher's question about the intent of the paper causes the writer to identify her purposes--to explain what letters meant to her. And again, in response to the teacher's question, the student notes that only on the second page does she really deal with her newly stated purpose. The writer is closing in; she admits that although she begins to deal with her focus on the second page, she doesn't "really dig into the mess." The teacher then pushes her in this direction by asking what things she was trying to say about getting letters; the agenda for the rest of the conference is set.

Or almost set. The student does offer up a concern early in the conference--a concern the teacher wisely ignores. In her first evaluation of this paper, the student says, "I don't think I did it the right way." This comment, common in an early writing conference, suggests that the student has been taught some ironclad rules for writing essays, and she wants to see whether these rules still apply. Toward the end of the conference, this concern once again surfaces as the student asks about her conclusion:

S: When you write a conclusion, is it supposed to be restating the beginning of the thing? I had a hard time. I didn't know how to end it.

The teacher responds that the writer must decide for herself and that each paper is different.

Finally, this conference illustrates the role of talk in revision. Revision is often used synonymously with rewriting; we change our writing by writing again and making changes. The student in this conference is revising by talking; she is creating an alternative text, an oral text that can be juxtaposed against the one she has written. The next draft she might write is not simply a nebulous possibility; rather, it is a draft that has, to a degree, been spoken. Near the end of the conference the teacher asks what she might do next, and the student answers, "I think I'll probably cut off the first page and a half and work on ....I don't know....giving examples. *Like what I told you a few minutes ago.*"

This emphasis on allowing students to speak these oral texts may seem almost insultingly self-evident. But in reading and annotating these transcripts, teachers were appalled at the opportunities that were missed--when they cut off students, and when they *told* students to expand a section rather than allowing them to expand orally. Students did not get a chance to hear what they know.

Implications

The lessons to be learned from this kind of self-examination are painfully obvious--but worth remembering because, in our eagerness to teach, we often forget the obvious.

1.   We all tend to talk too much. The little lecturettes that pop up in writing conferences usually bring things to a grinding halt.

2.   The opening minutes of the conference are critically important in giving the conference direction--they act as a kind of *lead*. The student's contributions in these opening minutes need to be used to give the conference a mutually agreeable and mutually understood direction.

3.   These agendas should be limited to one or two major concerns. Conferences seem to break down when a discussion about a "high-level" concern like purpose veers abruptly to a discussion of sentence structure.

4.   Potentially, student contributions to the agenda-setting process often are missed if the teacher has *fixed* on a problem early. It is particularly easy for the teacher to fix on the agenda if he or she takes the papers home and marks them up before the conference. Furthermore, a marked-up paper indicates to the student that the agenda has *already* been set.

5.   While the teacher must be responsive to the student's contributions in the writing conference, this does not mean that the teacher is non-directive. Students, like the one in the

first conference, may at first be unfamiliar with the evaluative-analytic language of the writing conference. These students often need to see how the teacher reads so they might get an operative understanding of what a term like "focus" means. The modeling described by Richard Beach (this volume) is vitally important in this type of conference. Unfortunately, listing conclusions like this implies that the difficulty of conferences can be smoothed out and problems prevented. This is not my position.

I see the writing conference as a dialectic encounter between teacher and student, in which both assume complex roles. The teacher, in particular, cannot escape the difficult choices between praise and support, suggestion and silence, each choice carrying with it a risk. For that reason, I am uncomfortable with some of the metaphors increasingly used to describe this complex relationship, many of which echo private property and contractual law. The writer, we are told, "owns" the text, which should not be "appropriated" by the teacher (Knoblauch and Brannon 1982). Graves (1983) has similarly urged that the student has "ownership" of the text. Knoblauch and Brannon (1984) describe the ideal reading of a student text as follows: It is the rare composition teacher who reads student writing with the assumption that composers legitimately control their own discourses, who accepts the possibility that student intentions matter more than teacher expectations as a starting-point for reading, and who recognizes that the writer's choices are supposed to make sense mainly in terms of those intentions, not in proportion as they gratify a reader's point of view of what should have been said. (120) The polarization of terms in this description is striking: student intentions/teacher expectations, student control/teacher control. And the term "legitimately" introduces, once again, the implication that in defining the role of the teacher we are working within clear, almost legal, boundaries.

But if we push on these metaphors a bit, they wobble. Ownership implies clear property lines guaranteed by legal statutes that are (at least to lawyers) clearly spelled out. For the most part, those who own property can do what they want to with it, so long as the owner is not creating a major inconvenience to others. Those of us who view the property may have opinions about the esthetics of the house built on it, but the owner need not listen, and we need to be very careful about passing on these judgments.

The metaphor of ownership is not slippery enough. To a degree, the student owns his or her paper, but the paper is *intended* for others in the way property isn't; and so, to a degree, the writing is also owned by its readers. No one (I hope) condones the practice condemned by Knoblauch and Brannon in which students must guess at some Platonic text that exists in the teacher's imagination. But by the same token, the expectations of the teacher, the course, and the academy must interact with the intentions of the student. Intention, in other words, cannot be an absolute, a "God-term."

Let's take this paragraph you are now beginning to read. Who owns it--you or I? Does my intention *matter* more than your response? Questions. like these divide the writing act in an unhelpful way. The text is neither mine nor yours--no one owns it. Even in writing it, I didn't feel that I was putting *my* meaning into language that would fit *your* needs. Rather,: there was a constant interplay between audience and intention so that I can no longer disentangle my meanings from your expectations. I did not feel set against you, my audience; rather, you became part of me in the act of writing. And so it is in a good writing conference, like the third one I quoted, where the teacher becomes an active instrument in the student's search for meaning.

I began this chapter by claiming that few courses at the university push freshmen to assume responsibility for their own learning. I'd like to close with an instance of one that did, a philosophy course, which caused an almost Copernican shift in the writer's view of what it is to be a student. It is, I believe, the same kind of shift that a good writing course can initiate. The paper, written for a freshman English course, is entitled "Philosophy Is Messing Up My Life," and it begins with the anxiety the student felt about taking an introductory philosophy course. At first the professor appeared intimidating, with a "strong philosophical nose, and eyes that could eat a question mark right through you." When the roll was called the writer barely managed an audible "here." Once the class started, the student opened his notebook and expected the instructor to begin by writing a definition of philosophy on the board. But he didn't. He asked questions to show the students that philosophy is, in this student's words, a "process of questioning and answering things you don't understand in an attempt to arrive at the `right' answer, which usually doesn't exist anyway."

This process of questioning has taken hold and started to "mess up his life":

I start out by asking myself questions about life. I've come up with some disturbing answers.... The reason I called this paper "Philosophy Is Messing Up My Life" is because most of the answers make me look bad. I don't like that at all. Realizing that I have a philosophy has opened up a whole new world for me that I never knew existed. I'm not sure I'm ready for the truth yet. But I've made truth my responsibility. . .

When we push students to speak, to evaluate; when we listen and don't rush in to fill silences, we may be able to transform the rules of studenthood in the way this philosophy professor did. And when we pose this challenge, we will be working at the very epicenter of a liberal education.

Acknowledgments

I would like to acknowledge the help of graduate students who recorded, transcribed, and annotated the conference excerpts used in this chapter. Thanks also to Elizabeth Chiseri Strater for her help on this project.

References

Carnicelli, T. 1980. The Writing Conference: A One-to-One Conversation. In *Eight Approaches to Teaching Composition,* edited by T. Donovan and B.McClelland, 101-32. Urbana, IL: National Council of Teachers of English.

Freedman, S., and M. Sperling. 1985. Written Language Acquisition: The Role of Response in the Writing Conference. In *The Acquisition of Written Language: Response and Revision,* edited by S. Freedman, 106-30. Norwood NJ: Ablex.

Graves, D. 1983. *Writing: Teachers and Children at Work.* Exeter, NH: Heinemann.

Knoblauch, C., and L. Brannon. 1982. On Students' Rights to Their Own Texts: A Model of Teacher Response. *College Composition and Communication* 33:157-66.

Knoblauch, C., and L. Brannon.1984. *Rhetorical Traditions and Modern Writing.* Upper Montclair, NJ: Boynton/Cook.

TEACHING COMPOSITION TO SPEAKERS OF OTHER LANGUAGES: AN OVERVIEW

Joy Reid

Even experienced teachers of composition whose students are generally native English speakers may experience discomfort and puzzlement when they find nonnative speakers of English (ESL students) in their classes—even before those ESL students submit their first writing assignment. New or less experienced composition teachers of native English speakers may face those same feelings as they first begin to teach, but they usually have the advantage that, at the very least, *they* have been native English-speaking students before they became teachers. Their experiences as students in U.S. classrooms have prepared them to understand both the expectations of their students and the nonverbal clues that native English speakers (NESs) offer in the classroom: heads nodding notetaking, raised eyebrows, shifting in seats, shrugged shoulders, and the like. In contrast, teachers who encounter ESL students may have only limited knowledge about and experience with diverse cultures. The expected protocols for asking questions, teacher-student exchanges, indicating understanding, and even group work that seem so "normal" in a class of NESs may be foreign to ESL students.

When composition teachers encounter the writing of their ESL students, their confusion and irritation may increase. A single ESL student paper may contain word-and sentence-level errors that differ in kind (if not in number or level of severity) from NES errors. In addition, there may be differences in the writer's percep5tions of the effective presentation of ideas in an academic setting. These differences between ESL and NES errors and perceptions may well make the ESL errors more visible (in the words on one teacher, "They seem to jump off the page") and so seem even more egregious to the teacher-evaluator. This essay discusses several major areas in which the needs of ESL students differ from those of NESs; it also provides information from experienced ESL composition teachers concerning the identification of typical ESL writing problems and suggests some solutions.

"Ear" Learners and "Eye" Learners

In much the same way that NESs differ in background knowledge, motivation, and perspective, it is important to realize that ESL students are not a homogeneous group. In addition to the clear diversity in language and cultural backgrounds, ESL students in U.S. colleges and universities can also be described in terms of the scenarios in which they acquired their second language. Specifically, most of the international (or "visa") students—students who travel to the United States from their homelands to attend post secondary institutions—differ from ESL students who have grown up in the United States, who have graduated from U.S. high schools, and may be permanent U.S. residents or citizens.

Students who have studied English as a second language outside the United States and have entered postsecondary institutions here have, for the most part, acquired English *visually*: They have read and studied about the structures of the language. However, their practice in producing written English has been limited to occasional tests and papers in the classroom. Moreover, because cultures evolve writing styles appropriate to their own histories and the needs of their societies, many international students have assumptions about the presentation of written ideas that are appropriate for their native discourse communities but not necessarily to the United States. A great majority of the students have not articulated or even considered those assumptions. As Ilona Leki [20] points out, not many educational systems appear to teach rhetorical patterns or the use of specific language structures for different communication purposes directly in the school setting. Indeed, in most countries outside the United States, there are virtually no courses in writing. Therefore, many international students have limited awareness of their writing strategies and underdeveloped rhetorical skills, even in their first languages.

In contrast, U.S. residents (that is, ESL students who have lived and attended secondary schools in the United States) have acquired much of their English through their *ears*. Although they may have had ESL classes alongside their regular public school work, their English has been learned mainly through immersion in the language. As a result of this aural basis, their spoken language may be fluent and comprehensible, and their writing may appear fluent. However, because these students have limited knowledge of the structures of English, their writing may appear more or less phonetic, with limited and perhaps incorrect use of the structures (verb tenses, prepositions, word forms) of the language.

This single difference between international and U.S. resident ESL students—whether they acquired their English principally through their ears or their eyes—bears directly on the strengths and weaknesses these students bring to their writing classes and significantly affects the ways teachers can approach writing processes with the ESL students in each group.

Intercultural Communication in the Classroom

Initially, the experience of teaching ESL students may parallel the "blind-random" setting on an exercise step machine. At this setting, the rhythm of the stepping slows and speeds up automatically and randomly, and so the stepper is "blind," not knowing when the rhythm will change or in what direction. Almost certainly, the inexperienced teacher of ESL students encounters periods of "randomness," of surprising incidents, time frames, and rhythms. Furthermore, because of the cultural differences between teacher and students and among the students themselves, the randomness is frequently not preceded by any clues—it occurs "blindly." The results: frustration and misperceptions for both teachers and students.

At the same time as composition teachers are struggling to accommodate their ESL students' needs, the ESL students may also be struggling to adjust their perceptions to a "foreign" classroom environment; that is, "blind-random" occurs on both sides of the desk. Even ESL students who have attended U.S. public schools and have lived in the United States most of their lives carry many of their first-culture values, needs, and expectations into their second-language classrooms. Researchers have shown that cultural differences between (and among) ESL students and their teachers may involve how students view teachers and student attitudes toward teaching and learning [1,2,12]. The degree of authority invested in and expected from the teacher, as well as the degree to which the teacher directs and dominates class activities, depends to a large extent on culture. For example, many Asian cultures (both in North American populations and in Asia) have

315

a tradition of deference: questioning a person in authority—a parent, a teacher—is disrespectful, and receptive, as opposed to proactive, learning is the key to success. In a U.S. college composition class, however, such behavior may be seen as inappropriately nonparticipatory.

In contrast, the strong cooperative values and high level of social responsibility of many Latin societies (in both North America and South America) make the highly individualized and competitive values of many U.S. students seem unpleasantly aggressive. For the newly arrived international student, the adjustment may be even more jarring: A class in the United States must seem a structureless, anarchical situation for learning. In the United States, composition students are expected to take an active part in the learning process, asking questions, challenging each other and their teachers, working (often loudly) in small groups with peers they know only slightly. Consequently, many ESL students must identify and practice a variety of learning behaviors. In fact, a truly multicultural class can result in substantial classroom imbalance in perspectives and even cross-cultural tensions as students and teachers struggle to develop appropriate roles and interactions.

Contrastive Rhetoric and the Composition Teacher

Robert Kaplan first defined contrastive rhetoric when he sought to discover whether organizational patterns of written material vary from culture to culture [16]. In his investigation of six hundred student expository paragraphs, written in English by native speakers of many non-English-language backgrounds, Kaplan used philosophical, psychological, anthropological, and linguistic insights to describe the differences between the essentially linear English paragraph, which does not tolerate digression or repetition, and paragraphs that he classified generally as Semitic, Oriental, Romance, and Russian. He represented the differences graphically (Figure 1); at the same time, he cautioned that "much more detailed and more accurate descriptions are required before any meaningful contrastive system can be elaborated."

Figure 1: Kaplan's Contrastive Rhetoric Diagram

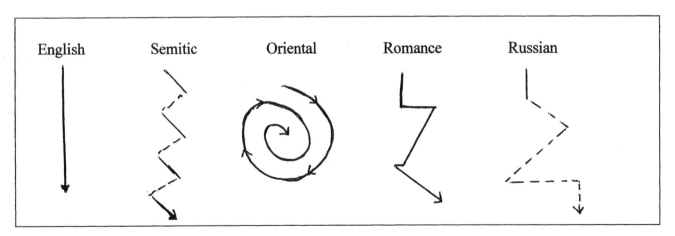

Since the appearance of Kaplan's article, the notion of contrastive rhetoric, along with the issues surrounding the transfer of rhetorical patterns in second-language writing, has grown into an area of study. Research reported by proponents of this theory, published in a collection edited by Kaplan [15] and a resource book by Ulla Connor [6] demonstrate that the style in which each culture organizes and presents written material reflects the preferences of that particular culture. As a result, ESL writers often intuitively employ a rhetoric and a sequence of thought that violate the expectations of the native reader. When they write for readers in another culture, they often have problems with identifying audience expectations and communicating effectively with different discourse communities.

Even within a language, there appear to be different rhetorical rules and conventions that govern different categories of texts. Leki [20] and John Swales [24] indicate that in U.S. academic classes, discipline-specific writing conventions differ in such diverse areas as length of sentences, choice of vocabulary, acceptability of using first person, extent of using passive voice, degree to which writers are permitted to interpret, and amount of metaphorical language accepted. According to William Grabe and Robert Kaplan [12], the ESL writer is also likely to have a different notion of what constitutes evidence, of the order in which evidence should best be presented, and of the amount of evidence needed to explain a topic or persuade the reader.

Background Information in the Composition Classroom

Successful communication rests on background knowledge and experience that is shared by writers and readers; that is, the prior knowledge of student writers necessarily influences what, and how, they write. Consequently, ESL students can face misunderstanding and even failure in their academic written work not just because of second-language errors but also because they are often unaware of the content expectations and of the rhetorical problems in their prose.

Unfortunately, there is no reason to assume that ESL writers will acquire the conventions of written academic English without assistance. Because ESL writers often organize and present material in ways that are different from NESs, providing necessary cultural information about the rhetorical organization of U.S. academic expository text and audience expectations of such text will help ESL students' writing be more effective. In other words, teachers must help their ESL writing students acquire appropriate linguistic, content, and rhetorical background knowledge.

For ESL students, then, the composition course is much more than a skills course; it is also a content course in which they need to learn about audience and purpose, levels of content specificity, general writing strategies, and academic formats, perhaps for the first time. The students need to know that writing involves not only linguistic processes but social and cognitive processes as well: when it is appropriate to write, what is appropriate to write for an identified audience in a specific situation, and how to organize ideas appropriately for that audience and purpose. In addition, ESL students (and less experienced NES writers as well) need to learn repertoires of strategies to generate ideas, draft pieces of writing, and encounter feedback from peers and teachers. To assist their ESL students toward those goals, composition teachers may well need to be more didactic; certainly they must become cultural informants for their students, by doing all of the following:

317

- Identifying and explaining the rhetorical and contextual variables in U.S. academic writing
- *Researching* U.S. academic writing assignments and the expectations of the discourse communities that design, assign, and evaluate those assignments
- Investigating and discussing the writing conventions of U.S. academic discourse genres
- Providing opportunities for students to practice and experiment with the rhetoric and language that fulfills the expectations of U.S. academic readers

Recognize that although such differences between ESL and NES writers may affect communication in a U.S. academic discourse community, they should not be stigmatized as deficiencies. As Alan Purves and his colleagues reported, differences among rhetorical patterns do not represent differences in cognitive ability but rather differences in cognitive style [22]. After all, arrangement and presentation of ideas, as well as style, can all be defined, practiced, and valued in many ways. However, ESL writers (like NESs) must acquire the background knowledge necessary to identify and fulfill the expectations of the U.S. academic audience; knowledge about appropriate language use, content, and genre can empower ESL students.

Accuracy, Fluency, and the Issue of Error

Teachers of ESL writers will almost certainly face student essays with linguistic and rhetorical problems that are related to the first languages of the students or "developmental" problems that are the result of limitations in students' previous education. Barbara Kroll describes a useful way in which ESL writing proficiency can be broadly divided into categories: *plus-syntax* and *minus-syntax, plus-rhetoric* and *minus-rhetoric* [17]. "One paper can provide insightful commentary on a substantive topic while replete with problems in spelling and punctuation [+rhetoric and –syntax]. Another paper can exhibit wide range of sentence structures, flawless syntax, adherence to mechanics, yet lack development and support of its central thesis [-rhetoric and +syntax]." Still another paper may be hard to read because it contains both second-language errors and a lack of coherence [-rhetoric and –syntax]. In terms of the two broad categories of ESL students described in this essay, typical international student ("eye" learner) writing, will demonstrate limited coherence, particularly a limited knowledge of academic forms and audience expectations [-rhetoric]. In contrast, typical resident student ("ear" learner) writing will often demonstrate some knowledge of expected U. S. rhetorical forms and fluency but may also contain many language errors [-syntax].

The perceived dichotomy between fluency and accuracy has been discussed in language teaching for decades: Should the language teacher concentrate on one or the other? Traditionally, accuracy has been defined as the focus on discrete elements of the rules of language, while fluency has been defined as the focus on the communication of ideas without consideration of discrete language elements. This is probably a false dichotomy. A focus on fluency does not necessarily exclude consideration of the systematic properties of language; after all, it is not possible to communicate successfully without some knowledge and monitoring of the language of the message. Similarly, a focus on accuracy demands concentration on discrete points of language but does not necessarily curb creativity and self-expression, ignore cognitive processes, or overlook personality traits of the learner.

At the basis of the accuracy-fluency controversy is the question of error. Once thought to be deviant behavior, error—in both first- and second-language acquisition—is now regarded as a natural phenomenon. Research has demonstrated clearly that ESL errors are generally neither random nor sporadic nor deviant. Instead, they are systematic, regular, and rule-governed, the result of intelligence, not stupidity. ESL errors come from a conscious or unconscious attempt by students to use what they have learned.

The Foundations of Error

Of course, errors in written language can be due to inattention, memory lapse, or indifference. Moreover, in an in-class writing situation, NESs as well as ESL students will make hasty "performance errors" that they may have neither the time nor the ability to monitor. More serious errors that interfere with clear communication are unacceptable in both NES and ESL writing. However, an understanding of the logical bases for second-language error in writing may mitigate the visceral reaction that excludes other components of the student writing.

For many ESL "ear" learners, error can occur as a result of often unconscious rule formation that is based on their oral-aural experiences or of their misinterpretation of a rule half-learned. Some of these "rules" may be partially correct; others may be incorrect. Following are examples of incorrect "rules" cited by U.S. resident ESL students:

- Capitalize all nouns.
- Always put a comma after *but*.
- All the verbs in a paragraph have to be in the same tense.

In addition, these oral-aural acquirers of English often mix formal and informal language and use ear-based (phonetic) spellings that may involve, say, omitting verb inflections. Here are some examples, with informal language in boldface and incorrect spelling/word forms in italics:

Young folks usually get a better **kick out of** trips than older people
It is imperative to **hang around** a large number of **kids**.
They will want to **take off ASAP**.
The students are *taken* their time.
Some of the reasons *while* **guys** getting jobs.
Students are *awared* of these matters.

In many ways, these "ear" learners are doubly disadvantaged in their writing. First, because their "eye" study of English has been limited, they may not have the necessary background knowledge to frame the structures of the language or even to talk about and understand the structures they are using. In addition, the"rules" they have used to categorize their language experiences must be analyzed, "unlearned," then relearned and habituated, a time-consuming and often frustrating experience.

Many NESs have experienced the process of unlearning and relearning a language structure on a much smaller scale. Consider the NES child raised in a relatively standard American English atmosphere who, as an adult and an English teacher, learns that she uses one English structure incorrectly: *lay/lie*. Having habituated that error for a quarter of a century, she spends the next twenty-five years "monitoring" for that error, thinking about the rules governing *lay* and *lie* before she uses those words, "unlearning," relearning, practicing, and, more often than not, avoiding that structure. Such habituated or "fossilized" language behavior, whether a single grammatical structure or an inappropriate oral response, is easy to identify but difficult to monitor, and that behavior is nearly impossible to change permanently, at least in a short period of time. For the ESL student (and especially for the "ear" learner), with not one but dozens of habituated language errors, writing flawless English prose is at best an overwhelming prospect.

Yet for many international students, grammatical error may come not so much from unconscious rule formation as from overgeneralization of rules they have learned through their eyes. That is, international ESL students may hypothesize, consciously or subconsciously, about a language form by extending the use of a rule they have learned in the second language. For instance, if the rule says that third-person singular verbs must take an *–s* ('he *runs*"), ESL students may overgeneralize the rule to include second-person singular verbs (you *runs*"). The hypothesis is incorrect, but it does reflect the systematic application of a rule. In these cases, students who can identify or monitor for language errors can learn to reformulate new hypotheses and adopt new learning strategies to correct the errors.

When ESL students who have studied the structure of English encounter a language form, they often infer rules from previous knowledge of their first language; they "transfer" that knowledge into a hypothesis about the second language. For that reason, students from the same language background may well make some of the same types of errors, though their hypotheses (and therefore the resulting language) may not be exactly the same. For example, native speakers of Spanish may use adjectives that have both gender and number and that follow, rather than precede, the verb (the flowers *reds*") because those rules apply in Spanish. Such first-language transfer occurs not only with grammatical structures but with first-language writing skills and strategies as well. ESL writers often transfer both good and weak writing skills from their first language into English, and many ESL students who have not developed good strategies for writing in their first language will not have appropriate strategies to transfer to their second language.

Next, if a language rule is particularly obscure, complex, or difficult, students may make errors as they attempt to construct the language form, or they may avoid the form altogether. For example, why is one of these sentences incorrect?

- People, who are against the English-only movement, might say that . . .
- Anne, who is against the English only movement, might say that . . .

Level of difficulty is a complicated concept, for it is in part dependent on both first-language differences and prior student experience. For example, while English is a subject-verb-object (SVO) language, Korean is a subject-object-verb (SOV) language, and word order is relatively free. A sentence in English, translated into Korean and then retranslated, word for word, into English, shows the differences:

English: Even though I told John not to take the chemistry class, he took it.
Korean: Even though I John chemistry class not to take told, John it too.

In addition to word order, many Asian languages are "tonal." That is, they have few or no inflections (such as verb tense and plural markers). Chinese, for instance, is a language that has no verb tenses and no articles; learning the complex rules for English verb tenses is an enormous task, and implementing those rules expands the task geometrically. Article use in English is often arbitrary and filled with exceptions; consequently, correct use of articles for an ESL student whose native language does not have articles is extremely difficult. For instance, try formulating the rules needed for the following examples, and consider the consequent decisions Asian ESL students must make. (X) indicates that no article is needed.

She considered him (a) genius.
(X) (The) number seven is lucky.
(The) only girl at (the) party was Nan.
(A/The) funny picture on (a/the) page

going to (a/the) church	versus	going to (X) church
going to (a/the) store	versus	going (x) (X) home
going on (a/the) journey	versus	going to (X) work

Some English-language structures are more difficult for learners of one second language than another. For Arabic speakers, relative clauses are easier to use than auxiliary verbs in English because relative clauses in Arabic parallel use in English (though in Arabic, the relative clause requires the use of a personal pronoun, resulting in such structures as "The man who likes coffee *he* . . ."). In contrast, there are no auxiliary verbs in Arabic, so a structure like "She taking a class" is a common error. And native Chinese speakers tend to avoid relative clauses in their writing because that structure does not occur in their language. In short, ESL students are similar to NES students of foreign languages: nativelike accuracy in nonnative-language writing is a lifelong struggle, so both students and their teachers must expect language errors in student writing.

Finally, because most international ("eye"learner) students have had many opportunities to practice written English at the single-sentence level but only limited practice with writing English in extended discourse, they will discover that they make grammatical and sentence structure errors even while they are following their "eye"-learned rules. For example, recent work in genre studies has shown that narrative writing, which occurs in history textbooks, research reports, newspaper articles, and in background sections of textbooks in many fields, is usually taught as occurring in the past tense. Yet work by Doug Biber [2], and expanded on by Pat Byrd [3] and Katherine Bardovi-Harling [1], demonstrates that the "backgrounding" in narrative (seen, for instance, in backgrounding and interpretation of the narrative) uses other verb forms, including past perfect and present perfect tenses.

In light of this discussion, teachers should consider the following points:

- Although ESL writing errors rarely approximate those of NESs either in number or in kind, their visibility should not immediately trigger negative responses.
- Looking beyond the irritating errors to rhetorical and contextual successes or problems, as teachers commonly do with NES writing, is essential.
- Habituated errors are difficult for students to see and even more difficult to supplant with habituated correct forms.
- Even ESL student writers who both comprehend and are able to produce correct English grammar and sentence structures in discrete exercises often cannot manage the complexities of language use in extended English discourse.
- Most ESL errors are a normal, natural, and necessary part of the learning process.

Teachers of ESL students who are interested in their students; errors may fruitfully investigate contrastive analysis studies that examine features of a native language (e.g. English) that contrast with features of another language (e.g. Spanish, Japanese) to determine what areas of second-language learning are most likely to cause difficulty for their students [25, 26]. In such an investigation, teachers may well discover that the students themselves are the best sources of contrastive analysis information and, more important, that asking students to analyze (and perhaps to log) their errors may prove beneficial to their learning processes.

Another interesting area for examination is "error gravity" studies, in which researchers investigate the "irritation" or "acceptance" levels of NESs—usually university non-ESL faculty—to specific second-language errors. To help teachers and students prioritize language errors and edit more successfully, error gravity studies focus on what second-language errors either interfere most with NES comprehension or irritate the NES academic reader. For example, Roberta Vann and her colleagues investigated the responses of 164 faculty members to twelve typical ESL errors [27]. They found that most respondents did not judge all errors as equally severe; incorrect word order (as in the direct translation of our sample Korean sentence) and incorrect word use were considered the most serious, and spelling errors the least severe.

Evaluation

Given the problems any second-language learner can have with accuracy in writing, the problem of evaluation facing the composition teacher with ESL students is substantial. "Lowering standards" or asking less of ESL student writers is not a viable solution, yet language errors must be seen in perspective: ESL students (and any writers in a second or foreign language) may have adequate knowledge of correct usage but find it difficult to produce accurate prose consistently. There is more, much more, to successful written communication than the use of articles. Liz Hamp-Lyons notes that evaluation works best and is most fair to learners when it takes into account who the learner is, the situation in which the writers produce writing, and the overall context in which educational success is to be measured for the student writer [13].

Therefore, as teachers carefully develop evaluative criteria—as they develop the writing assignment and before they assign the writing—the criteria should be realistically grounded in the discourse communities the students will face outside the classroom. The composition teacher might then consider giving a separate grade for language or perhaps three grades for each assignment: organization, content, and mechanics. Or teachers might even give several grades for each paper in areas of focus for that paper: coherence, use of detail, audience awareness, and so on. Such a grading scheme would allow students to identify their writing strengths and weaknesses more easily. An average of those grades, some of which might be weighted differently, might be the overall grade for the paper. Finally, the evaluative criteria must be explicitly articulated: Students have the right to know the bases on which they are being evaluated.

Moreover, students learn to do best what teachers can demonstrate. Dana Ferris's seminal large-scale study with ESL students and revision indicates that because "a significant proportion of the comments appeared to lead to substantive student revisions" [9], teachers should be careful in developing their responding strategies, explaining their responding strategies to their students, helping students learn to revise, and holding students accountable for considering feedback they receive. In short, feedback without follow-up (in the form of discussion, practice, and graded revisions) will be less than effective. Researchers Ann Fathman and Elizabeth Whalley [8], as well as Ferris [10], found that students can become independent editors of their own written work when teacher response and intervention during the writing process and t4eacher correction of error are clear. In other words, the response or correction must adequately describe the problem and then suggest a means of correction. And of course, early intervention and explanation feedback can help students identify and solve language problems before evaluation occurs.

In contrast, in any teacher intervention, marking local (discrete) errors or commenting on global alternatives must occur with consideration of the student and the writing context. For example, marks that do not identify errors are ineffectual; after all, virtually no student intentionally turns in an error-ridden paper for evaluation. For the same reason, comments asking students to "organize" when they think they already have done so are at best confusing for the students. Instead, teachers might begin by marking, but not correcting, language errors and then asking students to distinguish between errors that they immediately recognize (and can therefore monitor) and errors that they do not recognize (and so need intervention and explanation). Identifying and then prioritizing language errors ("Work on X first because those errors interfere with reader comprehension") can make monitoring for error easier for ESL students.

Next, careful planning of peer response groups and teacher intervention throughout the writing process can help ESL students identify problems and solutions. Conferencing, individually or in small groups, is another intervention technique that can prove useful for ESL students. Lynn Goldstein and Susan Conrad discuss the problems and the benefits of conferencing with ESL students about specific language and rhetorical problems during the drafting process; they advise prior training of students to prepare them for the different role of a conferee, and they agree that successful conferencing can strengthen writing skills and develop independent decision making, so vital in successful writing [11].

Finally, as Rebecca Oxford points out, ESL students (and NESs as well) must be trained in necessary strategies to deal with peer and teacher feedback and to correct their errors and must be given the time to digest appropriately and then to practice corrections [21]. Students must also acquire effective strategies in the processes of composing, drafting, and editing that facilitate student learning. Knowledge of resources other than the teacher (reference books, World Wide Web, interviews and surveys, textbooks, peers, the campus writing center) will enable students to seek help with their academic writing outside of class, even after the course has ended.

Conclusion

Identifying and studying the differences in communication styles and strategies between cultures is worthwhile, even necessary, for both ESL students and their teachers. The more understanding that exists, the better prepared teachers will be to communicate effectively with their students; the more students understand about those differences, the more easily they will fulfill their academic readers' expectations. Building background knowledge about academic writing can facilitate student success by enabling students to learn the social processes, the appropriate use of language, and the rhetorical conventions for written communication within academic discourse communities.

How teachers focus on ESL students in their classrooms depends, at least in part, on their goals for all students, on how and for whom they want to empower those students. If, as Robert Land and Catherine Whitley suggest, the objective of a composition class, particularly a class with ESL students, is "to acquire enough facility with Standard Written English (SWE) to succeed in school and in the workplace," an effective pedagogy would include teaching composition not only as a skills course but also as a content course [19]. Grabe and Kaplan have indicated that for ESL students, the content of a composition course must include such areas as composing and revision strategies, coherence systems and mechanisms, language features, rhetorical patterns, audience characteristics and expectations, and genre conventions [12].

Annotated Bibliography: Suggested Readings

1. Bardovi-Harling, Katherine. "Tense and Aspect in (Con)Text." *Grammar and Discourse* 3 (1996): 19-33.

2. Biber, Douglas. *Variation across Speech and Writing.* Cambridge: Cambridge UP, 1988. For this original research, Biber wrote a computer text analysis program, then gathered a large corpus of spoken and written English. His computer text analysis of this corpus revealed that the grammar of spoken and of written English differ in several ways and that the grammar in each is used in "clusters." For teachers interested in language and genre, an essential book.

3. Brislin, R. W., K. Cushner, C. Cherrie, and M. Yong. *Intercultural Interactions: A Practical Guide.* Newbury Park, CA: Sage, 1986.
   The most practical volume in the Sage Series on Cross-Cultural Research and methodology, this book contains "100 Critical Incidents." Each situation focuses on some common (and perhaps universal) characteristic of interpersonal interaction. Following are essays that integrate and interpret the points made in the critical incidents. Accessible, discussible, and eminently educational.

4. Byrd, Pat, ed. *Teaching across Cultures in the University ESL Program.* Washington, DC:NAFSA, 1986.
   An excellent collection of articles that provides background discussions of relevant issues in cross-cultural communication, useful descriptions of cultural programs developed at several institutions, and explanations of materials and methods developed by individual teachers for use in cross-cultural classrooms.

5. Byrd, Pat, and Joy Reid. *Grammar in the Composition Classroom.* Boston: Heinle and Heinle, 1998.
   Insights into the paradigm that demonstrates grammar from context and grammar "clusters," as well as additional information about responding to and evaluating ESL writing, offer teachers both theoretical and practical ideas.

6. Connor, Ulla. *Contrastive Rhetoric: Cross-Cultural Aspects of Second Language Writing.* Cambridge: Cambridge UP, 1996.
   Draws on a wide body of interdisciplinary literature to define and explain contrastive rhetoric. Using a variety of languages, she demonstrates how ESL writers draw on a range of cross-linguistic and cross-cultural influences. Of special interest to teachers of ESL writers are Chapter 2, "Contrastive Rhetoric in Applied Linguistics,' and Chapter 8, "Genre-Specific Studies in Contrastive Rhetoric."

7. Connor, Ulla, and Robert B. Kaplan, eds. *Writing across Languages: Analysis of L2 Text.* Reading, MA: Addison-Wesley, 1987.
   Describes the concept of contrastive rhetoric, discusses empirical research in the contrastive rhetoric of many languages with English, and suggests applications of such research in the teaching of ESL writing.

8. Fathman, Ann, and Elizabeth Whalley. "Teacher Response to Student Writing: Focus on Form vs. Content." *Second Language Writing: Research Insights for the Classroom.* Ed. Barbara Kroll. New York: Cambridge UP, 1990. 178-190.

9. Ferris, Dana R. "The Influence of Teacher Commentary on Student Revisions." *TESOL Quarterly* 31 (1997): 315-339.

10. Ferris, Dana R. "Student Reactions to Teacher Response in Multiple-Draft Composition Classrooms." *TESOL Quarterly* 29 (1995): 33-53.

11. Goldstein, Lynn M., and Susan M. Conrad. "Student Input and Negotiation of Meaning in ESL Writing Conferences." *TESOL Quarterly* 24 (1990): 441-60.

    A detailed description of an ethnographic study that demonstrated the problems of group work and, particularly, student teacher conferences with ESL students. The authors provide advice and activities for training ESL students to assume appropriate roles in conferences and small group settings.

12. Grabe, William, and Robert B. Kaplan. "Writing in a Second Language: Contrastive Rhetoric." *Richness in Writing: Empowering ESL Students.* Ed. D. Johnson and D. Roen. New York: Longman. 263-83.

    In this article (in a book that contains many valuable articles about teaching ESL writing), the authors summarize and synthesize prior and current research in contrastive rhetoric, the detail suggestions for raising awareness and informing teachers about the fundamentals of contrastive rhetoric. In addition, they offer specific pedagogical advice for teaching writing to ESL students from different language and cultural backgrounds.

13. Hamp-Lyons, Liz, ed. *Assessing ESL Writing in Academic Contexts.* Norwood, NJ: Ablex, 1992.

    This collection of articles written by the growing number of researchers in ESL testing, focuses on the testing of ESL writing. It follows a clear, carefully written explanation of the issues in this research area; the assessment issues discussed range from validity questions concerning commercial writing tests to practical questions concerning classroom testing. Other issues discussed include cross-cultural assessment, academic literacy, criteria and scoring models, needs assessment, and models of feedback.

14. Johnson, K. *Understanding Communication in Second language Classrooms.* Cambridge: Cambridge UP, 1995.

    Using data from authentic classroom discourse, Johnson examines teacher-student interaction from both teacher and learner perspectives. By investigating classroom dynamics, teachers can recognize the patterns of culturally based classroom communication and the effect these patterns have on second-language learning.

15. Kaplan, Robert B., ed. *Annual Review of Applied Linguistics*, 1982. Rowley, MA: Newbury House, 1983.

    The third volume of the series is directed toward studies related to written text, more specifically to rhetorical differences between English and such languages as German, Hindi, Korean, Mandarin, and Marathi. Kaplan introduces the collection and provides an integrative essay in conclusion.

16. Kaplan, Robert B., "Cultural Thought Patterns in Intercultural Education." *Language Learning* 16 (1966): 1-20.

Kaplan's seminal article on contrastive rhetoric has influenced a generation of researchers. Though not empirically based, it provided the basis for understanding the principles of the body of research that followed.

17. Kroll, Barbara. "The Rhetoric-Syntax Split: Designing a Curriculum for ESL Students." *Journal of Basic Writing* 9 (1990): 40-55.

18. Kroll, Barbara, ed. *Second Language Writing: Research Insights for the Classroom*. New York: Cambridge UP, 1990.

This seminal collection of thirteen articles is addressed to teachers in training and to experienced teachers in the field of ESL teaching as well. The first of two sections presents "the current state of thinking on what the teaching of writing to normative speakers entails"; the second presents a "variety of specific studies, each focused on a different aspect of writing and/or the writing classroom."

19. Land, Robert, and Catherine Whitley. "Evaluating Second Language Essays in Regular Composition Classes: Toward a Pluralistic Society." *Richness in Writing: Empowering ESL Students*. Ed. D. Johnson and D. Roen. New York: Longman, 1989, 284-93.

20. Leki, Ilona. *Understanding ESL Writers: A Guide for Teachers*. New York: St. Martin's, 1992.

Written particularly for NES teachers of NES freshman English classes in which there are ESL students, the focus of this book is on immigrant students rather than international students. Their problems with reading and writing, and the problems faced by their teachers, are discussed in clear and cogent detail, with practical suggestions offered that are based on second-language acquisition research and composition theory.

21. Oxford, Rebecca L. *Language Learning Strategies: What Every Teacher Should Know*. Boston: Newbury House, 1990.

Oxford bases her practical suggestions in this volume on theory and fieldwork that she explains with clarity and simplicity. Her objective is to train teachers to train students to be more successful language learners by learning about, experimenting with, and practicing learning strategies. Especially useful for composition teachers of ESL students.

22. Purves, Alan, ed. *Writing across Languages and Cultures: Issues in Contrastive Rhetoric*. Newbury Park, CA: Sage, 1988.

The collection of research articles from scholars of several countries addresses the issue of cultural expectations in the assessment of ESL writing. How these writers deviate from the norms of the foreign culture in the kinds of material they choose, the style, and the organization of their prose is examined.

23. Samovar, Richard, and Larry Porter, eds. *Intercultural Communication: A Reader*. 6th ed. Belmont, CA: Wadsworth, 1991.

Interesting and informative articles by a large number of international educators in the field of cross-cultural communication. Each chapter examines current issues in the field, on such wide-ranging topics as the sociocultural necessity of effective communication, the impact of Confucianism in East Asia, Arabic concepts of effective persuasion, and the cultural patterns of the Masai.

24. Swales, John. *Genre Analysis: English in Academic and Research Settings*. Cambridge: Cambridge UP, 1990.

Focuses on rhetorical conventions and discourse styles employed in various academic settings and how such norms are effectively taught to NES and ESL writers. Swales analyzes specific text types, specifically research-related genres, and addresses the pedagogic issues involved in preparing students to achieve the purposes of each for its intended audience.

25. Swan, M., and B. Smith, eds. *Learner English: A Teacher's Guide to Interference and Other Problems*. Cambridge: Cambridge UP, 1987.

26. *Thirteen Language Profiles: Practical Application of Contrastive Analysis for Teachers of English as a Second Language*. Vancouver, BC: Vancouver Community College English Language Training Night School, 1983.

   Presents the basics of thirteen languages in sections that range from borrowed vocabulary and potential phonology problems for speakers of that language who are learning English to the written script and writing problems that those students might have. Very easy to understand and very worthwhile reading for teachers of ESL writers.

27. Vann, Roberta, D. E. Meyer, and F. D. Lorenz. "Error Gravity: A Study of Faculty Opinion of ESL Errors." *TESOL Quarterly* 18 (1984): 427-40.

   One of the first empirical studies to examine the response of university faculty to ESL essay errors. The authors clearly describe the research methods, and the results have been widely used to prioritize error monitoring in ESL writing.